IQ

IQ

How Psychology
Hijacked Intelligence

Stephen Murdoch

Duckworth Overlook

This edition 2009
First published in UK in 2007 by
Duckworth Overlook
90-93 Cowcross Street, London, EC1M 6BF
Tel: 020 7490 7300
Fax: 020 7490 0080
info@duckworth-publishers.co.uk
www.ducknet.co.uk

© 2007 by Stephen Murdoch

First published in the US in 2007 by
John Wiley & Sons, Inc.
111 River Street, Hoboken,
New Jersey 07030-5774

A catalogue record for this book is available
from the British Library

ISBN 978 07156 3447 9

Printed and bound in Great Britain by
Creative Print & Design, Blaina, Wales

For Melissa,
whom I love immeasurably

Contents

Acknowledgments

Many people were kind enough to help me in the course of this book. William Clark, my agent, has always believed in my writing and has represented me flawlessly. I'm lucky to have him. Duckworth editor Dan Hind purchased the book in the United Kingdom, and I'm so glad he did. The writer-publisher relationship can be notoriously lousy, but working with Duckworth has been all pleasure. I'd like to include a special thanks to the editor Caroline McArthur and the best publicist in London, Suzannah Rich. With them, it doesn't feel like work.

I periodically spoke to my father, William Murdoch, about the project, and at the end he turned his incisive brain to the entire manuscript, aiding me tremendously. I also relied heavily on my writer's group in Washington, D.C. They provided crucial feedback to early drafts. They are Melanie Kaplan, Cate Lineberry, Matt McMillen, Joan Quigley, Lori Nitschke-Hansen, and Amy Serafin. In particular I'd like to thank Peter Gwin, who took far too many angst-ridden phone calls from me. He is a terrific writer, and the world awaits his books.

Many thanks to my two favorite professors, Drs. George Higgins and William Mace. They made psychology interesting when I was an undergraduate at Trinity College, Connecticut; in particular, this book would not have happened without Dr. Mace's history of psychology class. After many professional meanderings, this book is a return to this early interest. These two fine gentlemen should not be held accountable for my opinions or factual errors.

As a group, the librarians at the Library of Congress are amazing, but there were a few who helped me repeatedly, and always energetically and professionally. They are Cheryl Adams, Abby Yochelson, Darren Jones, and David Kelly. Tim Wells, author and editor of the *Washington Lawyer* magazine, taught me how to write a book proposal at the Writer's Center in Bethesda, Maryland. Dr. Susan Bachrach, exhibition curator at the United States Holocaust Memorial Museum, opened up her files to me in her museum offices. Tamara Koch did a great job translating Ursula H.'s medical file. Whitney Dangerfield did some helpful research at the Library of Congress after I had moved to California. Others who helped in various ways were Jay Carlander, Evan Gottesman, David Lubitz, Nicholas Lapham, and Bob Lang.

The history of IQ testing is so varied and complex that no outsider could write about the field without relying on the heavy lifting of previous gifted researchers and writers. I'd like to acknowledge expressly a few of them here: Raymond Fancher, Leila Zenderland, Paul Lombardo, Adrian Wooldridge, and Henry Friedlander. I enjoyed reading your works very much. Paul Lombardo spent much of one day with me in Charlottesville, Virginia, explaining the intricacies of *Buck v. Bell*, and he generously provided me with legal documents he had spent years tracking down. He is the paragon of what an academic should be.

Finally, I'd like to thank my wife, Melissa, and three daughters, Ainslie, Serena, and Annabel, who helped in more ways than I can list.

Preface

When I was in the sixth grade, I went to my local public junior high in Santa Barbara, California, where I grew up, to take an IQ test to see whether I would be admitted to the Gifted and Talented Education program. My mother dropped me off, and I walked with trepidation to a man with a large black drooping mustache in a little office who asked me a series of very strange questions. He seemed bored and preoccupied and at one point during the test asked me to step outside so he could take a phone call. Part of the test was a series of flash cards with pictures on them, and he asked me what item was missing in each one. In the picture of an umbrella I noticed that it lacked the little spokes at the top of the pole that fan the fabric out. I pointed that out to him.

"That was good," I remember him saying, sounding surprised. "Most people don't get that one right." His comment, rather than emboldening me, put me off. Was he surprised that I had gotten it correctly because my other answers had been stupid?

He then asked me to organize colored blocks into various patterns and shapes that he presented to me. The task was perfectly fine, but he was holding a watch the whole time, which put me on edge. But then, to my relief, he asked me questions about the world, and I seemed to know the answers.

"Who was Charles Darwin?"

My father was a biologist at the local university, and I had just watched a TV show with my parents about Darwin's trip to the Galapagos on the *Beagle*.

"He was a biologist who went on a trip to South America," I said.

I left the exam feeling very mixed and shaken. Weeks later, I was surprised to learn that I had been accepted into the gifted and talented program. This positive outcome, however, affected my view of the experience barely at all. I remained convinced that I hadn't passed and that my mother—who was active in the PTA—had gotten me into the program behind the scenes.

While I was working on this book, people asked me how I got interested in the history of IQ testing. To them, the subject seemed so esoteric that they expected a personal story. I often wished I'd had an obvious answer—for instance, that I had an IQ of 69 but nonetheless graduated from Harvard; neither of those facts, however, is true. My personal introduction was pedestrian and yet at the same time ubiquitous. No one comes to the subject of IQ tests without personal biases, assumptions, and experiences—the subject is so emotional that it is literally impossible—and like many people, I disliked taking these tests. In particular, as a child, I never liked being judged, and the whole purpose of an IQ test is to scrutinize. The very idea that one quick test could sum me up frightened and irked me.

The truth is that the ideas behind IQ tests were too interesting for me to ignore, and that's how I came to write this book. I had learned about some of the historical figures who had created the exams as a psychology undergraduate, at Trinity College, in Connecticut, and their hubris had stuck with me years afterward. I didn't study to become a psychologist after leaving Trinity, but strayed into law, doing human rights work in Cambodia for a couple of years and practicing civil litigation briefly in Washington, D.C. In my early thirties I became a freelance writer, and after writing about the law for a while I began going to the Library of Congress to learn about how the exams came to be. Someone with a more scientific bent would have produced a more technical treatise on the subject. I have always liked history, however, and my inclination was to try to discover the origins, stories, and people behind the exams.

IQ history turned out to be so fecund, fascinating, and important that I stayed a lot longer at the Library of Congress than I had originally intended. I began by reading about the first mass intelligence testing, which the U.S. Army administered during World War I. A total of 1.7 million men took them, and it wasn't long before I realized that this obscure testing affected how decisions have been made about people throughout the world, during the twentieth century to today. Very quickly, I realized I had a book.

Over a few weeks at the outset of America's involvement in World War I, seven men in rural New Jersey banged out questions to put to America's young men. They asked questions like "Why do we use stoves?" and "The **Armadillo** is a kind of **ornamental shrub   animal   musical instrument   dagger**" and presumed that the recruits' answers revealed useful differences in innate intelligence. After the war, they convinced a nation—and then a world—that such presumptions were true.

As I learned how quickly these World War I tests were cobbled together, I began to wonder how these seven men and their exams were connected to today. At first I assumed, because the exams seemed so antiquated, that they wouldn't be very connected, but it turns out that they are to an extent that most people don't know about. While psychology has become far more sophisticated since the early twentieth century, the astounding aspect of the story is how little its tests have changed. From these New Jersey tests came exams and beliefs that have affected all of us in one way or another at different stages in our lives.

My book, I thought, wouldn't be full of charts and graphs and long explanations of statistical analyses, but one that explains to people how it came to be that they were placed into a high-, middle-, or low-flying life track by a single test. We are put into gifted school programs (or not) and into one university over another based on exams that came from World War I and before. As adults, people qualify for jobs, promotions, government benefits, and death by injection and gas, or are barred from any of these based on the New Jersey tests. Over the past century, the exams have affected people's right to live, have children, or reside in the country of their choice, and they have not changed significantly since their inception. They have been one size fits all in almost every setting where people need to be sorted according to mental ability. I want to tell you why. The reasons will surprise you.

Chapter 1

The Problem with Testing

When Tim was just three years old his mother, Janet, knew he was going to have problems getting into one of the elite private schools in Washington, D.C. Tim's father had gone to one of the best and was eager for his son to go there, too, but the competition among the children of Washington politicians, scientists, lawyers, and business families was fierce. Janet worried most about the IQ test Tim would have to take to get into kindergarten.

"There's something about [testing] three-year-olds that makes you feel dirty being involved," said Janet, an easygoing, pretty woman in her late thirties.

Worse than feeling dirty, Janet got an inkling early that Tim was a bad test-taker when she took him to an independent school consultant, an expert who would guide Tim's family through the complicated process of applying to private schools. Such consultants charge thousands of dollars, promising to evaluate the tiny candidates and explain the differences in philosophies among the schools. They also often administer an IQ test—or at least bits of one—to see how the child is going to perform and then recommend schools they think would be a good match. The higher the score, the fancier and more competitive the school. At the very outset of the process, IQ test scores are dictating where the children will apply.

The consultant asked Janet to leave her office while she tested Tim. After about half an hour, she called Janet back in with some bad news. The only school she could recommend for Tim was one

1

for children with language disorders in the remote suburbs. To a family like Janet's—all East Coast–educated at the best schools—it was like shooting for the Ivy League but ending up studying agriculture at a satellite campus of the University of Nebraska.

"I felt terrible," Janet said, remembering the experience. "I cried for three days. She told me he was a moron," she said, unwittingly using a term that long ago entered the vernacular from technical, IQ-based classifications. Then Janet paused and realized that the consultant hadn't actually said Tim was a moron; it just felt as if she had. "She basically told me he was kind of limited in intelligence."

The consultant had also recommended that Tim should be in speech therapy, so while Tim was still in preschool Janet signed him up for it twice a week. Early on in his therapy the therapist asked Tim to make up a story, but he was completely stumped, coming up with nothing. And when he did speak, the "ums" flowed like bullets from a Gatling gun.

"Um, no, no, um, um, um, um, my, um, I, I don't have a farm. Yeah, yeah, I have a farm at my house. Yeah. Um, no. Know what?! I have a, um, um, I have a um, um, um, um a, I have a no, no no farm."

Even an articulate kid of that age can sound like a cold motorcycle in need of repeated kick-starts, especially when answering questions from someone he doesn't know (and about a farm, of all things). But Tim often had problems expressing himself, and on a test of verbal ability administered by the therapist he scored in the 2nd percentile—just a wee step from those scoring the worst. This boded ill for Tim, and Janet knew it, for in Washington, private schools rely heavily on IQ tests for admissions. And for a hundred years, IQ tests have largely been based on verbal ability, so the outlook for Tim wasn't good.

Washington parents receive mixed messages from school administrators about the importance of tests in the elementary school admissions process. On the one hand, they're told to relax: IQ scores aren't that important, there are many factors in admissions. At the same time, administrators tell parents not to take their child in for testing if she is sick, grumpy, or sad on the day of test-ing—a clear implication that the tests matter. In fact, test scores matter more than parents are told, but school administrators know that parents will become tense if their fears are not assuaged. To the schools, relying heavily on IQ scores makes institutional sense. After all, most of the very young children applying are well groomed, well spoken, and bright, and come from white, wealthy, and hypereducated families. How else are these schools supposed to "weed out," as one local psychologist put it, the overabundant attractive and able three- and four-year-olds?

A parent's nightmare is if her child simply isn't in the mood to play along with the psychologist administering the test, as exempli-fied by Mary, a brown-haired young girl in Washington, D.C. Mary walked out of a psychologist's office and into the waiting room, with a therapist in her early thirties in tow.

"Mary, what's the difference between a horse and a pony?" the therapist asked earnestly.

Mary paid her no attention, but simply sat down on a couch to play with her doll next to me as I waited for an interview.

"Mary, what's the difference between a horse and a pony?" she was asked again, but Mary knew the value of selective hearing bet-ter than someone married for thirty years. There's no convincing a stubborn young girl that although the pony-horse distinction may seem frivolous, this is a test, and it's important. By the time the psychologist doggedly posed her taxonomic question a third time, Mary had had enough. She turned to me and said, proffering her playmate in a pointed snub to the tester, "Will you put a diaper on my doll?"

Who knows how Mary's score was affected? For tests that are supposed to measure innate ability in large part, it's an open secret that a child's mood will affect her score. For generations, critics of IQ tests have worried that it's the good kids, those willing to follow adult rules, who do well on the tests. Good psychologists try to take a child's mood and energy level into account when administer-ing these tests, but there's only so much they can do when they see her only once.

As Tim's speech therapy moved along, Janet was unsure how it was progressing. She thought the therapist was good, "but not a warm and fuzzy woman. Once [the therapist] was watching him draw and she said, right in front of him, 'That's not normal.'"

"They want you to draw a stick figure at a certain age and he couldn't," Janet explained. So Janet sent Tim to an occupational therapist to do fine and gross motor skill work as well, although she found it a little odd. She had heard that occupational therapy helps, but she wasn't convinced it had been "scientifically proven." The therapist gave her a brush to use on Tim's skin, essentially so he would get comfortable in his own skin. Janet and her husband were supposed to do it every day, but they wondered at its efficacy and didn't do it very often.

"So at one point," Janet said, "he was going to speech therapy twice a week and occupational therapy twice a week." Either despite or because of all this therapy, Tim began to stutter. "His face would get all contorted," she said raising both hands near her face, so she asked the speech therapist to work on stuttering as well.

The IQ test outlook was really not looking good for Tim. Nevertheless, most families like Tim's don't view the Washington public school system as a tenable option for their children. The schools are mainly for the working class, and their statistics are often depressing: fewer than half of the students are at grade level in reading and mathematics, and only about 60 percent make it to high school graduation. And so, amid all this therapy and with considerable trepidation, Janet made an appointment with a local psychologist for an IQ test. A few months before his fifth birthday, Tim's first IQ test was the WPPSI, pronounced "whipsee" and standing for the Wechsler Preschool and Primary Scale of Intelligence, which is the standard exam for young children.

"He was immediately talkative and curious about what we were going to do together, and rapport was easily established," the psychologist found. She asked him commonsense questions such as, What happens to water when it gets cold? She gave him a puzzle and a timed pegs-in-the-holes test. She asked him to name animals in pictures and build with blocks; she noted the size of his vocabulary.

Although Tim was at first open and enthusiastic, things quickly turned sour for him. "As items became tougher, particularly during question-and-answer periods, [Tim] was reluctant to take a guess, and frequently struggled to find words. At those times he became very frustrated, asking his mother if they could go home 'now,' and on at least two occasions [Tim] became tearful, throwing himself in his mother's arms and responding to comforting from her," the psychologist wrote about the meeting.

In the end, Janet's fears about Tim's IQ turned out to be well founded. Already at age four, Tim was very good with computers, but computer skills aren't on IQ tests. Ever since their inception, IQ tests for little kids have emphasized language and motor skills. In these two areas, compared to other kids his age (which is how IQ tests measure intelligence), Tim was bad. He scored in the 34th percentile, an improvement over the 2nd percentile on his verbal test, for sure, but by no means Washington private school caliber.

"If you're trying to get into one of the private schools and if [your children] don't do well on these tests, forget about it. You don't get in with a 34th percentile," said Janet. Most parents feel that for their children to attend one of the top schools they've got to be scoring in the nineties. School admission officers don't talk about whether there is a threshold, but there probably is. As one psychologist put it, if Sidwell Friends (one of the best private schools in the country and located in Northwest D.C.) "can have their pick of the kids who are in the 90th percentiles . . . they fill it with kids like that. I don't know why they wouldn't. The people that I know that go there are very well connected people who are the cream of the crop of the city."

After receiving his test scores, Tim's parents didn't bother applying to his father's alma mater for kindergarten; they just sent him to a public elementary school that doesn't have such a bad reputation. The facilities were not as nice as the private schools', and parents had to pool together their own funds to hire a music teacher. For years the administration had been asking the city for physical improvements, to no effect. But there were some excellent teachers, some of the best, Janet thought, especially in the lower years. Just before Tim started kindergarten, Janet decided to take him out of all his therapy.

"I will say that the therapy worked, but he might have just out-grown his problems, too," she said. Whatever the case, Tim stopped stuttering after leaving therapy. Nevertheless, when she met Tim's kindergarten teacher for the first time, Janet warned her that her son was a great kid but that he had lots of learning issues. A few weeks later, the same teacher made a point of taking her aside and telling Janet that she had got it wrong. "He doesn't have a lot of problems," said the teacher. Tim was just a normal kid. The relief Janet felt, and the frustration with the experts, were palpable when she recounted this story. All fears that Tim actually was a moron had melted away.

"He's pretty much thrived ever since," Janet said of Tim. One year, Tim's public school teachers wrote in his report card that he "continues to be extremely strong in all academic subjects such as reading, math and writing. In addition, we have noticed that [Tim] really seems to enjoy science. He is very inquisitive and is getting comfortable mastering the scientific process."

Tim was happy at the public elementary school, and Janet was happy to have him there. Besides, she felt sure Tim would "get in somewhere" when the time came for the inevitable switchover to private school, but her husband still wanted him at his alma mater as quickly as possible. There's a perception in Washington that the longer families wait to send their kid to the private school, the harder it is to get in. So Janet took Tim to a new psychologist and he retook the WPPSI test when he was six. This time he got in the 79th percentile, still not a stellar score, but perhaps within fancy private school striking distance, especially since the family had a legacy. Nevertheless, Janet and her husband decided to keep him in public school and have him tested a year later.

When Tim was seven, Janet took him back again, this time for the WISC (the Wechsler Intelligence Scale for Children, an exam for the next age group up from the WPPSI). In the four years since he had first started speech therapy, Tim had come a long way from his initial days of "um-ing" through an exam. The psychologist found him to be "intent, focused and eager to do his best, he was serious about his performance, determined and sometimes a little impatient with himself." Tim excelled, especially at nonverbal tasks such as duplicating designs with colored blocks and completing pictures.

On the WISC, Tim scored in the 98th percentile overall, fully 64 percentile points up from just three years previously. With this score, Tim was ready to apply to the fanciest schools around, and in a recent early spring he was accepted at his father's old school. The Ivy League, although years away, had just gotten a whole lot closer.

Tim had some verbal developmental problems, but he was the same kid when he scored in the 34th percentile and the 98th percentile. Such differences in scores are uncommon, say psychologists, although they admit that IQ scores generally don't "settle" until children are in adolescence.

"Any IQ estimate before the age of five is obviously going to be unstable because children are going through such rapid cognitive development," said Diane Coalson, who is senior research director at Harcourt Assessment, the company that produces the WPPSI and the WISC. According to Coalson, it's not until adolescence, "let's say age sixteen and up [that] IQ is more stable."

How did schools, businesses, and governments decide that these rough, narrow estimates of innate intelligence, these stress-producing tests consisting of a series of discrete little problems, are the best way to decide who is worthy and unworthy in countless settings? In a word, puffery.

Let's pause to think about the word puffery for a moment. It most often arises in legal contexts to describe the overselling of a product. Our toothpaste is the best in the world! While this is innocuous in the realm of oral hygiene, it's not, as you will discover, when it comes to ranking people by perceived intelligence. Many millions of people have been harmed by the uses of IQ tests in large part because, from the beginning, psychologists oversold what their exams measured. It's hard not to draw the conclusion that one of the main reasons psychologists over-promised what their exams could do was because it helped them to gain access and power at a crucial time for their fledgling field. Nevertheless, it's important to note from the outset that the problem isn't so much with the product they hawked, but with their hype, including the label "intelligence test" itself. A century ago, IQ tests were actually novel and amazing inventions. The sadness of the history you are about to read is that if they had been described more honestly and modestly, people probably would not have used them so nefariously or ill advisedly.

Chapter 2

The Origins of Testing

The science of modern intelligence tests and the theory that underlies much of the field started with a remarkable upper-class Englishman who liked to count and measure in almost any circumstance in which he found himself. Francis Galton is now a distant, obscure figure, but in the Victorian era he was a famous polymath, a cousin of Charles Darwin on his mother's side and on the other a descendant of a great-grandfather who made money in guns. His penchant for math and measuring in various forms led him to original contributions in geography, weather systems, genetics, statistics, criminology, and anthropometry, the field of measuring humans. Galton was intellectually tremendously fecund, and he contributed, even defined, many of the debates, tools, and constructs of modern psychology.

"Whenever you can, count," Galton would often say, an attitude perfectly designed to found a field about counting, ranking, and measuring people.

Galton also was highly strung. As a young man, he suffered a nervous breakdown after studying mathematics at Cambridge University, when he discovered there were better mathematical minds than his. His father wanted him to return to his medical studies, which Galton had done in his teens, but he didn't have much heart for it, and when his father died and left him a fortune, Galton quit university life altogether.

All of a sudden, and like rich people everywhere, Galton was blessed with the caviar curse of not having to make a living, and he waffled in the years after university, unsure what to do with his life. He took a trip down the Nile with some Cambridge friends, went shooting in Scotland, and generally partied and caroused. In embarrassment many years later, he claimed it was a period of deep thought, in which he read a lot of great books, but there is little indication of this. Finally, in his late twenties and tired of being directionless, Galton saw a phrenologist (a head shape and size expert) in London who told him he wasn't really suited for a life of the mind.

"As regards the learned professions I do not think this gentleman is fond enough of the midnight lamp to like them, or to work hard if engaged in one of them," the phrenologist concluded.

The phrenologist was wrong about Galton's intellect and capabilities, but after the visit Galton decided to become an African adventurer. Instead of just rambling around that continent showing a white face where there hadn't been many before, Galton turned his measuring nature to cartography. In 1850 he made a serious mapping expedition to Damaraland, in what is now in Namibia, in southern Africa. Even in a subsequent best-selling travel book, *Narrative of an Explorer in Tropical South Africa*, Galton was unable to leave out the subject of measuring. At one point he recalled admiring a young Hottentot woman who was married to a missionary's "sub-interpreter." Her figure was so remarkable that it sent him into a frenzy.

"The sub-interpreter was married to a charming person, not only a Hottentot in figure, but in that respect a Venus among Hottentots. I was perfectly aghast at her development, and made inquiries upon that delicate point as far as I dared among my missionary friends."

Galton thought she was stunning, but his inclination was to obtain her measurements, not to woo her. He could hardly go up and ask to measure her, though, for he didn't speak her language and the request would have come across as odd, anyway. Being a man of scientific bent, and on a map-making expedition, he quickly seized upon his sextant, which would allow him to size her up remotely.

"The object of my admiration stood under a tree, and was turning herself about to all points of the compass, as ladies who wish to be admired usually do. . . . I took a series of observations upon her figure in every direction, up and down, crossways, diagonally, and so forth, and I registered them carefully upon an outline drawing for fear of any mistake; this being done, I boldly pulled out my measuring-tape, and measured the distance from where I was to the place she stood, and having thus obtained both base and angles, I worked out the results by trigonometry and logarithms."

Galton's travel book became a best seller, and his mapping and exploration earned him membership in the coveted Royal Geographic Society. Galton was therefore successful by his late thirties, but he was still fairly conventional and not known as a great thinker. In 1859, however, his cousin Charles Darwin published a book, *On the Origin of Species*, that changed all that. The book would eventually cause Galton to analyze human mental abilities in terms of evolution and, in a logical extension, want to manipulate natural selection to improve the human race. That is, Galton wanted to breed people.

Before Galton read *On the Origin of Species*, he was a devout Anglican with no interest in biology. After reading it, Galton's entire worldview changed profoundly, although not quite as quickly as he later claimed. As an old man, Galton wrote that *On the Origin of Species* made him an agnostic at "a single stroke," like a plot point in a Thomas Hardy novel, but it wasn't true. The ideas in the book, and those of other scientists around him, actually did transform Galton, but the process was long and grueling.

The unorthodox ideas that began to form in Galton's mind after reading *On the Origin of Species* caused a three-year nervous breakdown. He convalesced at home, obsessive and anxious, barely able to work, and unable to meet friends for dinner in public. So when Galton wrote late in life that Darwin's book made "a marked epoch in my own mental development," it was an understatement: it was sufficiently life-altering to keep him home for three years.

When he recovered, Galton began to argue in published papers and in public that people inherit good or bad mental characteristics that dictate their success or failure in life. He would devote the rest of his life to this idea. To Galton, applying theories about physical attributes in animals to psychological ones in humans made perfect sense. After all, most families shared recognizable physical similarities—tall fathers, for instance, tended to produce tall sons. Since these physical characteristics were passed along from one generation to the next, Galton assumed that psychological characteristics, such as intelligence or laziness, were as well. The debate still rages about the degree to which this is true, but Galton's work laid the groundwork for modern controversies, beliefs, and even methodology.

Galton internalized *On the Origin of Species* by thinking about his personal experiences. "I began by thinking over the dispositions and achievements of my contemporaries at school, at college, and in after life, and was surprised to find how frequently ability seemed to go by descent," Galton wrote.

Even his travels in Africa bolstered Galton's view that blacks were innately inferior to whites, a subject that academic psychology is still interested in, often jarringly to those outside the field. Perhaps harking back to an encounter with a tribal African leader he had written about in *Narrative of an Explorer*, Galton believed that when European men and "native chief[s]" confront each other in the bush "the result is familiar enough—the white traveler almost invariably holds his own in their presence. It is seldom that we hear of a white traveler meeting with a black chief whom he feels to be the better man."

In short, Galton had no real evidence and instead relied on personal experience and even hearsay to prove the black-white ability differences. He wrote: "The number among the negroes of those whom we should call half-witted men is very large. Every book alluding to negro servants in America is full of instances. I was myself much impressed by this fact during my travels in Africa. The mistakes the negroes made in their own matters, were so childish, stupid, and simpleton-like, as frequently to make me ashamed of my own species."

In 1869, ten years after publication of *On the Origin of Species*, Galton decided to test statistically the idea that ability ran in the family in a book called *Hereditary Genius*. It was a radical use of statistics, for while they had been applied to physical human characteristics before, Galton was the first to apply them to mental abilities. The central inquiry of *Hereditary Genius* was whether "eminent" men were more likely than run-of-the-mill types to be related to other eminent men. If they were, Galton believed this would bolster his claim that ability is inherited. To test his hypothesis, Galton gathered names of men who had been recognized in various biographical dictionaries as having made positive contributions to society, ending up with a list of judges, military commanders, statesmen, poets, athletes, and many other worthies.

After analyzing their family trees, Galton discovered that an astonishing 10 percent of the pool—just shy of a thousand people—were related to one another, and that most of these relatives were from the same nuclear families. Although the vast majority of people in his study were not related to each other, the percentage of relatives was much higher than one would expect from a randomly selected group. Those who were related to eminent men also tended to achieve success, or at least a reputation (as evidenced by their appearance in the biographical dictionaries), in the same area as their relatives had, which Galton thought supported his argument that ability is inherited.

A man, wrote Galton, must "inherit capacity, zeal, and vigour; for unless these three, or, at the very least, two of them, are combined, he cannot hope to make a figure in the world." This explained why remote descendants of eminent judges, for instance, were less likely than the judge's immediate relatives to be successful. After "three successive dilutions of the blood, the descendants of judges appear incapable of rising to eminence," Galton concluded.

For centuries, European philosophers had been debating whether attributes such as intelligence were innate or learned. The argument was hardly settled in Galton's time, and the balance between environment and biology is not close to being settled today. Moreover, many of the successful and related men in Galton's study presumably lived in the same house (at least at some point during their lives) and helped one another's careers, as family members do. But for Galton, who came from a successful family, environment had very little effect on one's place in life. Look at America, he said, where they educate their middle and lower classes more than England does. And yet, despite this environmental difference, "America most certainly does not beat us in first-class works of literature, philosophy or art. The higher kind of books, even of the most modern date, read in America are principally the work of Englishmen. The Americans have an immense amount of the newspaper-article-writer, or the member-of-Congress stamp of ability; but the number of their really eminent authors is more limited even than with us."

Galton's privileged background could have led him to believe that the effects of environment matter more than heredity, but it did not. Francis was the youngest sibling of seven, not so odd in itself, but he was raised in large part by his sister Adele, who was twelve years older than he and an invalid who suffered from a debilitating spinal disorder. After Francis's birth, she contrived to have his crib brought into her room, threw her attentions on him, and commenced to tutor him at a very early age. Galton's odd upbringing created a precocious child. At age eight he could explain how the ancient Saxons had built their ships, and, according to family lore, he once reprimanded his mother for mistaking locusts for cockchafers, which he pointed out belong to different entomological orders. For Galton, however, his family's blood mattered more than how they had raised him.

Along with the belief that mental ability is inherited often comes the conclusion that society is structured the way it is for natural reasons, and so it was for Galton. For him, women, blacks, and the lower classes occupied inferior positions because of their lack of innate talent, and he published graphs illustrating this. On the far left of his bell curve lived people of low genetic worth; they were the "criminals, semi-criminals, loafers and some others." People with slightly more genetic ability, and higher up on the bell curve, were "very poor persons who subsist on casual earnings, many of whom are inevitably poor from shiftlessness, idleness or drink." Those who composed the bulk of the bell curve, in the middle, were the "respectable" working class: not too bright, but solid types. Finally, and inevitably, "the brains of our nation lie in the higher of our classes," at the far right end of the curve.

From this belief that social position resulted from innate worth, Galton made a most astonishing segue into public policy suggestions that reverberate even now. Galton believed that only those on the extremely gifted end of the curve—those who could "found great industries . . . and amass large fortunes for themselves"—should be allowed to have children. Those three years hiding at home and mulling over Darwin's *On the Origin of Species* paid off for Galton: the biggest idea of his life was purposefully to apply natural selection to human breeding.

The idea makes some sense at an intuitive level. Dogs have different attributes and can be bred for them; humans have different attributes and should be bred for them, too.

"Some dogs are savage, others gentle; some endure fatigue, others are soon exhausted; some are loyal, others are self-regarding. . . . So it is with men in respect to the qualities that go towards forming civic worth, which it is not necessary at this moment to define particularly, especially as it may be a blend of many alternative qualities. High civic worth includes a high level of character, intellect, energy, and physique, and this would disqualify the vast majority of persons from that distinction," Galton said in one lecture.

Through such reasoning, Galton created a new applied science of human breeding, which he called eugenics, a term he coined from Greek roots meaning "well" and "born." But one of the biggest problems for eugenics, Galton noticed early on, was recognizing people with talent when they are young enough to procreate. Most of the people listed in the biographical dictionaries Galton studied for his book *Hereditary Genius* were of middle age or older, which, from a breeding point of view, was a missed opportunity.

What Galton needed was an exam to figure out which young adults and schoolchildren were genetically worthy to reproduce. In a paper published in 1865, six years after the publication of *On the*

Origin of Species, Galton wrote of the need to create "public examinations, conducted on established principles." And those who scored well on his tests should be encouraged to marry and should be given proper respect in society. Young men should be paired with slightly younger women who had been tested for "grace, beauty, health, good-temper, accomplished housewifery, and disengaged affections, in addition to the noble qualities of heart and brain." If these high-scoring men and women chose to marry, they would be presented with £5,000, an astonishing sum at the time, and their children's maintenance and educational costs would be "defrayed."

"The Sovereign herself will give away the brides at a high and solemn festival . . . in Westminster Abbey," Galton wrote.

Galton's main problem was that neither he nor anybody else knew what tests of innate mental ability "conducted on established principles" looked like. IQ tests, or at least their precursors, the "mental tests," as they would later be called, were about to be born.

Francis Galton was the man to create such tests. Back home from Africa, he had continued to count and measure in a strange cocktail of the profoundly useful, useless, and idiosyncratic. He counted fidgets at dull Royal Geographic Society lectures to measure boredom, of all things. But he also created Britain's first weather map and was a pioneer in the use of fingerprints in criminal investigations.

He was not just an original thinker, but also a capable tinkerer who devised novel tools and devices to meet his own needs. When working on a "beauty map" of Great Britain, Galton created a number of little wooden and paper caps rigged with metal points that he would place on a finger to count and rate women as he traveled around the country. These small counting devices allowed him to keep a hand in his pocket and secretly poke cross-shaped pieces of paper he had prepared beforehand. Good-looking women would earn a prick on the top of the cross and average women on the arm of the cross; ugly ones were shoved down to the bottom. The results showed London with the best-looking women and northerly Aberdeen with an overabundance of unattractive ones.

All of his quirky yet sometimes genius ideas as well as his ability to build his own tools came into play when he devised the first mental test. At the London International Health Exhibition of 1884, twenty-five years after the publication of *On the Origin of Species*, Galton stuffed a little six-by-thirty-six-foot booth with seventeen devices to test physical abilities. He eventually tested nine thousand people there, and they even paid him for the pleasure: threepence each, which they gave to the doorman upon entering.

People loved it. They lined up for hours to be scrutinized, mainly orderly and curious, with only an occasional drunken visitor, swigging from his personal stone beer bottle of the kind that working-class men brought with them, requiring the boot. Galton's booth, just one among many at the exhibition, was a smashing success, so busy at times that people walked away, dissuaded by the long lines. But most visitors waited out the long lines, their curiosity magnified by what they spied through the outer latticework wall: men, women, and children of all ages and classes from around the country deliberating over, striking, staring at, and breathing into the weirdest of devices.

Whatever could they be doing? The big enigmatic sign in block letters above Galton's booth—"Anthropometric Laboratory"—probably didn't mean much to most visitors, although it sounded impressively scientific. In the poor lighting of the vast exhibition hall, people picked up and squinted into a sickle-shaped wooden box and read out snippets of scripture while a man took notes. He tested their hearing among the din of thousands of tourists by asking them to put a cylinder to their ears and then striking a coin at the other end. He weighed people, measured their height, and, oddly enough, the middle finger of their left hand, all the while taking notes on little cards.

At one point people had to punch the padded end of a rod to test the swiftness of their blows. One quick, straight jab was all that was required of them, but many bungled it, striking the rod on the side, breaking it, and damaging their knuckles and wrists in the process.

These bunglers led the tremendously competent Galton to remark exasperatedly, "It was a matter of surprise to myself, who was born in the days of pugilism, to find that the art of delivering a clean hit, straight from the shoulder, as required by this instrument, is nearly lost to the rising generation."

Galton thought that these measurements of physical ability and size offered insight into who had the most "natural ability." The more gifted the person, Galton argued, the more neurologically efficient he would be. Therefore Galton thought the way to discern who was talented and who was not was to devise tests that measured people's physical energy, reaction times, and sensory acuity.

"The only information that reaches us concerning outward events appears to pass through the avenue of our senses," Galton wrote, "and the more perceptible our senses are of difference, the larger the field upon which our judgment and intellect can act."

As with his views of blacks and the shape of society, Galton's theories about sensory acuity came from his personal experience. Men, he opined, were more able than women, and, surely not coincidentally, men's senses were sharper, too. Why else would there be no women in wine tasting and wool sorting jobs? "Ladies rarely distinguish the merits of wine at the dinner-table, and though custom allows them to preside at the breakfast-table, men think them on the whole to be far from successful makers of tea and coffee," Galton wrote.

Before the exhibition, Galton spent months masterfully designing and crafting many of the wood and iron instruments himself. He gauged people's keenness of sight with the sickle-shaped box people peered into, with passages from the Bible placed progressively farther away inside. He tested people's ability to distinguish different shades of green with bits of fabric. He measured their power to breathe and ability to hear, their power to pull and squeeze, and their "swiftness of blow." He had two men working full-time in the booth taking bodily measurements, noting people's scores and determining the size, shape, and abilities of Britons.

Speaking to a crowd at London's Anthropological Institute after the close of the health exhibition, Galton admitted that he might have failed to take one necessary measurement.

"One omission in the laboratory has been noticed by many," he said. "I had decided, perhaps wrongly, after much hesitation, not to measure the head."

Galton was unsure about the relationship between head size and intelligence. Many of the men he admired had unusually large heads. Women, he noted, tended to have smaller heads than men; that women were not as capable he was quite sure. Galton himself, though, had a smaller than average head and, well, how could that be? He had been a child prodigy, able to read children's stories and print his name at two and a half. By four he was learning Latin and French. As a young man he had a seat on the prestigious council of the Royal Geographical Society; he had created Britain's first weather map and had discovered the anticyclone. Francis Galton was a man of no mean ability, but he did have a small head, which had also quickly become bald as he entered manhood, but for the mutton-chop sideburns he always kept. (In keeping with good British genes, too, Galton had extremely thin lips, which gave the flesh between nose and mouth a prominent, simian appearance.) Galton eventually decided that head size must interact with other attributes to produce a man's abilities, but that it wasn't the sole deciding factor.

Dignitaries stopped by the lab in South Kensington to be measured and tested, including Prime Minister William Gladstone, a great Liberal leader of the nineteenth century. Galton chose to treat the prime minister rather snippily when the subject of head size came up. Gladstone insisted that hatters often told him that he had a head large enough to be referred to as an "Aberdeenshire . . . a fact, which you may be sure I do not forget to tell my Scottish constituents." He then asked Galton if he had ever happened upon a head as large as his, to which Galton replied tersely, "Mr. Gladstone, you are very unobservant," implying, apparently, that there were many larger craniums around.

Along with Prime Minister Gladstone, four million Britons visited the London International Health Exhibition, which was sponsored by Queen Victoria and set in London's intellectually vibrant neighborhood of South Kensington—its vast halls erected between

Royal Albert Hall and the Natural History Museum. As odd as it may seem today, the exhibition celebrated the new field of "sanitary science," which fascinated Victorians. Visitors attended lectures on health and pressed about mock shop windows and stalls, admiring physical objects at least putatively related to sanitation: clothing, shoes, ambulances, baths, heating and cooking appliances, all contrasted with older and presumably unhealthier versions. People toured an "insanitary house," realizing how similar it really was to theirs, and a "sanitary house" next door, which offered ways of making their homes healthier.

Among all of this, the tiny Anthropometric Laboratory had its place, for Galton was very much concerned with the health and well-being of Englishmen. But Galton's booth differed from the rest of the shops and exhibits in that it was not intended to educate the public, which, because of his belief in innate ability, he thought was a waste of time. As entertaining as it seemed to thousands of people, the lab was mainly a way to gather biometric information.

From the outset, his belief in eugenics often led to harsh views about how to solve social problems. Galton believed that what people traditionally think of as charity—say, tending to the sick and needy—was actually counterproductive. After all, these people are innately weak, and no amount of help will change that; charity may even help them to propagate, making matters worse. Instead, Galton thought, people with charitable hearts should encourage the gifted to marry by offering financial incentives. While traditional recipients of charity might continue to receive aid, it should be contingent upon their agreement to forbear having children, which would greatly reduce society's human impediments within just a few generations. Similarly, if ability—and therefore success—are biologically predetermined, then universal public education, like charity, is a waste of resources.

Galton also pointed out that those worthy of breeding were far outnumbered by those who were not: just look at the bell curve. One method of improving the situation would be to promote marriages between the meritorious, but another way would be to deter people of average and substandard ability from having children. This darker side of Galton's science was to become known as "negative eugenics" and, as can be imagined, would have disastrous consequences. But at the time, Galton idealistically believed that when common people learned about the inheritability of talent, they would voluntarily cease to have children. He also believed that people should be treated with "all kindness" as long as they forsook procreation. If they did not, however, "such persons would be considered as enemies to the State, and to have forfeited all claims to kindness."

Until the end of his life, in 1911, Galton continued to publish papers and speak publicly proselytizing for eugenics. He was such a gifted communicator that he captured the imagination and fervor of scientists, policymakers, notable figures, and regular citizens. In 1904, Galton concluded a lecture to the Sociological Society held at London University by saying that academics should eventually accept the tenets of eugenics "as a fact" and then give "serious consideration" to the practical development of the field. Eugenics, he said, should enter the "national conscience, like a new religion . . . for eugenics co-operate with the workings of nature by securing that humanity shall be represented by the fittest races. What nature does blindly, slowly, and ruthlessly, man may do providently, quickly, and kindly."

H. G. Wells, who published comments on Galton's remarks, claimed to have more faith in negative than in positive eugenics. "The way of nature has always been to slay the hindmost, and there is still no other way, unless we can prevent those who would become the hindmost being born." Rather ominously and prophetically, Wells went on to add, "It is in the sterilization of failures, and not in the selection of successes for breeding, that the possibility of an improvement of the human stock lies."

George Bernard Shaw expressed his support for eugenics, too, although he was less keen on the negative type. "It is worth pointing out that we never hesitate to carry out the negative side of eugenics with considerable zest, both on the scaffold and on the battlefield.

We have never deliberately called a human being into existence for the sake of civilization; but we have wiped out millions. We kill a Tibetan regardless of expense, and in defiance of our religion, to clear the way to Lhassa for the Englishman; but we take no really scientific steps to secure that the Englishman when he gets there, will be able to live up to our assumption of his superiority."

Galton hoped that his Anthropometric Laboratory moved him closer to achieving his eugenic visions. By the 1880s, he was arguing that mobile laboratories should be set up throughout the country, testing students and young men and women, wading through the human chaff to find those worthy of reproduction.

Rather than the actual testing methods and tools developed for the Anthropometric Laboratory, Francis Galton's greatest contribution was to statistics. He had been developing novel statistical methods long before his lab, but the task of working through the mountain of data it produced helped him to work through mathematical problems he had been struggling with for years. In 1889 he published the book *Natural Inheritance*, which laid out his statistical work of the previous dozen years: most notably the mathematics underlying regression analysis and the correlation coefficient.

Confronted by complicated data sets with variables he presumed to be interdependent and related (for instance, people's physical measurements; and the ability to hear, see, and strike), Galton found mid- to late-nineteenth-century statistics of little help. While statistics certainly existed at that time, it was not a stand-alone field as we know it today, nor did the word *statistics* necessarily have the same mathematical connotation it does now. Of the European countries this was particularly true in Britain, where Galton worked. True, there was a London Statistical Society, but it was more intent on gathering political information than on pursuing mathematically based analyses. And while scientists on the Continent did use statistics in the mathematical sense, they had very different research goals from Galton's. European physicists and astronomers, for instance, mainly employed statistics to make sophisticated estimates of errors when measuring something they did not have direct access to, such as planets and stars. They could usually, however, take repeated measurements of the celestial body in question, and thus their statistics could estimate a "probable error," usually by taking the mean of these measurements.

Galton had the statistics of probable error at his disposal, but his need for statistics was very different from the other Europeans'. While those on the Continent were trying to nail down error to get a truer measurement of celestial bodies, Galton was actually interested in the very differences—the variations or "errors"—his lab measurements produced. In other words, he was interested in how abilities were distributed among people, which he assumed was the result of genetics, not error.

Galton also wanted to understand, with mathematical precision, how ability was inherited, something that had not been attempted before. To do this, he had to measure the tendency of variables to be related. Surprisingly, no one had ever tried to do this. A scientist interested in genetics, though, would see the need immediately; after all, everyone knows that tall men tended to produce tall sons, but how strong was that tendency?

Ultimately, Galton wanted to prove that people's success in life correlated with their performance in his lab. By the 1880s, Galton had already introduced novel and handy statistical ideas—for instance, the rank ordering of subjects and percentiles—but he needed something more sophisticated to compare the variables produced by the Anthropometric Laboratory. He knew how swiftly people could strike an object and the strength of their pull, for instance. He knew, as well, the examinees' professions, because they had filled out biographical information on cards at the International Health Exhibition booth. But he did not know whether there was any correlation between performing well on the seventeen tasks and success in life, or even if each of the tasks was correlated with another. A strong correlation between success and the tasks in the booth was the linchpin of Galton's neurological efficiency theories, and without proving it statistically he simply had a pile of measurements of unknowable worth. Who is to say that differentiating between shades of green is a worthwhile measurement unless the people who are good at it are more successful in life than those who are not?

The tools of error theory would not help, but Galton's genius for math would lead him to develop the ideas that could, most notably the correlation coefficient. Although it took Galton's disciples to perfect the correlation coefficient, this mathematical invention allowed scientists and statisticians to measure the relatedness of two variables for the first time. Galton was so ahead of his time that it took decades for the scientific world to understand the import of his shift in focus from error theory to the study of the relatedness of variables. In fact, from the 1860s to the 1890s Galton toiled alone on his new statistics, with only the occasional help of mathematicians he managed to press into service.

Ironically, however, Galton's statistical inventions would be the downfall of the field he had created. They would prove that the physiological tests of the sort Galton had used in his Anthropometric Laboratory were not correlated with each other or with measures of worldly success. Less than twenty years after the Anthropometric Laboratory, the correlation coefficient would bring the entire field of "mental testing," as it became known, to an ungainly end.

One of Galton's most ardent supporters was James Cattell, an American who received his Ph.D. in Leipzig, Germany, in the 1880s and who met Galton while studying medicine for a brief time at Cambridge University. Galton hugely impressed Cattell— he called him "the greatest man I have ever known"—and Cattell was very taken with his Anthropometric Laboratory. Cattell had spent three years in Leipzig measuring people's reaction times, but almost mindlessly, for he hadn't extracted any psychological meaning from the test results. He was measuring for measuring's sake. The Anthropometric Laboratory and the study of human differences, as Galton's field became known, offered Cattell a way to put three years of mechanical measuring to use.

Cattell returned to the United States and is largely responsible for bringing Galton's work in anthropometry to America. At the University of Pennsylvania and later Columbia University, where he was a professor in the 1890s, Cattell created batteries of tests based on Galton's Anthropometric Laboratory and urged students and the public alike to take them. He improved upon Galton's devices and dropped many of the simple body measurements that had been included in the health exhibition lab. Cattell included the dynamometer, which measured hand-squeezing strength. Among other tasks, he asked examinees to judge ten-second intervals without reference to a watch or a clock and to bisect a fifty-centimeter line simply by eyeballing it. He even pressed a rubber tip against examinees' foreheads with progressive force until they showed or reported signs of pain, theorizing that people who were more sensitive to pain were more neurologically efficient (and therefore more naturally able).

At the end of the nineteenth century, the United States was ready for Cattell and his mental tests. In the antebellum years, there had been a tradition of itinerant phrenologists who would travel the country offering their services. For a fee they would analyze a client's head—its shape, size, and unique bumps—and offer advice on career and marriage. They would tell a client of the strengths and weaknesses of his character, and they were often sought after to give expert opinion when a family needed it, much like a therapist or guidance counselor today.

Although phrenology paved the way for physiologically based mental testing, by the 1890s Americans largely believed phrenologists to be quacks. And by the turn of the century, many Americans were searching for structural solutions to their societal problems, rather than seeking the individual advice phrenologists peddled. While some psychologists were therapists to individuals, in the late nineteenth century an American experimental and scientific psychology emerged based on a German model. Psychology began to market itself as a field that could be relied on to solve societal problems—in schools and ports of immigration and on the streets.

Psychologists claimed to have the tool—the mental test—that could help sort people in a newly industrialized, complicated society, and businessmen and educators began paying attention. As a result, a cottage industry of mental testing laboratories arose in Europe and in the United States in the 1880s and 1890s. The problem was, most psychologists—at least the cautious and prudent ones—were not quite sure how mental tests worked. They tested something, but were mental exams really that helpful?

James Cattell assumed that psychologists were on to something; they just had to figure out what. He compared their situation to that of the men working in electricity fifty years previously; at that time, investigators "believed that practical applications would be made, but knew that their first duty was to obtain more exact knowledge."

Other testers more outrageously proclaimed the usefulness and predictive powers of the physiological tests. One Boston man established a career guidance school and promised to match young men to careers by testing their "delicacy of touch, nerve, sight and hearing reactions, association time, etc."

Eventually, though, psychologists began to question the usefulness of mental tests based on physical tasks. Galton's correlation coefficient, too, had become refined by the 1890s, giving scientists a means to judge statistically whether the exams were testing anything worthwhile. The growing skepticism and improved statistics spelled doom for mental tests of the physiological sort. In fact, it was one of Cattell's graduate students who delivered the fatal blow. Cattell himself was, if not quite innumerate, pretty close to it: he would often add and subtract incorrectly. He knew, though, that his idol, Francis Galton, had created statistical tools that could be useful in analyzing his mental test data. Therefore at the end of the 1890s (after a decade of meticulously testing Columbia students and members of the public), Cattell confidently asked a graduate student named Clark Wissler to study the correlations between his physical tests and mental ability. Complying, the mathematically adept Wissler examined whether students who had performed well on Cattell's mental tests were also good students, the most reliable indicator of mental ability around.

Devastated does not do justice to how Cattell must have felt upon hearing Wissler's findings. After years of research and an entire career and professional reputation based on experimental psychology, he learned from Wissler that there was no significant relationship between his mental tests and academic performance.

By the turn of the century, correlations were represented numerically, as they are today, with +1 equaling a perfect positive relationship and −1 defining a perfect negative relationship between variables. A result of zero (0) indicates that there is no relationship between the variables at all, and of course there are many degrees of relationship between +1 and −1. People in the hard sciences, such as physics, tend to look for higher correlations than they do in the social sciences, but Wissler's numbers were too low for even psychologists to argue that the various measurements were meaningfully related. "Class standing correlated −.02 with reaction time, +.02 with color naming, and −.08 with" hand strength. These are trivial levels of correlation, and likely to have been produced by mere chance when in fact there is no correlation. Wissler even analyzed student head size, and it was no better at predicting academic success. In fact, mental tests did not even correlate with each other. The correlation between reaction time and color naming, for instance, was −.15. The correlation between color naming and hand movement speed was +.19.

Like a group of flat-Earth advocates in the age of satellite imagery, mental testers were doomed by advances in science—advances that Galton himself had put into motion. Wissler, having devastated the field, perhaps wisely opted to become an anthropologist. Cattell, for his part, gave up experimental psychology, relegating himself to administration, editing *Science* magazine, and running a company he called the Psychological Corporation.

Despite the demise of his testing methods before his death, however, Francis Galton remained widely respected and admired. One day in June 1909, when Galton was an infirm old man at home alone, Prime Minister Herbert Asquith—like Gladstone, another great British Liberal—sent him a confidential letter saying that Galton was to "receive the honour of Knighthood on his Majesty's approaching birthday."

In a letter of his own to a niece, Galton joked, "I have to live until November 9 and then shall blossom." Francis Galton managed to live two years more, but eugenics and one of its prime tools, the intelligence test, would continue to flourish well into the future.

Chapter 3

The Birth of Modern Intelligence Tests

At the turn of the twentieth century, the intelligence test was saved by Alfred Binet, a Frenchman who fell into psychology quite by accident and who failed miserably, repeatedly, and publicly until he created the exams that are the foundation of intelligence tests today. At age twenty-two, Binet convalesced in Paris's Bibliothèque Nationale after a nervous breakdown—a rather fitting recuperative locale for a young, independently wealthy intellectual. His emotional collapse came after years of educational meandering and uninspired study. Like many young men and women who are presented with too much choice and not enough direction, Binet had first been lured into law, a field that promised stability and respect, or at the very least something to do. He even earned his license to practice, but could not bring himself to actually work as a lawyer, concluding that law was "the career of men who have not yet chosen a vocation."

Binet fled the law and entered medical school, but couldn't tolerate the operating theater. It wasn't so much the blood and guts that put him off, but rather the memories of a sadistic physician father who had forced him to touch a cadaver when he was a small boy, with the intention of "curing" young Alfred of his shyness.

During his recuperative stay in the library, Binet became fascinated by psychology. Binet learned informally about the field on his own by reading and doing, though his doing was initially a disaster. He turned out to be abysmally bad at experimental psychology—at least initially. And his failures were grand, public, and humiliating.

Over a period of twenty years he published articles based on poorly constructed experiments that severely damaged his reputation. In particular, he conducted a terribly thought-out experiment involving a beautiful neurotic woman, a large horseshoe magnet, and hypnosis, which brought him mockery in serious journals. Part of Binet's problem was actually a strength: he was such a good writer that he got published more readily than his scientific methods warranted. Astonishingly, out of this personal and professional mess emerged a man who is now considered a giant in the history of psychology. As a result of his experiences, Binet also would become scientifically more rigorous and more conservative in his conclusions.

In the late 1880s, Binet began studying his two young daughters, Madeleine and Alice, who were both under age five. He published three papers about them, and while the papers were not recognized as groundbreaking at the time, they were in fact signal contributions to child psychology and the future field of intelligence testing. Like many parents, Binet noticed that his two daughters had very different personalities from an early age. When Madeleine "was learning to walk, she did not leave one support until she had discovered another near at hand to which she could direct herself." Alice, "on the other hand, advanced into empty space without any attention to the consequences."

Binet used the psychology of his day, some of it based on Galton and Cattell's work, to measure his children's capabilities and differences. He measured their hand movements and reaction times, their ability to recognize that lines were of different lengths, and their performance on many other tasks. Binet then compared Madeleine and Alice's results to adult performance on the tasks and discovered that his two daughters could perform as well as the adults when the tasks were simple. And when the children concentrated, which they had problems doing much of the time (no surprise to anyone who has had young children), their response times were often the same as adults'. This led Binet to conclude that one key difference between children and adults was the ability to concentrate, and that attention was key to the development of intelligence. This may now not sound like much of an insight, but it was of great importance in the development of psychology. All of a sudden, a psychologist was thinking about the higher mental processes behind physical tasks. And it took a man interested in children to think about human ability in this way.

Binet discovered that on tests that involved sensory acuity, such as comparing the length of parallel lines or sizes of angles, his daughters even outperformed adults. At the same time, though, his daughters' language was not as developed, sophisticated, or facile as adults'. The children could match colors almost as quickly as an adult, but they weren't as fast at naming them. His daughters' understanding of words, too, was functional and crude. When he asked them to define what a knife was, for instance, they just said it was used "to cut meat." Similarly, boxes were to "put candies inside," "A snail is to step on," and "A dog bites."

Clearly, if children could score as well as adults on sensory acuity tests, and if their reaction times occasionally equaled adults', then physiological tests aimed at measuring mental ability were misdirected. Mental tests ought to be able to distinguish between children and adults, Binet reasoned, and Galton and Cattell's tests did not. Henceforth IQ tests, thanks to Madeleine and Alice, would focus on higher reasoning, language, abstract thinking, and complex cognitive abilities.

After Binet, testers came to believe that the center of mental ability was in the brain and that they should be measuring the fruits of that organ. No more peering at snippets of the Church of England's Bible through a sickle-shaped box to test visual acuity, as Galton had his subjects do at the International Health Exhibition. No more measuring of arm spans or pressing rubber tips against foreheads to discover the pain threshold, as Cattell did. After Binet's test, psychologists focused more narrowly on intelligence rather than on a range of intellectual traits that determined success or failure in life, and they realized that to measure it they should test thinking. Binet's insights were a massive breakthrough.

Despite this theoretical breakthrough, Binet struggled without success during the 1890s to devise a two-hour exam that would test intelligence. Just after the turn of the century, though, Binet's interests in testing happened to coincide with an issue of French national concern. The French government passed a law requiring all school-age children to receive several years of education. One side effect of universal education laws was that, suddenly, mentally handicapped children were attending school. Up to this point, re-tarded children had simply stopped attending school when it became apparent they couldn't keep up with their classmates—or their parents had never bothered to send them to school at all. Now, educators and school administrators not only had to educate retarded kids, they also had to identify them. But they lacked reliable diagnostic tools for deciding who was and who was not retarded, and if the former, to what degree. The French government therefore created a commission to explore the matter, and it appointed Binet a commissioner.

The need for these diagnostic tools in France a hundred years ago led to the first modern intelligence test, published by Binet and fellow researcher Théodore Simon in 1905. In the test, Binet was able to put into practice all he had begun to figure out since testing little Madeleine and Alice. In creating the 1905 test, Binet and Simon initially floundered. They began with a scattershot approach, throwing heaps of questions at a group of "normally" developed children, as well as at a separate group that teachers and doctors alike had found unquestionably subnormal. Binet discovered that while these two groups of children scored differently on average, on particular questions some kids in the "subnormal" group did better than some in the normal group. That is, the groups' performances overlapped, which reduced the efficacy of the questions as a diagnostic tool.

Eventually Binet and Simon hit upon an idea that makes intuitive sense; they took the age of the child into account. It didn't matter if both mentally handicapped and typical kids could answer a particular question correctly; what mattered was the age at which they could answer the question. Binet and Simon therefore decided to develop questions that the so-called normal children could answer at an earlier age than their retarded counterparts.

In their first 1905 test, Binet and Simon devised thirty questions of increasing difficulty. Examinees would have to be severely mentally retarded to fail the first few tasks. The first was merely for the student to keep his eyes on a lighted match that the tester moved around. Binet and Simon were testing, simply and beautifully, the basic ability to concentrate. The next tasks were to distinguish a piece of dark chocolate from a white piece of wood (and eat the correct one), unwrap a candy, and shake hands with the tester. Binet and Simon found that the developmentally normal children could do these first, most basic tasks by age two. The most severely retarded children, regardless of their age, could not, and were officially labeled idiots.

In the next series of progressively more difficult tasks, children had to name different parts of the body; they had to define, only in a functional way, certain household words such as *fork*, *horse*, and *mama*; and they had to repeat back to the examiner numbers and simple sentences. Average five-year-olds could do these tasks. Imbeciles, those at the next level of retardation, could go no farther, regardless of their actual age.

The final group of questions, devised so that average five- to eleven-year-olds could answer them, were significantly harder and more abstract. For example, they required children to describe the differences between objects, such as paper and cardboard. They had to draw designs from memory, to rank identical-looking objects by their different weights, and to come up with words that rhymed with *obeisance*. The *débiles* (morons), the highest grade of retarded, didn't make it this far, only getting a few of the group of questions correct.

Binet and Simon's decision to compare mental age with chronological age gave teachers a tool they could use. If a student scored too far below his chronological age on the Binet-Simon exam, it indicated that he might have developmental difficulties. Binet and Simon also derived a means for arriving at a numerical result from each exam. A child who answered correctly all the questions that a six-year-old should be able to answer was given a score of 6, plus whatever additional questions he got correct toward the seven-year mark. As a result, children could end up with results calculated to a decimal point (6.2, for example). This made Binet uncomfortable, for he feared that his tests would seem more precise and scientific than they actually were.

"It must be well understood that these fractions in so delicate an appreciation do not merit absolute confidence, because they will vary noticeably from one examination to another," he wrote.

Unlike many of the psychologists who were to follow him, Binet also didn't believe that he was measuring a fixed quantity of intelligence. Intelligence testing wasn't the same as measuring and comparing wooden beams, where "one is six meters long, one seven, the other eight," Binet wrote. When it comes to wooden beams, "one really measures," but in testing how many digits people can remember, who knows "whether the difference between a recall of six digits and a recall of seven digits is or is not equal to the difference between the recall of seven digits and the recall of eight."

The young Alfred Binet, who had wielded a magnet over a hypnotized hysteric, had by middle age matured into a cautious and rigorous scientist. He had also finally become successful and respected. But in one of the most unfortunate twists in the history of intelligence testing, Francis Galton's eugenics theory would attach itself to Binet's superior testing methods.

* * *

At roughly the same time that Alfred Binet was working on his new kind of test, an Englishman named Charles Spearman made a theoretical breakthrough that would greatly help intelligence testers bind eugenics theory to Binet's testing approach. Spearman, an English army officer, had studied psychology in Germany. During the second Boer War (1899–1902), he was stationed on the English Channel Island of Guernsey—rather far from the action in South Africa, though Spearman later described it as "a position of some importance, owing to the dubious attitude of France at that critical period."

Being clear of the action had its advantages. His post was rather handily near "a little village school," and, "inspired" by Francis Galton's writings, Spearman started experimenting on the students there. To discover whether different intellectual abilities were correlated with each other and with sensory discrimination, he undertook a study similar to that of James Cattell and Clark Wissler at Columbia University (although he was unaware of their study at the time). But unlike these researchers, he discovered that there were significant statistical relationships between various intellectual and sensory abilities, such as grades in various classes (classics, French, English, math) and the ability to discern different musical pitches and to differentiate between varying weights.

Most importantly, Spearman found that the more that thinking was involved in the endeavor—for example, the study of classics requires more thinking than does differentiating musical pitch—the better it predicted other activities that involved thought. Thus, classics grades correlated quite strongly with grades in French, English, and math (in descending order), and not as strongly with grades in music. From these results, and subsequent studies elsewhere, Spearman postulated that there must be a "general intelligence" that operates within everyone that is important whenever thinking is required.

Most psychologists thereafter have believed that a person's level of g (the field's abbreviation for *general intelligence*) affects his ability to argue with his mother, devise witty ad copy, study physics, or play soccer. But as Spearman's experiment on Guernsey indicated, g was measurably more important in some activities than in others. Classics, for instance, was the best predictor of other grades, so Spearman considered that endeavor to be saturated with g. To be a good soccer player, on the other hand, requires more "specific intelligence"—smarts that are specific to the sport rather than general intelligence. Spearman thought of this as a two-factor theory of intelligence: general and specific.

Spearman had a theory, but no exam to test intelligence. He did, however, believe that the best way to test g was "by measuring promiscuously any large number of different abilities and pooling the results together." The average of these various tests, he thought, would approximately measure people's general intelligence. The method might seem random, Spearman wrote, but it was the best way to get at people's innate ability.

"In such wise this principle of making a hotchpotch, which might seem to be the most arbitrary and meaningless procedure imaginable, had really a profound theoretical basis and a supremely practical utility."

With the results of these "hotchpotch" tests of various abilities, decisions could be made about people based on their innate worth. "One can . . . conceive the establishment of a minimum index [of g] to qualify for parliamentary vote, and above all, for the right to have offspring." Spearman himself wasn't too concerned with such practical applications, but it's easy to predict that other eugenics thinkers would latch on to such ideas.

In 1905, just a year after Spearman first published his two-factor theory of intelligence, Alfred Binet and his partner Théodore Simon independently provided just such a "hotchpotch" test of mixed and varied test questions that resulted in a combined score. Moreover, their new test measured thinking, rather than sensory acuity, which comported with Spearman's ideas on how to measure general intelligence. Although Binet and Simon themselves did not believe that their tests measured a singular, innate intelligence, the majority of psychology would, thanks to Spearman's experiments and two-factor intelligence theory. This fusing of multisubject testing style and the concept of general intelligence has dominated psychology ever since, although there has always been a minority critical of this approach.

Chapter 4

America Discovers Intelligence Tests

Despite Alfred Binet's new intelligence test and his subsequent fame as an experimental psychologist (he eventually had his own psychology journal and a laboratory at the Sorbonne), his intelligence tests remained unknown in the United States for several years after he had published them. Somehow, no American had noticed his 1905 test, or if anyone did, he wasn't very impressed. It took an American troubled by the same problem—diagnosing mentally handicapped children—to discover Binet's tests and bring them over the Atlantic. And it was in America, with its crush of new citizens, and schools bursting with a motley mix of new students, where intelligence tests would really take root.

"My getting hold of Binet's work was the result of a series of lucky accidents," Henry Herbert Goddard wrote many years after the discovery and promotion of Binet's tests had made him famous. "Somehow there came into my hands a single printed sheet signed by an unknown Belgian by the name of M. C. Schuyten. Luckily I did not throw it in the waste basket."

At the time he happened upon this single sheet of paper, Goddard was an unknown forty-one-year-old New Jersey psychologist on the fringe of his profession. He was more an educator than a research psychologist, having worked at West Chester Normal School, in Pennsylvania, at the turn of the century. By 1906 Goddard was an isolated one-man psychology research department at the Training School for Feeble-Minded Girls and Boys in Vineland, New Jersey.

Goddard's school was a backwater of psychology. Physically, it was nothing but a few cottages around a pitched-roof administrative building set in the flat agricultural fields of southern New Jersey. It was just about the most unlikely place to spawn a movement. Yet the school's intelligence testing practices would radically alter how modern industrialized societies process people in schools, militaries, businesses, and, in certain instances, also how people are treated in medicine and courts of law.

Vineland was a place for educators who believed with religious conviction in the school's mission of training mentally handicapped kids. Unlike its depressing state-run institutional counterparts that housed a thousand or more children in big, impersonal buildings, Vineland was small—only two hundred or three hundred students at a time lived on campus—and suffused with an upbeat Christian ethos. Its motto was "Happiness first, and all else will follow."

"We have a little secret society in which the password is, 'We belong,' and the signal is a smile," said Edward Johnstone, the school's superintendent. "Wherever we go about the school, if anyone looks cross or sad, someone is sure to look at you and smile in your face, saying, 'Do you belong?' and you simply have to smile back because you are just as human as they are."

At Johnstone's invitation, Henry Goddard first visited this "Village of Happiness" in 1900. Goddard had never worked with feebleminded children before, but Johnstone noticed that Goddard was immediately at ease with them. Goddard spoke, Johnstone thought, as if he "were accustomed to talking to the feebleminded." It seems likely that Goddard could relate to Vineland's young, troubled, and oft-ignored charges because he himself had had a terribly lonely childhood. His father had died when he was young, and his mother became desperately poor and seized with religion. She packed him off to Quaker boarding school in Providence at age twelve while she visited Quaker meetings throughout the world. Despite the privileged, manicured school setting, the poor scholarship boy described his experience as "Quaker Jail."

In 1906 Johnstone asked Goddard to set up a psychology laboratory at Vineland. Although Vineland was obscure, the job offered Goddard a way out of pedagogy and into research, and he took it. In September 1906, he arrived at a big, empty space that was to be his laboratory. His first task was to cobble together with a meager budget the scientific equipment of his day. The machines Goddard wrote about in his diary reflect a technology and techniques based very much on the approaches of the Galton and Cattell era, despite their rejection at Columbia University years earlier. Goddard wrote about working on his ergograph, a contraption with pulleys and weights that could measure muscle power.

"Fixed an electrical attachment to metronome," he also wrote in one almost ominous-sounding diary entry: "This is used to test will power." He bought or assembled a spirometer for testing lung capacity, an automatograph (consisting of a wooden board on which subjects placed their arms, and a stylus that measured their involuntary movements), and a dynamometer to measure hand strength.

But Goddard discovered that working with feebleminded children had its peculiar difficulties. Unlike other children or university students, many of Goddard's kids could not speak or follow directions. Worse, even when he was able to take measurements, he had nothing to compare his results to. Goddard was measuring without a yardstick: there were no published data sets defining how normal or subnormal children scored on these various tasks.

In the end, Goddard, like Binet and Cattell before him, came to realize that physiological examinations didn't work. While Cattell had discovered this by the use of nascent statistical methods, Goddard came to his conclusion in a rougher, ad hoc manner. After measuring his students as best he could on his various machines, he asked Vineland teachers to assess them. Based on years of working with and living alongside the students, the teachers knew the kids well, and their assessments of their abilities matched Goddard's measurements not at all.

At this stage, American mental testing was stagnant and completely ineffective. Despite the fact that Cattell had learned of his methods' uselessness years earlier, no useful alternatives had been invented, and the old ones were still being mindlessly applied. In 1908, with nowhere else to turn, Goddard got on a ship and traveled to Europe to see what scientists and educators there had to offer. What he found, however, initially depressed him, for there were fewer institutions for the feebleminded there than he had hoped.

"No imbecile asylums in France, no kindergartens in Germany, no Christians in Palestine! It is the same old story," he noted in his diary.

He didn't even bother to visit the famous Alfred Binet and his laboratory, because other French psychologists had warned him off. "Binet's lab. is largely a myth," was another of his entries. The problem was, although Binet had the best tests around, he was also a hothead with strongly held views, which had hurt his professional standing and the dissemination of his ideas. As a result, Goddard didn't learn about the new tests directly from their author.

Goddard did learn about Binet's 1905 test on this trip, however, from an unknown Belgian, who handed him a single sheet of paper describing Binet's work and some of his questions. The contents of that page would transform Goddard from an unknown American psychologist in rural New Jersey into a world-famous psychologist.

In the end, Goddard returned to New Jersey with what he had set out to Europe to find: a new tool for diagnosing the feebleminded. He translated Binet's questions into English and tried them out on Vineland's students. To test the efficacy of his new tool, he compared exam results with teacher assessments, as he had with measurements taken from his machines, and was far more impressed with the results. Goddard had found his diagnostic tool. The difference between Binet and Goddard, though, was that Binet did not believe he was testing fixed, inherited intelligence, while Goddard did. He took a rough social measurement—teacher opinions—and claimed that it validated a tool for measuring something biological, called intelligence.

The effects of such a mental leap might not have been so far-reaching had Binet's translated "scale" of intelligence not fit pressing societal needs so perfectly. In the early twentieth century, America desperately required tools to categorize people in a systematic, almost automated and mechanical way.

Goddard first went to work to persuade the field of medicine to use his new exam. Doctors at the turn of the twentieth century were hopeless at diagnosing the mentally handicapped. Surprisingly, they had not focused on the retarded very much until fairly recently, because insanity had always been more fascinating. Why study the dumb when you can focus on the crazy? We've all heard of Bedlam, the venerable English insane asylum, but there is no famous equivalent institution for dim people. Characters like Forest Gump do appear in popular literature, but the insane—the psychopathic killer, the genius artist afflicted with visions, the brilliant mad scientist—crop up with more frequency than does the wise idiot. People have traditionally made links among insanity, genius, and creativity, but the village idiot is often ignored. He's just plain dumb (although, as the term "village idiot" indicates, people have been aware of subnormal intelligence for a long time).

It took French doctors at the time of the Enlightenment to study idiocy with any rigor, but they didn't make much headway. They had nomenclature and not much more, and this state of affairs continued to the end of the nineteenth century. Alfred Binet had very little patience for doctors' diagnostic terms and he let them know it, which is one reason why that profession never much liked him.

"The vagueness of their formulas reveals the vagueness of their ideas. They cling to characteristics which are by 'more or less,' and they permit themselves to be guided by a subjective impression which they do not seem to think necessary to analyze," Binet wrote.

Doctors of the time described children with small heads as microcephalic, those with abnormally large skulls as hydrocephalic (literally, water on the brain). They talked of cretins, epileptics, cripples, and "Mongolians" who had eyes that reminded them of Asians. But none of these terms was very precise, and they often didn't convey information about underlying pathology. They were simple physical descriptions.

Most puzzling of all to doctors, educators, and psychologists were the people who bore no outward markings of sickness or deficiency but who were cognitively inadequate for some unknown reason. Why couldn't some kids read no matter how much they were tutored? Why was a child socially maladroit and inept at almost all subjects at school but terrific at calculating vast sums in his head? At the turn of the twentieth century, doctors who worked at institutions that housed these populations could not agree on what their own nomenclature meant.

Binet argued that doctors had failed to comprehend that mental deficiency was the result of psychological problems, not physical ones. Therefore, the condition of mental subnormality, Binet argued, must be described in psychological, not physical, terms. For doctors and most everyone else, this was new.

American doctors had taken their cue from the French, and as a result the former were no good at classifying the mentally handicapped, either. Idiots and imbeciles, the Association of Medical Officers stated in 1877, were people with "a want of natural and harmonious development of the mental, active and moral powers." This wasn't a very useful definition if you had two hundred or three hundred feebleminded students to organize and study, as Goddard did at Vineland.

After a year of trying Binet's scale out on Vineland students, Goddard was ready to talk about it to American institutional doctors who worked with the feebleminded. It was an important step for, in the early twentieth century, institutes for the feebleminded were still primarily doctors' demesnes. Psychologists were often viewed as poorly trained upstarts. Luckily for him and for American psychology, Goddard's subtle, nonthreatening, and amiable approach proved far more effective at persuading doctors to adopt a new analytical approach than did Binet's abrasive and accusatory style. As a result, psychology, a brash young profession, would gain power in America's institutions for the retarded. It might not seem like much, but it was a small beachhead for a profession desperately looking to invade new territory.

At the 1909 meeting of the American Association for the Study of the Feeble-Minded, instead of going on the attack, Goddard voiced concerns that "we," meaning himself and all the doctors present, harbor about the present system of diagnosing the feeble-minded. It was as politically astute as it was true: many doctors were frustrated with their inability to quickly and effectively diagnose their patients. Goddard simply and tentatively described Binet's ideas as a possible "set of mental tests which might serve as a basis for [a new] classification."

Goddard's approach was immediately received warmly. "Here is a case of microcephalis or hydrocephalis—what does it mean?" a doctor asked the group rhetorically after Goddard was through speaking. They were terms that describe size only, he felt, and did not describe any particular sickness. Similarly, "Mongolian," he continued, "does not mean anything definite pathologically, it does not suggest any underlying condition. We have no intelligent pathological classification at present."

Instead of becoming angry at a finger-pointing psychologist in their midst, the doctors realized he was right and formed a committee to find better diagnostic tools. The doctors on the committee went away and promptly forgot about the matter (after all, who cares about committee work?), which actually helped Goddard. Between the annual meetings, Goddard was the only person to put forward any ideas about the classification of the mentally subnormal. In fact, Goddard was the only member of the committee to attend the association's next meeting, in 1910. This clearly had huge advantages: when asked to report to the association at large, one year after first introducing Binet's tests and all the more a believer, Goddard merely stated his own views clearly and forcefully as the opinion of the committee.

He supported his claims with a paper, "Four Hundred Feeble-Minded Children Classified by the Binet Method," in which he expanded on the method of relying on teacher impressions to corroborate his new tests. One day after his presentation, the association adopted the Binet tests as the means of classifying the feebleminded. What a Trojan horse! Goddard had won and, unbeknownst to the medical profession, so had psychology. The measuring of minds, at least feeble ones, was about to pass from doctors' hands to psychologists'.

Goddard's achievement was immense. For the first time, institutional doctors had a shared vocabulary about the feebleminded and a uniform way of measuring mental deficiency. It seems almost too obvious to state now (which just proves Goddard's success), but the mentally handicapped lacked sufficient intelligence, and this lack was measured by an intelligence test. Doctors now even had a way of defining intelligence: scores on an intelligence test. An "idiot" was a person who performed worse than the average two-year-old. An "imbecile" scored between the mental ages of three and seven. And the highest degree of feeblemindedness (not *débile* in the States, as it was in France, but "moron," a term coined by Goddard, a softer euphemism for "fool," which he felt was too harsh a word) scored between the mental ages of eight and twelve.

The idea made intuitive sense to doctors. As Dr. A. C. Rogers, a superintendent of an institute near Minneapolis, said, "Who is there that does not have a mental picture, always in view, of the activities and capacities of normal children at different ages? What more natural and rational than to compare the mind, backward in development, with a normal one?"

It was the first step in the way people in general, not just specialists, would think about intelligence in everyday life.

"Mental testing produced a change in the conceptual landscape," wrote psychologist Franz Samelson in the 1970s, "it transformed the idea of intelligence, itself a descendant of the idea of reason, from an amorphous, creative force to an 'objective' yet clearly value-laden dimension of individual differences consisting essentially, or 'operationally,' of getting the right answer on more or less clever little problems."

In America, this cultural sea change began with Goddard's subtle, socially adroit powers of persuasion at the American Association for the Study of the Feeble-Minded. But he also got lucky: just as he was promoting his new French tests, there was a great need for them, both perceived and real.

In the early twentieth century, mentally inferior people seemed to lurk everywhere, often undetected and burdening society with their poverty, prostitution, and crimes of every nature. At about this time, people began to link intelligence with moral agency, "the girl problem" (sexually active single women), and racial purity. That is, they believed that retarded people, because of their low intelligence, were more likely to commit crimes and be social burdens. As a result, while "idiot schools" in America had been around since the 1850s, institutions for the feebleminded became more important in the early 1900s as instruments for social protection from the dangerous.

As the medical superintendent of California's Sonoma State Hospital testified to a state commission on lunacy in 1904, "I do not believe that mental defectives have received the consideration from the State accorded to the insane and criminal class and yet public safety demands that these people be housed and cared for to prevent their multiplying their kind, as well as to cut off the source of supply that helps to fill our jails, reformatories, and insane asylums."

Henry Herbert Goddard found and translated Alfred Binet's tests at the right historical moment—just in time to capitalize on this fear of the feebleminded. He and other intelligence testers would be at the forefront of this movement to segregate the feebleminded, for they had a tool to penetrate people's exterior, to determine scientifically who was normal and who was feebleminded.

Underpinning the eugenics movement was a fallacious belief that parents passed down a single gene for feeblemindedness. Henry Goddard likened feeblemindedness to hair color. "No amount of education or good environment can change a feebleminded individual into a normal one, any more than it can change a red-haired stock into a black-haired stock," he wrote.

More than any other publication, Goddard's 1912 *The Kallikak Family: A Study in the Heredity of Feeble-Mindedness* ratcheted up fears of the "menace of the feebleminded" and bolstered eugenics' seemingly scientific footing. The book made Goddard famous and led to the vilification of the mentally handicapped for years in lay and scientific minds alike throughout the world. In it, Goddard purportedly proved that Deborah Kallikak, a pseudonym for a young woman at his New Jersey Vineland Training School, was the product of six generations of mainly feebleminded ancestors. These ancestors, Goddard argued, should have been stopped from passing along this one gene for feeblemindedness to poor, young, and pretty Deborah.

Goddard based his research for the book largely on the work of a zealous and imaginative fieldworker he employed for years named Elizabeth Kite, a woman who rather dubiously managed to ascertain the intelligence of 480 of the girl's relatives, most of whom were dead. Kite's methods were indirect in the extreme: she often couldn't administer IQ tests to Kallikak's relations directly, so she ascertained and defined intelligence by their behavior, but if even this were not possible, she relied on mere reputation for behavior and ability. To gather this information Kite zigzagged across New Jersey interviewing living Kallikaks and, to gauge the intelligence of the dead, she relied on families' memories, written records of occupation, marital status, health, and even, in one instance, on the condition of heirloom furniture.

Kite loved her work, for as she put it, "even the defective has experienced the truth of the saying that it is more blessed to give than to receive." But she didn't even tell her kind, if defective, hosts that the real purpose of her visits was to assess their intelligence. Whipping out a Binet test would have blown her cover, so her intelligence estimates had to be made during social interaction. Kite was aware that her methods weren't very scientific. "Subjective appreciation of mental states," she admitted, "in spite of the fact that Binet rigorously opposes, and in season and out of season reiterates his antagonism to this method—does enter into the diagnosis of most cases." Kite visited people and winged it, labeling them genetically "normal" or "feebleminded" as she deemed appropriate; and her boss, Henry Goddard, signed off on the methodology.

She certainly couldn't administer a Binet test to the dead, either, but Kite felt certain that she had overcome the obstacles of the great beyond in a scientific manner. "After some experience," Goddard wrote in *The Kallikak Family*, "the field worker becomes expert in inferring the [mental] condition of those persons who are not seen, from the similarity of the language used in describing them to that used in describing persons whom she has seen." In other words, people talked about dim dead people in the same way that they talked about stupid living people. Smart people got good jobs and unintelligent folks got bad jobs. To Goddard and Kite, reputation and social standing were sufficient tools for scientifically measuring intelligence, even if the subject had been dead for generations and was personally unknown to anyone living. Francis Galton, after all, had relied on reputation as a proxy for innate ability, so this was a venerable practice in intelligence research.

After two years of research into six generations of Kallikaks reaching back to a Revolutionary War ancestor, Goddard and Kite were stunned by what they'd unearthed. "The surprise and horror of it all was that no matter where we traced them [the Kallikaks], whether in the prosperous rural district, in the city slums to which some had drifted, or in the more remote mountain regions, or whether it was a question of the second or sixth generation, an appalling amount of defectiveness was everywhere found." Goddard and Kite found "conclusive proof" that 143 descendants of the Revolutionary War figure were feebleminded. They withheld diagnosis of 291 descendants, despite being fairly sure that they weren't "good members of society," and found just 46 normal people in Deborah Kallikak's family tree.

Among the demonstrably feebleminded Kallikaks were 36 illegitimate sons or daughters, 33 prostitutes and other sexually immoral types, and 3 epileptics. There were also 82 dead infants, 3 criminals, and 8 ancestors who "kept houses of ill fame." Just as bad, these feebleminded people had married into other families, exposing a further 1,146 people to the destructive feebleminded gene.

The message of the Kallikaks was clear: the social costs of allowing the mentally deficient to breed are measurably huge. Readers throughout the United States and Europe swallowed the doctrine whole, not questioning Goddard's methods, assumptions, or conclusions, but simply wondering what could be done to prevent the passage of the tainted feebleminded gene. Some people advocated killing all the idiots, the stupidest grade of feebleminded, but while Goddard referred to this group as the "loathsome unfortunate[s]," he did not approve of such a remedy. Goddard wanted to sequester and segregate the feebleminded, but he truly cared about his students at Vineland. The other alternative, murder, didn't sit well with his Christian values. More importantly, Goddard didn't believe people should be worrying too much about the idiot because he was too dumb to find or be appealing to potential mates.

"He is indeed loathsome," Goddard said of the idiot. "He is somewhat difficult to take care of; nevertheless, he lives his life and is done. He does not continue the race with a line of children like himself."

On the other hand, Goddard believed that the moron, the highest level of the feebleminded, was a creature worth worrying about, for the highest-performing retarded people could pass for normal. The frontispiece of his book, a picture of Deborah Kallikak, visually captured Goddard's argument. In Sunday school best, Kallikak sat on a wooden chair in the corner of a room at Vineland, smiling slightly, a large bow in her hair, a book in her hands, and a cat in her lap. Although she might be pretty and innocuous-seeming, as the picture implied, Deborah Kallikak was actually a menace to society. Take care of her and be compassionate, but stand vigilant and don't let her pass along her defective feebleminded gene.

Deborah scored poorly on Binet's Scale of Intelligence when Goddard tried her out on it. For example, when he asked her "How many are 12 less 3?" she was able to correctly say "9," but she took a few moments, and her eyes wandered the room while she thought about it.

"'Do you know how I did it?' she asked, delighted at her success. 'I counted on my fingers.'"

After repeated testing in 1910 and 1911, Goddard discovered that Deborah consistently scored at a mental age of a nine-year-old child, despite being twenty. She defined words by the object's use, as Alfred Binet had discovered that a child would. "Fork is to eat with," she would say, and "Chair is to sit on." She had problems arranging weights in rank order and constructing a sentence out of just three words given to her.

"This is a typical illustration of the mentality of a high-grade feeble-minded person, the moron, the delinquent, the kind of girl or woman that fills our reformatories," Goddard wrote in his book. "They are wayward, they get into all sorts of trouble and difficulties, sexually and otherwise. . . . It is also the history of the same type of girl in the public school. Rather good-looking, bright in appearance, with many attractive ways, the teacher clings to the hope, indeed insists, that such a girl will come out all right. Our work with Deborah convinces us that such hopes are delusions."

Goddard thought that not enough of Deborah's type—only a tenth—was currently institutionalized, and he advocated rounding up the rest of them. "We need to hunt them out in every possible place and take care of them and see to it that they do not propagate and make the problem worse, and that those who are alive today do not entail loss of life and property and moral contagion in the community by the things they do because they are weak-minded." While that might seem expensive, "such colonies [for the feeble-minded] . . . would very largely take the place of our present almshouses and prisons, and they would greatly decrease the number in our insane hospitals." And besides, once the feebleminded stop propagating, their numbers will greatly reduce from three hundred thousand to no more than a hundred thousand "and probably even lower."

In part due to Goddard's *Kallikak* book, the "menace of the feebleminded" gripped the nation. In the early twentieth century, state institutions for the feebleminded expanded and new ones sprouted up. Some states even established traveling clinics to administer intelligence tests at public schools. Regardless of parental consent or its absence, children who scored below normal could be sent to soul-deadening institutions to protect the rest of the population.

Having persuaded doctors to adopt his tests and his definition of intelligence, Goddard now needed to get Binet's tests into schools, which would provide a much larger (and eventually more lucrative) venue for psychologists. After all, schools were the most obvious locales for mass use of intelligence tests and where they would affect the greatest number of people. Luckily for Goddard, life in American schools was a lot more complicated than it had been in the nineteenth century, so the need for sorting tools was great. At about the turn of the century, especially in the cities, schools had a massive influx of bodies and minds that needed to be categorized and arranged.

American schools grew rapidly in the late 1800s and early 1900s for three reasons. First, like France and other European countries, many American states had enacted mandatory universal education laws. This trend began in the 1850s, requiring some school attendance for children up to age fourteen. But in about 1900, labor activists, school reformers, and philanthropists began pushing for stricter mandatory attendance, longer and more school days, and mandatory schooling to a later age, all primarily in the hope of reducing child labor.

School administrators of the time were not always pleased. In 1919, Ellwood Cubberly, the controversial head of Stanford University's Department of Education, complained about mandatory universal education burdening the schools with "not only the truant and the incorrigible, who under former conditions either left early or were expelled, but also many children of the foreign-born who have no aptitude for book learning, and many children of inferior mental qualities who do not profit by ordinary classroom procedure."

Second, school populations ballooned because people were moving from the countryside to the cities. Mechanized agriculture increasingly depended less on human labor, and urban industrial jobs also lured people away from the countryside. And third, the U.S. population as a whole grew tremendously because of immigration. Each large passenger ship to pull into New York Harbor carried hundreds of new students, many of them poorly educated and coming from the disdained southern and eastern parts of Europe.

In the quarter century before World War I, American public school enrollment increased by more than 50 percent, from 12.7 million in 1890 to 19.7 million in 1915. During the same period, high schools for the first time became an integral part of the public educational system, causing enrollment at those institutions to increase almost sixfold, from just 203,000 in 1890 to 1.3 million in 1915. School costs, of course, grew out of control along with their populations, from $141 million to $605 million annually.

The increases in numbers, diversity, and costs had far-reaching impacts on American schools that can be felt today. For starters, their goals changed. In the nineteenth century, few people went to high school, and those who did were likely to go on to college; high schools prepared students for further education. In the twentieth century, on the other hand, with essentially all children in attendance, schools began to see themselves as preparing people for work, for leisure time, and especially the newly arrived, for citizenship.

The rising costs and numbers also forced administrators to focus, in the industrial, modern manner, on efficiency. American schools had recently been grouping their students by age—the one-room schoolhouse had mainly died out by the mid-nineteenth century—but now stratification and compartmentalization of students greatly accelerated. For schools to run efficiently, it was thought that students needed to be fairly and cost-effectively ranked and sorted.

Finally, on top of demographic forces was political pressure. While the school population was exploding, a national debate about "laggards" erupted. Studies and popular articles warned that too many American students were behind their grade level, and were holding back everyone else. For instance, studies found that 7 percent of students in Medford, Massachusetts, were "overage," as it was called, while an amazing 75 percent of students in Memphis, Tennessee, were, too. All of a sudden, overage students—those big lugs at the back of the class who slow everybody down and just can't seem to learn to read or write—became a problem, despite the fact that mixed-age classrooms were as old as the republic. Education experts began to describe the situation in new and negative ways. They began to talk about school "failures," much as we do today; inefficiency, that progressive bugbear, wandered in every American school district, dragging all students down with it.

In response, progressive-era psychology and education strove to turn themselves into sciences. And science meant numbers, statistics, percentages, and measurements. Francis Galton would have loved it. The experts wanted to measure every mind and likened the attempts to earlier—and, of course, successful—scientific attempts to quantify other phenomena.

"The 'science of heat was made possible by the thermometer,' noted a Philadelphia school superintendent; 'astronomy was mere astrology before the application of the pendulum,' and 'chemistry was but alchemy prior to the perfection of the analytic balance.'" This superintendent warned that if educators could not find accurate mind measurements, as well, "pedagogy will remain—well, pedagogy will remain pedagogy." His field, of course, did remain pedagogy; it merely became infatuated with assigning numbers to students.

Considering the demographic forces at work, the political pressures on schools to fix the laggards problem, and education's desire to become scientific, it's fairly easy to guess what came next. Henry Goddard had just what science-aspiring pedagogy needed, just as he did for medicine. He argued that Binet's test would show educators just how far off a student's mental age was from the grade he occupied.

Goddard first needed a school in which to prove his tests' usefulness, and here again his appealing personality, political instincts, and people skills worked wonders. He wrote to a public school superintendent whose district was near Vineland, in New Jersey. Knowing that "there was a big difference between asking a favor of a man, and offering him a favor," Goddard didn't directly ask the superintendent if he could test the district's children. Instead, he pitched his French tests as an opportunity. He described how well the Binet tests had performed in classifying the students at Vineland, stating that he could "probably get permission from the Superintendent of the Training School [at Vineland] to give the test to every child in the Public Schools."

Goddard's approach worked exactly as intended, for the school superintendent wrote back straightaway to invite him to come. The very next Monday morning, five assistants from Vineland tested all the children in the district, about two thousand of them. They were the first public school students in the United States to take a Binet-Simon intelligence test. Before this exam, Binet tests were used solely to classify mentally retarded children. After 1910, "normal" children would take intelligence tests after just one friendly letter to a colleague. That Monday morning of testing would change American schools forever and would eventually spawn a vast testing industry.

When the testing was done, Goddard took the exams back with him to his laboratory at Vineland and analyzed them.

"To a person familiar with statistical methods," the existence of normally distributed test results (that is, when graphed, they form the famous bell curve) was "practically a mathematical demonstration of the accuracy of the tests," Goddard claimed.

Despite Goddard's confidence in his test results, many other psychologists were skeptical. Moreover, these early critics immediately saw many of the fundamental problems of intelligence testing. For instance, one critic pointed out that most of the exam questions tested verbal ability, reflecting the assumption on Binet and Goddard's part that "native ability to do can be tested by testing the ability to use words about doing." This critic also argued that many of the questions were vague and experience-dependent. As an illustration, he posed to businessmen a question that had been on the exam: "What ought one to do before taking part in an important affair?" Some of these men responded pithily with "ugly words" about how preposterous the question was. "Take a bath," was one response, while another said, "Put on your best clothes." Perhaps the best answer was "Transfer your property to your wife." Each man had answered the question according to his own life experience, and presumably the New Jersey students had, too: so much for Goddard's "objective" test questions.

As the field of intelligence testing grew, its critics did not fade away. By 1912, just two years after Goddard's foray into New Jersey public schools, intelligence testing had caused a big enough splash to warrant a published review of its scientific literature in the *Journal of Educational Psychology*. The author pointed out an amazing, if obvious, flaw in the field: no one, including Goddard, had thought to define intelligence, the very subject they were claiming to measure.

Binet himself, who had died unexpectedly the year before, had been aware of the definitional problem. "We have not attempted to treat, in all its scope, this problem of fearful complexity, the definition of intelligence," he wrote. American testers, however, were less forthright than Binet, and they became sharply defensive on the issue, as they can be today. In 1916 Lewis Terman, a Stanford psychologist, wrote that "to demand, as critics of the Binet method have sometimes done, that one who would measure intelligence should first present a complete definition of it, is quite unreasonable . . . electrical currents were measured long before their nature was well understood."

Intelligence testing had serious flaws, but it was the best technology around, and doctors and educators needed the tests. In the years before World War I, even lawmakers began to take notice of the new tests. In 1911, just a year after the tests were first applied in public schools, the New Jersey State Legislature passed a law requiring school districts to create special classes for students who were "three years or more below the normal." The idea that intelligence was defined by mental years—Binet's idea—was enshrined in law for the first time in America. The only available method for testing mental age, of course, was the Binet-Simon test.

Teachers around the country pressed Goddard for copies of his exams, which he sent out as quickly as the requests came in. By 1914 (just four years after he had introduced Binet tests to American public schools), 83 out of 103 cities were using mental tests to identify feebleminded students. This included all U.S. cities with populations over 250,000. No longer was poor performance in class the only reason why children were placed in special education classes. Now, they could be moved there if they scored poorly on one intelligence test.

If someone had predicted for him his future successes on the boat ride to Europe in 1908, when he was looking for tools to assess the feebleminded, Goddard would have been dumbfounded. In just a few years, Binet tests—designed with the limited goal of classifying French elementary school-age retarded children—were being used in the United States to diagnose mentally handicapped patients and to sort public school students of all abilities and ages. It would just be the beginning.

Chapter 5

Turning Back the Feebleminded

Standing in Ellis Island's Great Hall, undoubtedly with months of planning and saving, a life of poverty, and winding lines of Europe's hopefuls behind him, chubby Pat from Ireland had almost made it to America. Only a doctor stood in his way, and he kept asking silly questions.

"Pat, if I gave you two dogs and my friend here gave you one, how many would you have?" the doctor asked.

"Four, sir," Pat said.

"Did you ever go to school, Pat?"

"Yes indeed, sir."

"Now, Pat, if you had an apple and I gave you one, how many would you have?"

"Two, sir."

"And if my friend gave you one, how many would you have?"

"Three, sir."

The doctor then repeated the original dog question, but still received the answer of four. "How can you possibly have four dogs when I've given you two and my friend just one?" he demanded.

"Why, sure, I've got a dog at home meself," said Pat.

The doctor decided to let "the heavy-set son of Erin" through, onto a ferry that would take him to Manhattan or New Jersey, from where, along with the thousands of others who arrived that day, he might continue to anywhere in America. Whether fat Pat would make a fortune selling automobiles, become a failed troubadour, or gain tenure at Notre Dame the doctor would never know. He saw thousands just like Pat every day; poor people all, just trying to get their crack at New World opportunity.

One thing from the story is clear. Despite the difficulties in communicating (and they both spoke English!), the doctor thought there was enough going on in Pat's head to let America take a chance on him. The doctor's job wasn't easy. Starting in about 1890, and every few years thereafter, Congress handed the physicians of the U.S. Public Health Service a new list of types of people to exclude from America. By the early 1900s, the list had become comically long. Some days, more than five thousand immigrants came through Ellis Island, and the doctors had to cull out the lunatics, idiots, and the insane; the epileptics, beggars, and anarchists; all those afflicted with numerous so-called immigrant diseases; and finally the "imbeciles, feeble-minded and persons with physical or mental defects which might affect their ability to earn a living." Like streetwise cops picking criminals out of a crowd of law-abiding citizens, doctors had but a few seconds to spot these medical miscreants traipsing along "the line," up the steps from the landing, and into the Great Hall.

Considering the number of people to be sorted, it's not surprising to find intelligence tests on Ellis Island. The port of entry was like a quality control station at the door of a great ramshackle factory where everything, just at the very end, became orderly and efficient. The immigrants, in particular, noticed the abrupt segue from old chaotic Europe to scientific America—and nothing was more cutting-edge before World War I than an intelligence test. The change in culture was immediate. On the docks, officials tagged the immigrants with labels that revealed their location on ships' manifests, formed them into lines, barked at them to leave their luggage, and then herded them upstairs to Ellis Island's high-ceilinged Great Hall.

An English journalist entered Ellis Island on Easter Day 1913 with a large batch of sheepskin-wearing Russian peasants. "The day of the emigrants' arrival in New York was the nearest earthly likeness to the final Day of Judgment, when we have to prove our fitness to enter heaven. Our trial might well have been prefaced by a few edifying reminders from a priest," he wrote. The immigration process was startlingly industrial and dehumanized. "This ranging and guiding and jurrying and sifting was like nothing so much as the screening of coal in a great breaker tower. It is not good to be like a hurrying, bumping, wandering piece of coal being mechanically guided to the sacks of its type and size, but such is the lot of the immigrant at Ellis Island."

Uniformed medical officers of the U.S. Public Health Service watched the worn-out travelers. One young doctor scanned them—systematically from foot to head—at the top of the long flight of stairs to the Great Hall, just when they were most winded. If someone breathed too heavily the doctor would mark an H on his clothing in chalk, indicating a possible heart problem. The limping immigrant received an L (for lame), the squinting an E (for eye). Those deemed too sick saw the Statue of Liberty once more, on the way back to Europe.

The mentally defective presented the biggest problem for doctors. In 1914 E. K. Sprague, a surgeon in the Public Health Service, warned in a magazine article that high-grade defectives, in particular, could easily pass as normal. To prove his point, Sprague published three pictures of perfectly pleasant-looking immigrants. All were young, poor, and, presumably, uneducated (steerage class passengers, not the first- and second-class, passed through Ellis Island). The seventeen-year-old girl whose picture was on the far right was pretty and even smiling slightly. Perhaps a layperson would have passed her by, but Sprague was far too experienced for that. Upon further inspection, he discovered that "her common knowledge was meager; she did not know the date, the number of months or their names; she could name the days of the week forward but not backward; she could count from 1 to 20 but not from 20 to 1."

Some doctors became confident that they could spot the feebleminded just walking up the stairs among the long line of immigrants. Those morons had a certain look. "Should the immigrant appear stupid and inattentive to such an extent that mental defect is suspected, an X is made with chalk on his coat at the anterior aspect of his right shoulder," wrote one Ellis Island official.

Dr. Sprague admonished, however, that they shouldn't rely solely on appearances. "Facial expression may be a help in some instances, but from the accompanying photographs it can readily be seen that little dependence can be placed upon it in the selection of the higher grades of feeble-mindedness." For divining the brightest of the clinically dumb, the doctors needed tests of intelligence.

The U.S. Public Health Service doctors on Ellis Island were America's first defense against the foreign feebleminded. They were like a thin, white, semipermeable membrane designed to let the vast majority of poor people in but keep the toxic ones at bay. It was ultimately a Galtonian policy, using Binet's methods, of keeping out the genetically inferior.

"The object is not only to prevent the introduction into this country of a communicable disease," their official 1903 handbook read, "but also to keep out a class of persons from whom so large a proportion of inmates of institutions for the blind and recipients of public dispensary charity are recruited."

The problem at first was that the doctors didn't know exactly how to ascertain who was feebleminded and who wasn't. In the beginning they just conversed with slack-jawed, seemingly stupid immigrants to try to ascertain their mental abilities. The good thing about this early approach was that they could sometimes figure out the immigrants' thought process behind their answers. Pat knew how to add; he just had a dog at home and probably not too much formal education. He might not have been the brightest guy off the boat, but he probably wouldn't be a burden on the country, either; they let him in.

The Public Health Service doctors could be quite sympathetic to immigrants because they knew about the inhuman conditions shipboard in steerage, the large expenses they had incurred to make the trip, and the families they had left behind. They understood that to go through all of this and then to be confronted with strange officials asking them to do basic math problems must be taxing and intimidating. The doctors also understood the implications of sending someone home. If a school misclassified a student as particularly dumb, they believed, this was easily rectified: they just moved him back in with the normal kids. But in the context of immigration, a misdiagnosis of feeblemindedness was without recourse.

"An error which results in unjustly deporting an alien from New York to Eastern Europe is a grievous blunder and is without remedy," explained one seasoned doctor.

Knowing the personal consequences of exclusion, aware of the immigrants' exhausted, worried state, doctors only classified an immigrant as mentally defective when confronted with an obvious and extreme case. Therefore, most of the time, Ellis Island doctors were just trying to see if there was something working inside each immigrant's mind. They didn't look for the best or the fastest answer to a question, just an answer that reflected at least decent cognitive activity.

A doctor named Howard Knox, who did the most for creating tests for immigrants, used to ask people to imagine that a "man walked into the woods. He saw something hanging from a tree that frightened him, and he ran back to notify the police. What did he see?" Rather than answering "a person hanged," which Knox had hoped for, one working-class Londoner replied, "a brawnch." Regardless, the empathetic Knox did not classify the man as feebleminded; his answer was at least possible.

By talking to immigrants and giving them math and hypothetical problems, doctors could get a rough and ready feel for a person's mental abilities. But considering the travelers' anxiety level, the dangers of miscommunications while speaking through interpreters, and the cultural differences between doctor and immigrant, this method was fraught with problems. Knox and like-minded medical colleagues began to look for neutral, objective ways to measure immigrants' minds. They came up with "performance" questions—questions that would rely as little as possible on schooling, language, and culture.

In 1913, Knox devised a "cube imitation test," which required immigrants to copy the order in which a doctor had touched four wooden cubes laid out in a row. The doctor would touch the cubes slowly, allowing jittery-nerved immigrants to take the pattern in. If the immigrant got the pattern correct, he moved on to a new series of cube-touching. In another test, doctors would hold up for just a few seconds a board that had objects tied to it, such as a toy gun, a doll, and a fork, and then record how many objects the immigrant could remember afterward.

Educators and others, not just the Ellis Island doctors, were well aware of the problems in testing these populations and, like Knox, they often turned to everyday items to devise new performance questions. For instance, a couple of children's toy companies (Milton Bradley, for one) produced boxes of multicolored blocks that people could put together to make pretty designs and pictures. In 1911, two testers published an exam using these blocks to examine people by timing how quickly they could put various designs together.

The doctors on Ellis Island also asked Alfred Binet–style questions that depended at least in part on cultural and educational knowledge. These questions today are called "verbal" (as opposed to performance) questions. The doctors reasoned, for instance, that anyone more than twelve years old should be able to define "justice, pity, truth, goodness and happiness," and tell how many legs one horse and one man have combined. They also asked immigrants to count back from 20; do basic math; name the days of the week backward; and, at least for young children, tell the time.

Knox thought his tests were fair, even if "the subject has never been taught and that he has only acquired knowledge by the experiences of every-day life. The performance tests especially are not dependent on any previous experience, but the ability to do them is based on the inherent or native power to surmount slight obstacles with which the subject is born and they are applicable to the educated as well as to the illiterate."

There was clear evidence in some cases that this assumption was false. One night, an immigration official who had witnessed Pat, the Irish immigrant, being examined took some new exam questions home with him and tried them out on his daughter and her friends, most of them teachers, who had come over for dinner. The questions, he discovered, "stumped" them. Another time, while he was at his desk, a Public Health Service doctor walked by and said, "You ought to see the new jig-saw puzzle they have downstairs; it beat me all right."

Nevertheless, the new performance questions were most likely fairer to people without English and formal schooling. A downside to the technique, however, was that doctors lost the flexibility of their former conversational method. Instead of looking for the method behind problem-solving techniques, doctors began looking for correct answers. As a result, more people, though still not many, were excluded from the United States. In 1908, only 186 people out of a little less than 600,000 were excluded on the grounds of feeblemindedness. By 1914, after the doctors had adopted their new tests, immigration officials excluded 1,077 people out of about 800,000.

It's not clear if excluding these people helped the country in any way, but the rigidity of the new questions foreshadowed problems to come. For one, the false sense of scientific reliability allowed people to generalize speciously about groups of people and compare them. Were Hungarians and Italians coming off the boats innately dumber than the English? Inevitably the answer was yes, and intelligence research was there to corroborate this conclusion.

In hindsight, these hodgepodge testing devices seem to have been developed haphazardly—school questions originally devised to cull out the retarded were thrown together with children's toys—yet who can blame their creators? There was no direct test of innate intelligence, doctors needed tests, and these amalgams were better than their predecessors. James Cattell of Columbia University might have had immigrants gripping a dynamometer to test their hand strength. Francis Galton, too, might have asked the immigrants to blow into tubes or punch a rod. A generation before that, immigrants might have had their craniums measured. The performance questions used by Dr. Howard Knox, along with Alfred Binet's school questions, were marked improvements.

Chapter 6

The Tests That Changed the World

Two weeks after the United States entered the Great War—on April 6, 1917—American psychologists were a bickering and unfocused lot, like small, uncoordinated boys left unchosen on the sidelines of a pickup basketball game. As a profession, they'd been around for only about a quarter of a century, and they looked enviously at other sciences that were focusing their efforts against the kaiser. Chemists, physicists, biologists, and research doctors at university laboratories worked on wireless telephony, submarine detection, airplane construction, poison gas manufacturing, blood transfusion, and more. Psychologists had to do something to help the war effort. But what? Some of them thought they could improve soldiers' ability to aim, or their ability to recover from severe injuries. Others believed they could improve military recreation, select for better fighter pilots, or devise tests for courage and self-mastery under stressful conditions.

On April 21, 1917, seven psychologists met in a room at the Hotel Walton, an imposing twelve-story building in downtown Philadelphia, to address the problem of their relevance. Despite the meeting's obscurity, both then and now, it would be surprisingly important to the field of psychology and, in years, the entire world. Of all the ways psychology could have contributed to the war effort, these men successfully focused the field's attention on a limited, narrow kind of intelligence testing that would catch on after the war. They established Alfred Binet's methods (with some additions and supported by Galtonian theory) and ignored other, more flexible and broader approaches to testing people. We are still feeling the consequences today.

The seven psychologists, all white men ranging from their mid-thirties to late forties, quickly filled their hotel room with cigarette smoke and divisive anger. Robert Mearns Yerkes, president of the American Psychological Association (APA), had convened the late-night meeting at the Walton in the belief that the war could change people's attitudes toward psychology, and intelligence testing in particular. Despite Henry Goddard's success in promoting Binet's intelligence tests in the United States, psychology was still on the fringes of society and academia. Psychologists had so far failed to have their field accepted as a natural science, which is how they wanted to be perceived. Worse, most other psychologists thought intelligence testing was quackery akin to water divination. Laypeople, too, were often confused and hostile toward testing, equating the very act of having their intelligence measured with having its quality questioned.

The psychologists at the Hotel Walton saw the war as an opportunity to change all this.

"I hope we can all get together Saturday night in Philadelphia for a good discussion. The prospects are now excellent that we shall have opportunity to do something important, unless perchance the war should suddenly end," wrote Robert Yerkes to America's pioneering applied psychologist Walter Dill Scott.

Yerkes sounded almost fretful that men might cease the slaughter on the fields of France before psychology had been able to prove itself, and it was this attitude, as well as the fixation on a rigid testing scheme, that led to problems at the Walton. Walter Scott felt that his colleagues there—all primarily theoretical researchers— were more interested in helping themselves and their nascent field than their country. Their attitude made him feel "utter disgust."

Scott didn't fit in with his theoretically oriented colleagues. He was really a businessman in academic clothing, a practical sort who preferred solving problems to sitting around worrying about the nature of intelligence. He was affable and socially and professionally savvy, while Yerkes, the head of the APA, was stiff, academic, and pompous.

Working as a psychologist since the beginning of the twentieth century, Scott had spent a good deal of his professional life with businessmen, catering to their needs. He became the first person to write about the psychology of advertising and public speaking and, in the years just before the war, he had worked on a range of applied problems, from employee motivation and the persuasion of consumers to vocational selection and business management.

Robert Yerkes described himself as a "moody, strong-willed, unsuggestible child, difficult to control," a self-assessment directly relevant to his vision for wartime psychology. If it weren't for a mother he was devoted to, he would have left home early out of fear of and hatred for his father, who was an unhappy, unsuccessful man who never understood Yerkes' intellectual proclivities. Yerkes was often alone as a child, a situation exacerbated when a younger, beloved sister died of scarlet fever. Yerkes contracted it as well, but was brought back to health by a doctor who "made lasting impressions and deeply stirred [his] admiration and vocational hero-worship."

After the childhood bout of scarlet fever, Yerkes daydreamed of being a "physician, surgeon, or, in other guise, alleviator of human suffering," but he hadn't become a doctor because his parents couldn't afford to send him to medical school. In contrast to Scott, Robert Yerkes was a doctor in academic garb and craved the respect of medicine. For years Yerkes had worked part-time at Harvard as a lofty and theoretical scientist and part-time at Boston Psychopathic Hospital, learning the ways of doctors.

At the Hotel Walton in April 1917, Yerkes wanted to play out his childhood fantasy and make psychologists part of the Army Medical Corps, under the direction of doctors and psychiatrists. For Yerkes, the medical model and the prestige that went with it was the future of psychology, the field's ticket out of the intellectual ghetto. Scott bristled at the idea, believing that psychologists should be equal to and independent of doctors.

But they differed also on theory and testing styles. Like most psychologists of the era, Yerkes tested people one-on-one, to measure as precisely as possible their general intelligence—that central and singular trait discovered by Charles Spearman during the Boer War. Before the war, Yerkes had investigated the evolutionary development of intelligence by studying organisms from the simple, such as frogs and worms, up the intelligence hierarchy to orangutans, insane people, and the mentally retarded. As a result, he was neither practiced nor focused on the practical matter of sorting people for organizations, which is ultimately what working for the military needed to be about.

Scott, by contrast, wasn't much interested in g. He had spent the previous years creating tests for groups, which was a fairly radical notion at the time. These were tests not just of intelligence but also of other traits, such as character, designed to help businesses sort through large numbers of job applicants. Scott wanted to isolate and test whatever characteristics would help businesses, and now the military, to hire the right person for the job and to get the work done more efficiently. Not surprisingly, Scott thought Yerkes' work on the evolutionary distribution of intelligence was theoretical blather.

Yerkes thought intelligence tests should be used during the war primarily as a tool for weeding out the feebleminded, much as the doctors on Ellis Island had used them, whereas Scott wasn't convinced that men should be sorted solely by their intelligence or that psychology's main focus should be so narrow. Scott had spent years devising rating systems for companies to use when evaluating applicants for managerial positions, and he thought psychology could do much more than just stand sentry against, in a phrase that had become popular, "the menace of the feebleminded." He thought his rating scales, which had examiners subjectively rank applicants in terms of characteristics such as appearance, manner, tact, loyalty, and honesty, could easily be adapted to the rating of military officer candidates.

It wasn't that Scott thought intelligence tests were a waste of time. He, too, had developed such tests, and like everyone else, his were based in part on Binet's scales. But when working with businesses, Scott would often customize his exams based on the client's particular needs, and his definition of intelligence was loose. Unlike his more academic colleagues, he never thought he was testing anything as theoretical as general intelligence, some mystical physical force that hadn't been found but could nonetheless be measured precisely. Instead, Scott took a holistic, flexible approach to evaluating human beings; had he won the argument in the Hotel Walton, people might thereafter have taken fundamentally very different exams.

For the most part, the other psychologists at the Walton believed that intelligence was the only personal and mental trait worth testing and that it had to be measured with scientific precision. Nothing would make the military more efficient, Yerkes in particular thought, than freeing it from the feebleminded, those hidden human defectives that only intelligence tests could reveal.

Scott, proud and practical, could not tolerate such narrowness, the idea that psychologists would be commissioned in the military (and would work for doctors), his colleagues' self-promoting testing schemes, or the limited focus on the feebleminded. Sometime after midnight in that smoky Walton room, Scott huffily realized that Robert Yerkes' vision would hold the day.

"I became so enraged by these points of view, that I expressed myself very clearly and left," Scott later wrote.

Out went Scott, and with him his broad and flexible testing style and his business-oriented approach. But while Scott might have walked out of the Walton, he didn't give up on helping the war effort. As a result, the army ended up with two groups of psychologists working separately on personnel classification problems. Scott would focus mainly on the selection of officers, while Yerkes and his posse would measure the intelligence of incoming recruits.

The army responded much more positively to Scott and his rating methods than it did to Yerkes, his theoretically oriented colleagues, and their intelligence tests. Scott was able to network his way right up to the secretary of war and persuade him to use his Rating Scale for Captains, which was based on a test he had devised for hiring salesmen. Yerkes, on the other hand, tried to enter the military through the surgeon general but initially couldn't because he didn't understand the military mind-set. With Scott gone, Yerkes pitched impractical ideas in a report titled *Plan for the Psychological Examination of Recruits to Eliminate the Mentally Unfit.* In it, he posited that psychologists be commissioned as officers in the Medical Reserve Corps. (Scott, like a good business consultant, thought psychologists should be civilian advisers to the army; unlike Yerkes, he would never put on a uniform.) Worst of all, Yerkes proposed that psychologists test recruits one at a time. To an army receiving, processing, and training thousands of recruits a day, it was an abysmal proposition.

In hindsight, with the ubiquity of nationwide standardized tests, the idea of testing huge numbers of army recruits one by one is a laughably inefficient idea, but for Yerkes it made sense. Doctors and psychiatrists at Boston Hospital, where he worked before the war, hadn't diagnosed patients in groups, and at the time the vast majority of intelligence tests around the world were administered one on one. Doctors pulled immigrants at Ellis Island out of line if they looked or seemed dim; psychologists pulled individual kids out of class to evaluate their mental states. Group testing was a new way of thinking for most psychologists, and initially they thought it unscientific.

Yerkes hadn't yet made the mental shift to large institutional needs, and as a result the army took no interest in his report and he got no funding to develop tests. Under Yerkes' leadership, if psychologists wanted to develop tests for processing recruits, they would have to make do on their own and on a very small budget. Henry Goddard yet again came to the rescue. He brought together at Vineland a group of seven psychologists from prestigious universities and institutions around the country who—starting on the afternoon of May 28, 1917, unpaid and on a total budget of $800 for two two-week sessions—hammered out the world's first large-scale intelligence tests.

With the conflagration at the Walton Hotel still fresh in his mind, Yerkes did not invite Walter Scott, a man with rare experience in creating group tests. Thus it was eugenics theoreticians who created the model for the first large-scale intelligence test. Ironically, many of Yerkes' own ideas didn't survive the meetings at Vineland either, and he immediately ignited intense debate by arguing that the tests should be used "to identify 'intellectually incompetent recruits,' 'the psychotic,' 'incorrigibles,' and 'men for special tasks.'"

By now, though, as with Scott, the others didn't want to focus only on the "misfits"; they also thought his idea of one-on-one testing was untenable. They wanted to test the entire set of new recruits, from the dumbest inductee to the smartest, and this meant group testing. Lewis Terman, a Stanford psychologist in attendance, argued that the German army needed only to assemble the human "parts of the machine . . . in order to begin work," while the U.S. Army, by comparison, was simply "an assembled horde." America had too much ethnic diversity, he thought, which was antithetical to efficiency, and intelligence tests could help. By the end of the first day the group had persuaded Yerkes of the narrowness of his vision and that one-on-one testing, in the face of universal conscription, simply was not feasible.

Walter Scott could have helped the Vineland group tremendously, since he had been creating and administering group tests for years, but the task would fall to Terman, a more academic-minded man with fixed theoretical ideas about intelligence, race, and class and with a background in teaching rather than business.

Like Henry Goddard, who also attended the Vineland meetings, Lewis Terman was a successful promoter and reviser of European ideas. Terman would become far more famous than Goddard, due to Terman's publication of the "Stanford-Binet" in 1916, which was a more sophisticated revision of Binet's tests. Terman's exam would quickly become the gold standard in intelligence testing and include the now-famous Intelligence Quotient, which was based on a German psychologist's idea of dividing the subject's mental age by his chronological age. Terman decided to multiply the ratio by 100, thereafter endowing intelligence test results with accessibly round numbers. For instance, a ten-year-old student who scored like an average fifteen-year-old would end up with a score of 150—in words, a genius. Inevitably, the quotient and even intelligence tests in general became known by a handy moniker—the IQ—and Terman's IQ test would become the standard by which future intelligence tests would be measured.

Terman had developed his IQ tests for Galtonian, eugenics purposes: to reveal the most and least intelligent in society. In 1916 he was confident that he had developed the right tool for identifying the feebleminded.

"It is safe to predict," Terman wrote, "that in the near future intelligence tests will bring tens of thousands of these high-grade defectives under the surveillance and protection of society. This will ultimately result in curtailing the reproduction of feeblemindedness and in the elimination of an enormous amount of crime, pauperism, and industrial inefficiency."

In his initial Stanford-Binet revision of Binet's tests, Terman introduced ninety more questions that tested school-related knowledge such as vocabulary, reading comprehension, and word definition. He threw test questions at thousands of (mainly urban, middle-class) students in California and Nevada, discovering that questions such as "Can you tell me, who was Genghis Khan?" and "What is the boiling point of water?" differentiated between children of different grade levels. That is, the average third-grader could answer some questions, for instance, but not others. The average fourth-grader could answer more than the third-grader, but not as many as the fifth-grader, and so on.

Despite the scholastic content of his questions, Terman didn't believe that his Stanford-Binet tested students' educational and cultural background. He claimed that his test was able to isolate and measure innate intelligence—a fixed, inheritable trait. It was a supposition that had clear political and social implications, as revealed in his description of two low-scoring Portuguese boys who "represent the level of intelligence which is very, very common among Spanish-Indian and Mexican families of the Southwest and also among negroes. Their dullness seems to be racial, or at least inherent in the family stocks from which they come. The fact that one meets this type with such extraordinary frequency among Indians, Mexicans and negroes suggests quite forcibly that the whole question of racial differences in mental traits will have to be taken up anew and by experimental methods."

These IQ tests allowed Terman and others to believe they were precisely assessing "high grade defectives," like the young Deborah Kallikak at Goddard's Vineland School in New Jersey. Morons had IQs between 50 and 70, Terman believed, while imbeciles scored "between 20 or 25 and 50," and idiots dwelled below even these scores. Applying numbers had a scientific appeal to it, but, like the Kallikak study, numerical test results could be put aside or supplemented by other data, such as reputation and social standing.

The slippery use of IQ tests came in handy when certain people who behaved like the feebleminded, such as unwed mothers and prostitutes, didn't perform as poorly on intelligence tests as it was thought they should. This happened in California when the state hired Terman and two fellow academics to survey "Mental Deviation in Prisons, Public Schools and Orphanages." Confusingly, some of these unworthy types scored above moron and occasionally even above average. Such results could cause unease among the experts. Thus, when California's Sonoma State Hospital learned that some of its feebleminded inmates scored better on Terman's IQ test than it was thought they should have, the hospital hired a psychologist to "explain the fact that there are certain high grade morons who test normal but yet are feebleminded."

Rather than question the assumption that social behavior reflects mental ability, or that the IQ was a useful tool, one of Terman's colleagues working on the California survey claimed to have discovered five different "Social-Intelligence Groups" among orphans and unwed mothers. Social intelligence, which he defined as "the extent to which the subject is mentally capable of 'managing himself and his affairs with ordinary prudence,'" was handily more malleable than intelligence test scores. It allowed him "to classify persons as feeble-minded whether or not the test results show them to fall within the usual I.Q. limits of that group."

Terman, earlier than most other psychologists, also saw the potential uses for group intelligence tests in schools, rather than the one-on-one versions, and he lobbied hard at the World War I Vineland meetings to offer the army a group version of his Stanford-Binet. While he hadn't yet refined his group exams by the time of America's involvement in the war, his graduate student, Arthur Otis, had been working on the problem, so Terman simply took Otis's tests with him to Vineland to use as a model. Apparently, it pays to arrive with documents in hand at a negotiation, which is what the Vineland meetings were in part. After just two weeks in Goddard's laboratory, with the sound of feebleminded children playing outside in the muggy New Jersey summer, the group of seven had largely signed on to Terman's tests. A couple of years after the war's end, Terman was able to brag in a letter that the resulting tests at Vineland "include[d] five tests practically in the form in which Otis had used them in his own scale [test]."

One reason for Terman's success at Vineland was a curious, ingenious, and novel testing method employed by Otis, which he, in turn, had picked up from a man named Frederick Kelly, dean of education at the University of Kansas. Kelly had wanted to improve upon the efficiency and objectivity of reading comprehension tests, and the result was an exam called the Kansas Silent Reading Test. The simple thirty-seven-page test included the following sample question that the teacher was to read to her class: "Below are given the names of four animals. Draw a line around the name of each animal that is useful on the farm: cow tiger rat wolf."

Seemingly obvious and insipid to us now, Kelly's question was actually hugely innovative. It was probably the first published multiple-choice question and the rest of the instructions sound amazingly familiar despite the passage of time.

"This exercise tells us to draw a line around the word cow," teachers were to explain to their class. "No other answer is right ... study each answer carefully ... do [the questions] as fast as you can, being sure to do them right. Stop at once when time is called. Do not open the papers until told."

The students in Kansas couldn't have realized that they were at the beginning of countless tests with bubbles to be filled out with number two pencils. With the invention of multiple-choice testing, institutions made a quantum leap forward; students no longer had to write, and teachers no longer had to read long student answers, or make subjective decisions. There was one correct answer, and teachers could skim their eyes down the page quickly and correct an exam in just moments, thus satisfying the goals of efficiency, fairness, and objectivity in an era when school populations were exploding.

Considering how many standardized multiple-choice tests now exist, Kelly deserves to be much more famous, or infamous, than he is. Within the next decade, this test method, as well as its weaker cousin the true-false question, would change American schools forever. From the get-go, multiple-choice questions allowed for no ambiguity or shades of gray, as evidenced when Kelly asked Kansas school superintendents to suggest additional test questions, which should "(1) ... be subject to only one interpretation (2) ... call for but one thing ... wholly right or wholly wrong, and not partly right and partly wrong."

In the words of the historian Franz Samelson, "This piece of educational technology is as American as the assembly line, and perhaps as alienating." People have complained about multiple-choice questions ever since: often that they reward compartmentalized learning and not critical thinking skills. But, outside of schools, institutional efficiency can rightly be more of a priority than understanding individuals, especially in times of war and universal conscription. These circumstances and the need to test hundreds of thousands of men quickly pushed the Vineland group to create in just two weeks an intelligence test very different in form from those of the past, and Lewis Terman's newfangled educational method allowed them to do so.

The men at Vineland also had to create two kinds of tests, because many of the army recruits couldn't read, or were foreigners who didn't speak English. They called the exam for literates the "Alpha," and a picture-based performance test called the "Beta" was for the illiterate and non-English-speakers. (Young adult men, of course, were different from schoolchildren, so the exams had to be tweaked. The test creators didn't care what facts examinees knew at a certain age, but rather whether they knew what they thought every intelligent adult should know.)

This new ability to test many people efficiently and simultaneously meant that psychologists were no longer forced to focus solely on the feebleminded. That everyone could be tested made this a pivotal moment in the history of intelligence tests. Ever after, psychologists such as Henry Goddard, who had made his reputation on the menace of the feebleminded, would recede in prominence, making way for the next generation, most notably Lewis Terman, to take his place. Of wider importance, psychology's power, through its ability to help institutions sort groups quickly, was about to grow immensely.

To prevent cheating, the Vineland psychologists banged out five different versions of the Alpha and Beta exams, as well as a guide for examiners. The exams could be administered in less than an hour and consisted of eight sections, each with eight to forty questions that ascended in difficulty.

"It was agreed," wrote Robert Yerkes, "that the aim should be to test native ability rather than the results of school training," but that wouldn't be apparent from reading the questions. They asked recruits to unscramble sentences, memorize number sequences, and do arithmetic. The Vineland group tested vocabulary by asking if words had the same or opposite meaning ("empty—full," "vesper—matin"). Recruits had to know the color of chlorine gas, where silk came from, and who commanded Union troops at Mobile Bay.

They tested "Practical Judgment" with multiple-choice questions such as "Why should food be chewed before swallowing?" "Why is tennis good exercise?" and the wonderful:

Why ought every man to be educated? Because:
>Roosevelt was educated
>It makes a man more useful
>It costs money
>Some educated people are wise

The Beta exam, on the other hand, required no writing. There were maze tests and form-matching questions, which asked examinees to find a matching shape, such as a particular triangle. Beta examinees had to finish pictures that were missing one key element—a lady's arm in her reflection in the mirror, or steam coming out of a teakettle, for instance. They had to number a series of out-of-order pictures to make an intelligible story: for instance, pictures of a horse-drawn hearse, a doctor ringing the front doorbell, a priest ringing the doorbell, and a coffin, should have been numbered to reflect a sick patient visited by a doctor; then a priest; the coffin (presumably with the dead patient inside); and finally the hearse.

After two weeks at Vineland, the seven psychologists dispersed to try out their new exams around the country. Terman tested high school kids and inmates in California. Yerkes examined feeble-minded students and patients at the Boston Psychopathic Hospital. Others tested U.S. Marines and civilian men at the Carnegie Institute of Technology. Back at Vineland on June 25, 1917, the psychologists analyzed the results and satisfied themselves that their new tests were quite good. Yerkes, in an 890-page report published after the war entitled *Psychological Examining in the United States Army*, concluded that "the correlations which the tests gave were therefore in the main satisfactory. They were [correlated] high with outside measures of known value; they were high enough with one another to indicate that all were reasonably good tests of general intelligence."

By "outside measures of known value," Yerkes and his colleagues meant that performance on the Vineland tests correlated with previous intelligence tests, such as the Binet-Simon and the Stanford-Binet. It's not as if they had a physical measurement of intelligence with which to compare their results, though you could be forgiven for thinking that they did, with all their talk of general intelligence. From the beginning of intelligence testing in the United States, psychologists measured the worth of new exams, in large part, by correlating them with previous exams. That new exams measured intelligence relied (sometimes tacitly) on the assumption that old exams measured intelligence.

The completed and vetted exams allowed Yerkes to procure a grant for a private trial. Psychologists traveled down to Georgia and gave, without the official imprimatur of the military, four thousand soldiers the new exams. After the tests were administered, Yerkes sought to prove their validity again by asking officers to rank their men in terms of intelligence—"*avoid being too much influenced by his rank,*" their instructions read. (Apparently it was okay to be influenced by rank just a bit.) Just as previous test results had been compared to teacher evaluations, now the army exams were corroborated by officer opinions. Yerkes calculated that officer rankings correlated between 0.5 and 0.7 with intelligence scores, depending on the camp.

"The results suggest," Yerkes concluded, "that intelligence is likely to prove the most important single factor in determining a man's value in the military service."

The psychologists were relying on a social barometer—in this case, officer opinion—to validate their intelligence tests, which would have been fine had Yerkes not claimed that the decent correlations proved that they had tested innate intelligence. Yerkes' tautology went as follows: because officer opinion correlated fairly well with test results, his exams tested general intelligence. Therefore, intelligence was of primary importance when classifying men.

What was good enough for the social sciences was good enough for the army, and it also helped that in 1917 the U.S. Army was hopelessly underprepared for the war and that it needed help processing all the incoming recruits. In its own words, before World War I, the army was "scarcely more than a national constabulary," and it knew that a large police force would simply not suffice for the gruesome, complicated warfare that was taking place in

Europe. In March 1917, the U.S. Army totaled only 190,000 men. In less than two years it would process and train roughly 3.5 million men, swelling its ranks to 3.665 million, by November 1918. In the end, psychologists would test almost half of them.

The army needed not only vast numbers of men, but also men with specialized skills demanded by a war between industrialized nations. In March 1917, the army had 22,000 men in its cavalry, zero soldiers in its air service and chemical warfare bureau, and no tank and motor transport units. Even at the end of the war, a history of the World War I army personnel system written by the adjutant general's office stated that "among three and a half million American soldiers there are plenty of barbers, tailors, and lawyers for all military needs, but there are not anywhere near enough experienced men to meet the demands of the Army for soldiers who can drive a truck, send a wireless message, or supervise the training of a dispatch dog."

The army signed on to Yerkes' testing program in August 1917, and he received a commission as a major, along with the promise of commissions for forty to fifty psychologists to test recruits around the country. Unfortunately for Yerkes, he and his intelligence testers would be commissioned in the comical-sounding Sanitary Corps, which did not even require its officers to hold professional degrees. He had desperately wished for commissions in the more prestigious Medical Corps, but had been refused.

Once these Sanitary Corps officers got in full swing they would administer up to 200,000 Alpha and Beta tests to recruits monthly. By war's end the psychologists had tested 1.7 million men. The recruits represented all ethnicities in America: Choctaw Indians, Asians, "Hebrews" (as the army referred to Jewish men), African Americans, immigrants from all parts of Europe, and young white men from every American state. The rich, the poor, the middle class, the educated, and the unlettered were all represented; the psychologists, measuring tapes in hand, had access to American male minds.

Chapter 7

Alpha and Beta

Official instructions told examiners, mainly graduate students in education and psychology, to put the literate recruits at ease by explaining that they were "not looking for crazy people. The aim is to help find out what we are best fitted to do." The instructions also warned examiners to be as "genial" as possible to the illiterate men because they would "sometimes sulk and refuse to work."

Despite the admonition to be friendly, the psychologists often administered the army tests—the Beta, in particular—terribly, frequently breaking their own rules of test administration. Foreign illiterates were often not given the Beta, despite poor performance on the Alpha. And many white officers simply marched entire groups of black recruits directly to the Beta exam without bothering to find out whether they were literate. Official instructions required that the examiners retest, one on one, recruits who had received a zero on any subtest, on the assumption that something must have gone wrong with the administration of the exam. But the white examiners often did not retest black recruits who had received zeros, even with the knowledge that other African Americans had scored significantly higher when they were given individual tests.

The racist misapprehension of African Americans by white examiners was systematic, as evidenced by the Beta exam's official explanatory introduction, which was wacky beyond belief. The examiners were ordered to explain the test silently, in pantomime, regardless of whether the group before them was composed of non-English-speakers or English-speaking illiterates, as many African Americans were. Not surprisingly, many of the recruits, especially those who had never taken a test before, were completely confused about what was expected of them. They simply saw a bunch of white Sanitary Corps officers flapping their arms about silently and meaninglessly in front of them. Then they were given an exam.

According to one dissenting army psychologist, the examiners "had been forced by superior authority to make the tests as incomprehensible to the subjects examined as possible. . . . The examiners were ordered to follow a certain detailed and specific series of ballet antics, which had not only the merit of being perfectly incomprehensible and unrelated to mental testing, but also lent a highly confusing and distracting mystical atmosphere to the whole performance."

Apparently one group of African American recruits was so bemused by the white officers' pantomime that they fell asleep "en masse." Not surprisingly, blacks scored worse than whites. Robert Yerkes, however, blamed black recruits' inability to concentrate on their "relatively lower intelligence." This, despite noting in the same breath that when the examiners tried giving verbal instructions—rather than the pantomime—at Camp Sevier, South Carolina, the "procedure seemed to yield more satisfactory results."

Sanitary Corps test administrators at Camp Travis, Texas, reported back to psychology headquarters that the Beta was "a splendid examination for negroes. Every negro should be given beta." Without mentioning the test-taking conditions, white officers reported that blacks had on average a mental age of ten.

Many, if not most, regular army officers thought the intelligence tests were a waste of time, regardless of administration details or how blacks were treated. They considered the intelligence testers themselves to be "mental meddlers," "pests," and worse. Camp commanding officers often didn't see the point in the testing and were sometimes purposefully slow to help the psychologists round up examinees. The very phrase "psychological examining," both new and odd to people's ears, made the psychologists seem like quacks. Many officers didn't know the difference between psychiatrists and psychologists and, whoever these people were, the officers resented them poaching on their traditional territory—promoting and classifying men—especially given the sketchy methods.

The commander at Fort Dix, New Jersey, claimed that psychologists were as helpful to him as "a board of art critics to advise me which of my men were the most handsome, or a board of prelates to designate the true Christians." Recruits, he noted, who had received low intelligence test scores often turned out to be fine soldiers. One man who had received a D (they issued letter grades along with raw scores to help officers understand the results) was "a model of loyalty, reliability, cheerfulness, and the spirit of serene and general helpfulness. . . . What do we care about his 'intelligence'?"

In the face of negative officer reaction, Robert Yerkes knew how to spin bad press. In his postwar monograph *Psychological Examining in the United States Army*, he described this same Camp Dix commander as having "exhibited keen interest in the work and [having] effectively facilitated it."

Walter Scott aside, the psychologists weren't good at making friends in the army. For example, psychologists let slip that, as a group, doctors scored lower than other officers on the Alpha exam. At Camp Lee, Virginia, they noted, 66 percent of engineers and 57 percent of artillery officers received an A grade ("very superior; intellectually competent to command"), while only 27 percent of doctors did. Doctors, it turned out, were as dumb as the dentists and the vets, which couldn't have settled well with the doctors' professional self-image.

Worse, Walter Scott had read Yerkes and his intelligence-testing colleagues right: they were in it as much for themselves as to help the army. During the war they took time out from their duties to meet in Washington, D.C., to discuss publicity, and they didn't hesitate to use the war as an opportunity to collect data for their own research purposes. Alpha test instructions, for instance, required inductees to write down personal information—race, country of origin, salary before the war, occupation—that was unnecessary to the administration of the exam and superfluous to army needs, but of great interest to scientists interested in how intelligence differs among groups of people.

This attitude led the commander at Fort Meade, Maryland, to conclude that while the psychologists were careful and conscientious, and while their work would be "of great scientific interest at some future time," their tests nonetheless had "very little, if any, practical value in furthering the production of training of a draft army."

The psychologists didn't even wait for the cessation of hostilities to begin analyzing their data, and one finding became immediately apparent: far more Americans were illiterate than had previously been thought. After testing more than 1.5 million soldiers, Yerkes discovered that 25.3 percent could not "read and understand newspapers and write letters home." A further 5.7 percent did so badly on the Alpha test that they, too, had to take the picture-based Beta exam. Yerkes and his crew, imbued as they were with nativist assumptions, were shocked to learn that more than half of this 31 percent of illiterates were not immigrants, but had been born in the States.

They were also stunned to learn that the more formally educated a recruit, the more likely he was to score well on the Alpha test. Some researchers estimated the correlation between education and test scores to be as high as 0.81. The finding uncomfortably indicated that the tests were biased toward the educated examinee and that environment might matter as much or more than biology when it came to intelligence test results. Lewis Terman explained away the high correlation, however, by reasoning that smart people stayed in school longer than their less-gifted schoolmates.

But what really got the intelligence testers excited and concerned was how poorly most recruits performed. For the first time, psychologists had access to a cross section of society, and most Americans were alarmingly stupid. In fact, about half of them would be technically classified as morons: specifically, 47 percent of white and 89 percent of black servicemen. The average mental age of white recruits was 13.08 years—just one measly year above psychology's official demarcation for feebleminded. They had previously thought the average mental age of Americans was 16, and now they stood corrected.

"It appears that feeble-mindedness, as at present defined is of much greater frequency of occurrence than had been originally supposed," Lewis Terman concluded.

With the proverbial scratch of the head, though, psychologists realized that they couldn't exclude half of all recruits from the draft. Who would fight the Bosch? They would have to lower the mental age acceptable to the military. In some camps, examiners decided to recommend that men with a mental age of less than 10 be barred from service, but even that proved too high. Later they lowered the bar to a mental age of below 8, and that seemed to keep enough bodies in the military.

Psychologists also thought their test results indicated that they were scientifically testing intelligence, based on the fact that charted recruits' scores formed a rough bell curve. Again, the psychologists engaged in a remarkable syllogism. They assumed that intelligence was distributed normally, as Francis Galton had posited. Army test scores were distributed normally, too, they pointed out. Therefore army tests measured intelligence.

The U.S. Army didn't care about the shape of the results curve, but officers' concerns about the testing program were somewhat assuaged when the results comported with their own class and race prejudices. Officers (75 percent of whom had gone to college) performed better than enlisted men on the Alpha test. Also, southern African Americans (20 percent of whom had no formal education) scored the worst on both exams. These findings allowed decision-makers to at least tolerate the testers for a while, if not rely much on their product.

Yerkes did manage to persuade the military to consider intelligence test scores when promoting men, but with little result. Before World War I, officers would promote men beneath them based on their personal knowledge and assign duties to enlistees almost randomly. One intelligence tester explained that military classification before World War I had not improved much since "the British colonel in the Boer War who stood at the gangplank of a troop ship in Capetown and tapped each descending recruit with his riding crop, diagnosing by some process of occult divination: 'Infantry! Cavalry! Artillery! Er—Medical Corps!'"

To bring the army up to date on personnel matters, the top brass turned to Walter Scott and put him in charge of the Committee on Classification of Personnel. Scott and others created the army's first qualification card, which stated what a man was professionally qualified for, as well as systems for rating officer candidates and tradesmen's abilities.

"The old [personnel] system resembled a craftsman's shop where each article is made by hand and finished by one individual," the army's official personnel history stated. "The new system had to be like a great factory where each process is separated and volume production is assured through rigid functionalization and organization. Men had to be sorted, recorded and assigned as goods in some great warehouse are received, checked, sorted, stored and shipped on order."

In other words, this modern processing was ripe for intelligence tests, which offered hope for ranking men's intellectual ability along a continuum, but because of the Hotel Walton schism, Yerkes was on the outside of this process. Just a few months after the Hotel Walton fight, Yerkes realized that Scott was making better headway with Army decisionmakers than he was, so he ingratiated himself onto Scott's committee by eating a little crow. "I fully believe that by holding things together we shall do much more for our science, as well as for national defense, than by working through divers channels," Yerkes wrote to Scott. As a result, Alpha and Beta test scores were included on each person's qualification card. At least in theory, if not often in practice, men's measured intelligence was to be used in all personnel decisions.

Some personnel officers did allocate men based on their intelligence scores, by assigning each company "its pro rata share of superior men, average men, and inferior men." Sometimes, too, the army used the mental tests to help select officers from the masses of new recruits, but this process was never systematic. It would not be until well after World War I that the military would routinely assign men and women to jobs based on IQ test results.

In the end, the army was never impressed by Robert Yerkes' uptight, self-serious academic personality, his profession's ponderous style, or their intelligence tests. Army brass consistently commissioned psychologists well below other professionals. At the beginning of the war, psychologists were often made lieutenants while doctors were made captains, majors, or lieutenant colonels. Yerkes was palpably indignant over the personal and professional treatment they received throughout the war. "Indeed, the low rank assigned to competent, experienced and adequately trained psychologists in the Sanitary Corps is one of the most serious injustices to this new service, as well as to the individuals concerned with it," he wrote.

The army never understood the intelligence testers. Before the war was over, the War Plans Division had ruled that psychologists could not take part in the elimination of mental defectives, surely their main use. At the same time, the army awarded Walter Scott the only Distinguished Service Medal received by a psychologist. In what must have been construed as a not-so-subtle insult, the secretary of war thanked Yerkes for all his hard work—not in person, but via Scott, who might have enjoyed that moment.

Ultimately it's difficult to know how or if the tests helped the U.S. Army in World War I. Were men who knew what product "Velvet Joe" advertised (tobacco) braver when running headlong into enfilade during the bloody Meuse-Argonne offensive? Or, more plausibly, did the men who correctly answered the question "Why are cats useful animals?"—as the Alpha exam asked—read maps and understand instructions better than other recruits? It's possible, but we don't know.

Of the five million recruits the army examined, eight hundred thousand were rejected, 42,000 of them for mental or emotional reasons. According to Robert Yerkes, psychologists recommended that less than eight thousand men be barred from service based on feeblemindedness (the ultimate decision was up to a discharge board, and psychologists only occasionally sat on those). It's not clear if the army ultimately paid attention to these recommendations—or, if they did, that the army was rendered any more efficient.

The highest possible numbers affected by the massive testing regime were remarkably small. As the historian Franz Samelson calculates, "Altogether the testing *at best* screened out 1/6 of 1% of the total manpower pool, 1% of all rejects, or 10% of those rejected/discharged as mentally unfit; it may have screened out practically none while *at worst*, it eliminated a relatively small number of men who the army could in fact have used."

The use of intelligence tests during World War I was very similar to their use on Ellis Island: in the end, many people were processed, but few were actually affected. During and especially after the war, psychologists made a big deal about how useful and important mental tests were, but in fact the testers were more successful in promoting their fledgling field than improving the army or protecting the country.

While the tests may not have helped the American war effort, there were four extremely important consequences. One, psychology established its reputation on the basis of the exams. Two, whereas before the war mass testing could have taken many different forms, including tests of many different personality characteristics, psychology rallied mainly around measuring intelligence in a single, rigid way. Three, because of the use of tests during the war, American schools would flock to intelligence testing, and a lucrative testing industry would be born. And four, analyzing Alpha and Beta exam results became an intellectual cottage industry in the 1920s that bolstered racist, nativist, and xenophobic tendencies.

Despite the army's dim view of intelligence tests and their practical relevance, Robert Yerkes, Lewis Terman, and the ex–Sanitary Corps colleagues used the war to catapult their careers and field. From then on, American students have taken IQ tests and their standardized test progeny, such as the SAT and graduate school entrance exams. Very few of them, on the other hand, have ever heard of Walter Scott or his *Scientific Selection of Salesmen* test. If the Alpha and Beta tests weren't as useful to the army as the *Salesmen* test was, how did the IQ test not only survive but also flourish after the war and for the rest of the century?

As with other products, it wasn't necessarily a question of quality, but rather a combination of chutzpah, self-promotion, and timing. Before the war, Yerkes, Terman, and other intelligence testers had warred over small scraps of funding for their research, everyone ultimately receiving very little support. The war taught these psychologists that it was better to band together and cooperate than to just scrape by individually. As a result, unfortunately, many psychologists lost their critical edge. Before World War I, Robert Yerkes had been thoughtfully critical of Lewis Terman's IQ test and his testing methods. He argued that Terman's test was inflexible and wouldn't allow for near-right answers, as Yerkes' own scale of intelligence did. He also felt that Terman placed too much emphasis on chronological age, when other factors, such as sex and ethnicity, were just as important. Foreshadowing modern critics such as Stephen Jay Gould, Yerkes even pointed out the dangers of comparing different groups of people—for instance, blacks and whites—with a yardstick that didn't take into account their dissimilar environments.

After the war, it was as if Yerkes suffered from battlefield amnesia: he seemed to forget not only his criticisms of Terman's Stanford-Binet, but also his own methods and tests. In this way, World War I acted to restrict the range of testing products in the United States—and therefore eventually the rest of the world. Gone were Scott's and Yerkes' tests, leaving just one successful, and soon to be lucrative, model: Lewis Terman's Stanford-Binet IQ test, modified by the army's Alpha. By rallying behind it, psychologists gained fund-

ing, power, and respect, but at the price of squashing other, potentially better, tests and ideas.

After the war, Lewis Terman not only had the tool and the
backing of his profession (he became president of the APA in
1922), but he also had the vision. He knew where his tests were
most needed—in schools—and how to pitch the product. Like
many good salesmen, Terman saw reality in a slanted way favorable
to himself. A few years after the war, he argued that the army Alpha
and Beta exams "demonstrated beyond question that the methods
of mental measurement are capable of making a contribution of
great value to army efficiency. . . . That their universal use in the
schoolroom is necessary to educational efficiency will doubtless
soon be accepted as a matter of course."

To the public, the U.S. Army seemed to endorse intelligence
testing during the war. In the words of one intelligence tester,
"Before the World War, the average intelligent layman probably
had little confidence in the value or the use of mental tests. After
the War, he believed that psychologists had devised a simple and
relatively perfect method of measuring intelligence." Nothing had
changed, of course, except the public's perception.

World War I allowed intelligence testing to grow from a narrow
field used primarily to test the feebleminded in limited situations to,
Americans thought, one capable of sorting and ranking all types of
human beings, be they smart, dumb, or average. And in a phrase
that has become famous in the history of intelligence testing, James
McKeen Cattell—the Columbia professor who discovered that his
physiological tests were useless at the turn of the century—said that
World War I "put psychology on the map."

Terman and Yerkes' biggest accomplishment was not convincing the army to test recruits, but persuading America of the usefulness and success of the army tests, despite the dearth of supportive
evidence. At war's end, Terman said he was immediately "bombarded by requests from public school men for our army mental
tests in order that they may be used in school systems."

Over the next year, using Rockefeller Foundation funds, Yerkes
and Terman oversaw the creation of "National Intelligence Tests"

for use in grades three to eight. They were aided by many former army intelligence testers, who helped to convert the army tests into a tool that was ideally suited for use in large, funds-strapped public schools crammed with students of all stripes. The transition was easy.

"The army and the school, of course, represent similar forms of organizations," Joel Spring, a historian of psychology, argued in the early 1970s. "The superintendent sits as commander of the armies, the principal acts as field commander, the teachers as officers, and below this command is a vast army of pupils. Orders flow from above, and pupils like soldiers receive privileges but are without rights."

Also like the military, schools were inundated with bodies they didn't know how to sort. Colleges snapped up the Alpha exams when the army unloaded them at reduced, fire-sale prices. Primary and secondary schools across the country clamored for the National Intelligence Tests to track their students into low, medium, and high classes.

In large part it was the multiple-choice question, the most radical and innovative testing technique employed during World War I, that excited educators. They were so easy to administer and grade it almost didn't matter who the school administrators put in front of the class.

By 1921, Terman and his colleagues had sold four hundred thousand copies of the third- to eighth-grade National Intelligence Tests, causing him to predict, in Henry Ford fashion, that there would soon be "a mental test for every child" in America. Aided by Terman's determined hand, science merged with mass marketing and production, and education colluded with industrial standardization. By the mid-1920s, psychologists would create more than seventy-five different mental tests for schools, and up to four million students a year would take one.

Terman promised schools that his tests revealed students' innate and immutable ability: a single, testable trait called intelligence. "The limits of a child's educability can be fairly accurately predicted by means of mental tests given in the first school year," he said. And when schools knew children's innate ability, he argued, they became much more efficient. Instead of grouping children by age, they could group them by ability—or, in psychology's terms, mental age. Children could learn material appropriate to their inborn ability: gifted children would be stimulated, while slow children would not be discouraged by classes that move too quickly.

With the National Intelligence Test, the examiners told schools they could detect the "subnormal" and the "unusually bright" and begin to provide vocational guidance (in ascending order of worth) "as among labor, trades, and professions." In 1922, Terman broke the vocational guidance down with scientific precision in a paper. The really dumb students, those who scored below 70, would break rocks and take other unskilled jobs. Those between 70 and 80 might be more capable of wielding a simple tool or two. Moving up the intelligence ladder, students who scored between 80 and 100 could manage skilled labor jobs or basic clerical work. Between 100 and 115, the student could become a semiprofessional (imagine a low-level salesman). The final and favored group, with scores above 115, would compose the professional and business class.

Terman and his colleagues had established themselves as the Brahmans of sorting. The psychologists successfully persuaded others that only they were able to divine—in just fifty minutes!— children's future civic worth. This boy will be a gardener, that boy an architect. At their urging, schools in the 1920s began to talk about "ability grouping," "homogeneous grouping," and "tracking." Each caste had its place in school, and therefore society. The low-scoring groups were not taught the same subject matter as the gifted classes at a slower rate, which would have been possible for most less-gifted students. No: many of the students were trained to fix cars, wield a pick, and work with wood. This is ultimately the radicalism of intelligence testing; the psychologists thought—and some still think—that they could rejigger society along one easily tested attribute called intelligence.

In addition to getting the tests into schools, experts had a field day with the 1.7 million test results gathered during the war. Writers extracted political and policy lessons, in particular, from Robert Yerkes' conclusions about national intelligence in his lengthy report *Psychological Examining in the United States Army*. Thanks to the extraneous personal information gathered from recruits during the war, almost every conceivable group could be categorized and compared according to their intelligence. And when the studies were written up in the popular press, Americans were stunned by how stupid they apparently were (remember, according to test results, almost half of them were morons).

Admen were among the most interested. The army test results worked their way into the ad industry's publications, becoming slightly warped, like an urban myth. "Most of us have the mind of a child of ten," one man wrote. And, "Remember, the average citizen has the mentality of a child of twelve," said another, as if American advertisers needed prompting to dumb down their pitches.

Cultural critics said the test results explained the popularity of tabloid newspapers and lowbrow movies. Newspapermen debated whether to write intelligently or to write for people in language they could understand. *Time* magazine decided to take the high road and not include "a multitude of features dedicated to Mr. and Mrs. Moron and the Little Morons."

Yerkes' postwar report *Psychological Examining* also allowed psychologists, racists, eugenicists, and xenophobes (sometimes all rolled into one person) to compare social groups, like a family seated in the parlor critiquing snapshots of cousins. African Americans, it turned out, had average IQ scores about fifteen points lower than whites. This was so unsurprising to 1920s America that newspapers of record didn't bother reporting on the finding. Of more concern to commentators at the time were the southern and eastern European immigrants arriving in America every day. In *Psychological Examining*, Yerkes had spent pages full of charts, graphs, and statistical analyses explaining how the least socially desirable peoples had lower average IQs than those people smiled upon, such as English immigrants. Although the media attention given them was new, the ideas were familiar to intelligence testers. In 1912, for instance, Henry Goddard started measuring the minds of immigrants on Ellis Island and found that only about 3 percent of northern Europeans coming off the boats were feebleminded, whereas up to 9 percent of the southern Europeans were.

The army tests corroborated these findings about groups on a grand scale. In *Psychological Examining*, Yerkes used a bar chart to illustrate the rank order of roughly 13,200 foreign-born test takers. England topped the list with the highest number of men who had scored an A on the Alpha test, followed by men from Holland, Denmark, and Scotland. After working its way geographically southward and eastward, the chart revealed that Russia, Italy, and Poland provided the stupidest white recruits in the land.

Like teenagers at a horror flick, Americans of the time were game for a good scare, and experts of the day, happily gobbling up and regurgitating Yerkes' book, were only too willing to comply. Writers such as Carl Brigham, Yerkes' assistant during the war (Brigham later created the SAT, which was based on the army tests), warned that 46 percent of the men from Poland, 42.3 percent of Italians, and 39 percent of Russians were as dumb as, and in some cases dumber than, "negroes." Blacks as intelligence benchmark: Brigham knew his audience.

When researchers interpret tests as reflecting inherent differences among groups of people, they often claim to be simple messengers reluctantly fulfilling their civic duty by reporting the cold facts to the public. They'd really rather be doing something else, but they feel honor-bound to inform the public of the results. Brigham was no exception. "I am not afraid to say anything that is true, no matter how ugly the facts may be, and am perfectly willing to stake whatever position I have on the outcome," he explained in a letter to Yerkes about his new book *A Study of American Intelligence*. "If the 'Conclusions' are published approximately as they stand, I shall invest everything that I can scrape together on short-term life insurance in the hope of leaving an estate."

America was in a particularly tight spot, Brigham argued. Now that World War I was over, hundreds of thousands of poor European immigrants were again clogging Ellis Island's Great Hall. These dullards were mixing with pure American stock of northern European descent and causing the race to deteriorate. Worse, there were already Negroes in the States, and they were also dragging the average intelligence down. Blacks and constantly arriving inferior whites were a gene pool–threatening double whammy that European countries did not have to contend with. "We must face a possibility of racial admixture here that is infinitely worse than that faced by any European country today, for we are incorporating the negro into our racial stock, while all of Europe is comparatively free from this taint," Brigham wrote. "The decline of American intelligence will be more rapid than the decline of the intelligence of European national groups, owing to the presence here of the negro."

For Brigham and like-minded thinkers, the U.S. Congress had a duty to protect America's national intelligence. "The steps that should be taken to preserve or increase our present intellectual capacity must of course be dictated by science and not by political expediency," Brigham wrote. "Immigration should not only be restrictive but highly selective."

Congress was far ahead of Brigham. Lawmakers had already established an immigrant-quota system by the time Brigham published *A Study of American Intelligence*. His writings as well as others' were known on Capitol Hill, but really the army intelligence test results simply offered legislators a scientific justification to make xenophobic immigration law permanent. Psychologists didn't create the policy that greatly reduced the number of southern and eastern Europeans entering the United States, but they were an important part of the scientific wing of the anti-immigrant movement.

When given an opportunity to help the country during World War I, most American psychologists thought their best weapon was the intelligence test. The version they chose to employ—mainly a combination of Terman's Stanford-Binet and paper-and-pencil versions of performance questions—more firmly established the field of psychology. But in the process of overselling what their tool measured, the psychologists bolstered harmful lawmaking and educational policy. Young students were now tracked into classes based on one test score, and the innate inferiority of African Americans and certain immigrants was supposedly proven scientifically.

Chapter 8

From Segregation to Sterilization: Carrie Buck's Story

In the 1920s, a young Charlottesville, Virginia, woman named Carrie Buck had many problems, mostly of the sort she couldn't control. Her father was dead and her mother, Emma, was poor and uneducated. When Carrie was very young, the county decided that her mother was feebleminded and ordered her institutionalized, leaving Carrie and her siblings without parents. At age three, Carrie was sent to live with foster parents, John and Alice Dobbs, who lived near the gracious Thomas Jefferson–designed University of Virginia campus. They sent her to elementary school for five years, and then she stayed home with them.

In 1923, Alice Dobbs went out of town for the summer, and her nephew took the opportunity to rape the seventeen-year-old Carrie. She became pregnant, and this seemingly local, familial event would change the course not only of Carrie's life, but eventually that of many others throughout the world.

The Dobbses decided to cover up their nephew's crime by initiating institutionalization proceedings against Carrie. John Dobbs contacted the Red Cross office in Charlottesville and said that they had a pregnant "girl" living with them and that he "wanted to have her committed somewhere—to have her sent to some institution." John and his wife also petitioned the local family court, saying that they had "residing with them an epileptic and feeble-minded person, one Carrie E. Buck, a white female child of the age of seventeen years." She hadn't always been this way, they said; her malaise came on when she was about ten or eleven and seemed to be getting worse. "Your petitioners," they wrote, "have cared for her as an act of kindness so long as they were able," but it was time for her to be sent to the State Colony for the Epileptic and Feeble-Minded, where her mother, not so coincidentally, was already incarcerated.

On January 23, 1924, a Charlottesville family court judge issued a warrant commanding Carrie and her biological and foster parents to appear before a commission to determine whether Carrie was feebleminded or epileptic. The court empowered John Dobbs, who worked for the local streetcar company, to bring Carrie in. The hearing was held the same day the warrant was issued, but only the Dobbses and Carrie showed up, as her mother was already incarcerated in Lynchburg and her father was dead. From the get-go until the end, three years later in 1927, when her court case would reach to the heights of the U.S. Supreme Court, Carrie was left to fend for herself.

Carrie Buck's legal case is important not only in terms of its impact on how IQ tests came to be used in medicine and law during the first half of the twentieth century, but also because it illustrates how intelligence—particularly in cases concerning the feebleminded—was often amorphously and flexibly defined by behavior, sometimes corroborated by IQ test results, but not always. In the past, poor women had been incarcerated for frowned-upon behavior, such as poverty or prostitution, but in Carrie Buck's case, the stakes were about to rise considerably.

The family judge at Carrie's incarceration hearing appointed two Charlottesville doctors—one of whom was the Dobbs' family physician—to form the commission along with him, and they found Carrie to be in perfectly fine health, at least physically. The Dobbs's family doctor, however, certified that he had "examined Carrie E. Buck and [found] that she is feeble-minded within the meaning of the law, and is a suitable subject for an institution for feeble-minded." In terms of expert medical testimony, that was it: there is no evidence that the doctor had even administered an IQ test, but just deemed her feebleminded within the law, whatever that meant. (The doctors also found her, despite a dearth of evidence, epileptic.)

The rest of the court's decision to commit Carrie was based on the Dobbs's brief answers to a set of boilerplate questions, not on any real evidence of feeblemindedness. To the question "How was the peculiarity manifested?" they responded simply "Peculiar actions" without elaboration. "Is patient honest and truthful? If no, give particulars," one question requested, but the Dobbs's only response was a singular "No." Worse than merely insufficient, their responses were inconsistent. At the beginning of the deposition they said that Carrie had never had "epilepsy, headaches, nervousness, fits or convulsions of any kind," but later they must have forgotten this when they stated that her epilepsy had existed "Since childhood."

Despite the brevity, the inconsistencies, and the lack of evidence, the commission found Carrie was "feeble-minded, or epileptic" and decided to institutionalize her. Carrie herself, a big-boned girl with dark hair cut short and high cheekbones, uttered not a peep, at least as far as the written record reflects. The same day that the warrant was issued and the hearing held, the judge ordered Carrie to the State Colony for Epileptics and Feeble-Minded in Lynchburg, Virginia.

This behavioral and circumstantial assessment of intelligence, with no real ties to biology or cognition, allowed mainstream Americans to treat her and, in the years that followed, tens of thousands of others, as lower-grade humans. Although she was soon to be tested with the Stanford-Binet exam at the state colony, in essence Buck was institutionalized for being poor, pregnant, and vulnerable, not on the basis of any real gauge of her mental abilities. The only hiccup in institutionalizing her was what got her into trouble in the first place: the Dobbses would have to wait until after Carrie gave birth—to a daughter, named Vivian—before the colony would admit her. In the cruelest of twists, the Dobbses were allowed to adopt Vivian when the state incarcerated Buck.

Soon after giving birth, Carrie boarded a train on the morning of June 4, 1924, with Caroline Wilhelm, a Red Cross social worker who would reemerge malevolently in Carrie's story just five months later. Wilhelm delivered Carrie to the colony at Lynchburg, her new one-thousand-acre home along the James River north of town. The setting was bucolic, but the colony was horribly oppressive to its inmates, who were mainly poor, unwanted children and young teenagers. The boys were forced to work in the fields and the girls to do domestic work in the dining halls and kitchens for as little as 25 cents a week. Punishments for perceived infractions at Lynchburg included being sent to a "blind room" for up to ninety days at a time, where shaved-headed inmates stayed alone, wearing nothing but a hospital gown and with just a mattress and a bucket for company.

In the 1920s, the "menace of the feebleminded" still existed in the United States and Europe, and Carrie, her mother, and newborn daughter were caught up in it. By this time, however, the political and economic landscape had changed, making expensive incarceration policies less tolerable. And despite the segregation of the feebleminded for some time, there had been no great reduction in crime, poverty, alcoholism, and other social ills, as promised by eugenicists.

Segregation of the feebleminded as a theory had lost some of its appeal, too. After all, at the end of World War I, psychologists had revealed that almost half of all Americans were morons, and almost half the country couldn't be locked up. Anyway, most people seemed to be law-abiding and getting along all right, morons or not. By the late teens, directors of institutions for the feebleminded had discovered that patients with a mental age as low as five were able to work outside institution walls without causing problems, so the feebleminded couldn't be quite as scary as previously thought.

By the 1920s, too, science had debunked the idea that a single gene controlled intelligence. Most significantly, geneticists began to understand just how complicated traits were, even in lowly creatures such as the fruit fly, let alone in human beings. To these scientists, the idea that intelligence, an undefined but surely complicated trait, was controlled by one gene—unaffected by environment—became laughable. In 1925, the geneticist Herbert Jennings wrote that eugenic arguments that complex human traits were defined by single genes are "an illustration of the adage that a little knowledge is a dangerous thing. The doctrine is dead—though as yet, like the decapitated turtle, it is not sensible of it. . . . Neither eye color, nor tallness, nor feeblemindedness, nor any other characteristic, is a unit character."

Given this research, it may be surprising that people still worried about the feebleminded at all, but social scientists, professionals, and policymakers still obsessed about how dangerous the retarded were. Only now, given the economic climate, they had to keep institutional costs low, so they needed a new fix for the feebleminded that didn't involve locking them up for their entire childbearing years. This reality led them to forced sterilization, which had been talked about and even practiced for years, but now took on more importance. People saw sterilization as a remedy neither as extreme as death nor as expensive as incarceration; it was the epitome of progressive moderation.

Until Carrie Buck's case, however, coerced sterilization often had to be conducted secretly because in most states it wasn't legal. Nevertheless, it happened, even where it was illegal, and people outside institutions knew it was going on. Before Carrie was institutionalized, George Mallory, a poor, uneducated man with twelve children living in Richmond, Virginia, figured out that Dr. Albert Priddy, the superintendent at the State Colony for Epileptics and Feeble-Minded, had been quietly and illegally sterilizing his patients for years. In September 1916, Mallory was out of town working at a sawmill when his wife, Willie, was arrested for allegedly operating a brothel, and their dozen children were rounded up. After a hearing in Juvenile Court, the youngest of the children were sent off to the Children's Home Society for being "exposed to vicious and immoral influences." A court found two of the older girls and

Willie Mallory herself to be feebleminded and sent them to the colony at Lynchburg. Six months later, Willie and one daughter were released, but only because Priddy had sterilized them, thereby supposedly rendering them harmless to society.

The Mallorys' fourteen-year-old daughter Nannie remained at the colony, incarcerated but with her Fallopian tubes still intact. In November 1917, Mallory wrote to Priddy, demanding that she be released, without the unnecessary surgery.

"Dear sir," he wrote, "one more time I am go write to you to ask you about my child I cannot here from her bye no means." Mallory had written to Nannie and sent her a package of supplies, but hadn't heard back. "I want to know when can I get my child home again my family have been broked up on false pertents same as white slavery, Dr what busneiss did you have opreateding on my wife and daughtr with out my consent. I am a hard working man can take care of my family and can prove it and before I am finish you will find out that I am. . . . My wife is 43 years old and to be treated in that way, you ought to be a shamed of your selft of opreateding on her at that age. . . . I am a humanbeen as well as you are I am tired of bein treated this way for nothing I want my child [back]."

The letter greatly angered Priddy. "I have your letter of the 5th of Nov. which is insulting and threatening in its tone and I want to say to you that if you dare write me another communication I will have you arrested and brought here [to the colony] too."

Unswayed, the sawmill worker sued, seeking the release of his children, who were still at the Home Society, and Nannie from the colony. On these causes of action he was successful, but he did fail in his attempts at trial to receive pain and suffering compensation for his wife's coerced sterilization. Priddy, who for years had been an advocate for eugenic sterilizations, successfully defended himself on the grounds that the surgery was necessary for Mrs. Mallory's health—that is, non-eugenic grounds. Despite Priddy's victory, however, the judge had a word with him after the case. Better not perform any more eugenic sterilizations, he advised, until Virginia had enacted a law legalizing the procedures.

Years later, Albert Priddy would pin his hopes on Carrie Buck, who arrived at the colony just in time to be the trial case for legal coerced sterilization. In the meantime, before her arrival, he would have to sterilize women quietly. Whereas, before Mallory's lawsuit, Priddy had crowed about the eugenic sterilizations he had performed (such as when he talked of surgery on "twenty young women of the moron type"), after *Mallory v. Priddy*, colony records reflected many more pelvic diseases, operated upon "for the relief of physical suffering." Nothing had changed; he was still sterilizing the feebleminded, but in official records he had to call it something else.

Priddy had been embarrassed at the very public *Mallory* trial, and he wanted to operate on young women with impunity in the future, so in 1920 he began lobbying for the passage of a Virginia law legalizing eugenic operations. According to Paul Lombardo, a historian and biomedical ethics professor at the University of Virginia who works within walking distance of where Carrie Buck grew up, "This is tort reform 1920s style. [Priddy] got sued and he wanted an immunity statute." Priddy would succeed, and the world would never be the same.

Paul Lombardo knows more than anyone else about Carrie Buck because he's been obsessed with her case—off and on, but mainly on—since 1980, when he was a history graduate student at the University of Virginia. He stumbled across her story while reading the newspaper across the street from the campus during a late breakfast one day. He talked to his adviser, who said, Lombardo remembered, "'That's a famous old case, you know.' And I nodded and said, yeah I knew, but I didn't. I mean I'd seen it in the article, but I didn't know anything about it."

Lombardo began uncovering records about Carrie Buck that few, if any, had looked at, and he turned them into his Ph.D. thesis. But back in the early 1980s, nobody else seemed to care. "The funny part was, at the time I wrote my dissertation . . . nobody was really interested in the topic." People thought, "who wants to talk about people having operations on their body like this and it was kind of a dark history. Nobody was paying any attention to this."

Carrie Buck's story wouldn't let Lombardo alone. He attended law school at the University of Virginia after getting his Ph.D., but he ended up spending far too much time away from his studies, roaming around Virginia looking for Buck-related sources. After a while, Lombardo found that the paper trail kept pointing to Lynchburg, home of the Virginia colony (still there today but under a different name) and its superintendent, Dr. Albert Priddy. What he untangled from a complicated paper trail was a truly great American legal scam propagated by a small group of Virginia men intent on achieving their personal and ideological agendas.

"It is a quintessential American story about government officials behaving badly, the poor and the dispossessed being treated poorly; about the clash between people of different world views and different classes. And it's about a little girl who ends up being a symbol of something that is totally false and then she dies. It's got all of the elements of a great epic," Lombardo said.

Lombardo discovered that Priddy initially failed to get a eugenic sterilization bill passed in the state legislature, so in 1924 he turned to a longtime friend, a state senator and fellow eugenicist named Aubrey Strode. Strode agreed to draft legislation legalizing eugenic sterilization for submission to the state Senate. He knew that for years state courts across the country had been striking down eugenic sterilization legislation as unconstitutional, so after considerable analysis of other states' laws, he drafted a Virginia bill that would overcome any foreseeable constitutional arguments. By March 1924, Strode had successfully brought the law through both houses of the Virginia General Assembly, meaning that Albert Priddy and the colony at Lynchburg were almost ready to sterilize their inmates legally.

The timing of Carrie Buck's June 1924 arrival at the Virginia colony couldn't have been worse—for her. In August, just two months later, Dr. Priddy stood before the colony's board of directors requesting that eighteen inmates be sterilized, including Carrie Buck. But remembering the public humiliation of *Mallory v. Priddy*, he requested that "as a matter of precautionary safety . . . a test case of the constitutionality of the [new] Sterilization Law be made before any operation is performed." The board agreed that such a legal case was necessary and told Priddy to consult with Aubrey Strode, who discussed the matter with the board a month later. Strode agreed that no sterilizations should take place until the constitutionality of the procedure had been settled by the Virginia State Court, and possibly even the U.S. Supreme Court. Otherwise, the colony and its management were vulnerable to being sued—again.

Priddy told the board during this meeting that Carrie Buck was a perfect candidate for the procedure. He had examined her with the Stanford-Binet and concluded that she was a low-grade moron with the mental age of nine (he made a mistake—a mental age of nine should have placed her as a middle-grade moron). Despite Lewis Terman's belief that the questions on his Stanford-Binet primarily tested "native intelligence, not school knowledge or home training," it's hard to believe that Carrie wouldn't have done better with more than just five years of elementary school. In part, the Stanford-Binet measured vocabulary and how well examinees could repeat a series of digits ("4-7-1-9-5-2") backward.

Although there is no record of Carrie's actual test, Priddy would have asked her to differentiate between words such as "laziness and idleness" and "evolution and revolution." He even would have presented her with a written code used during the Civil War and asked her to write, in code, the words "come quickly." It's unlikely that Alice Dobbs, Carrie's foster mother, had spent much time with her on such school-like activities.

At this colony board meeting, just as at her incarceration hearing, Carrie's family circumstances and supposed behavior were equally as damning as her test results. Priddy said that no one knew who her father was (which wasn't true) and that "her mother, Emma Buck, is and has been for several years a feeble-minded patient in the Colony of low mental grade." Priddy also claimed that Carrie "had one illegitimate, mentally defective child," although it isn't clear how he could have known, considering the baby was only six months old and he had never seen her. When he concluded that Carrie was "a moral delinquent, but physically capable of earning her own living if protected against childbearing by sterilization," the board agreed.

Rather than taking her straight to the operating room, which was handily on colony grounds, the board decided to make Carrie's sterilization a "test case" to see if the courts would uphold Virginia's sterilization law. The board members charged Aubrey Strode, the man who had drafted the sterilization law, with bringing Buck's case to trial. He would represent the defendants, Albert Priddy, in his role as superintendent, and the State Colony for Epileptics and Feeble-Minded. It was a remarkable reversal of how the American legal system is supposed to work. In general, plaintiffs bring suits and defendants try to avoid and defend them. In Carrie's case, the defendant, Albert Priddy and the colony, decided that Buck, the plaintiff, should sue them. They even chose her attorney for her and paid his legal fees. It's hard to imagine a bigger conflict of interest for Buck's attorney—never raised by any court in the three years of litigation—and the outcome would be unsurprisingly dire for her and hundreds of thousands of others around the world whose surgeries were often rationalized by Carrie's eventually famous legal case.

The colony hired a friend of Strode's and a former board member to be Carrie Buck's defense counsel. Irving Whitehead had been friendly with Strode through law school, World War I (Whitehead had helped Strode secure an army commission), and the practice of law. Whitehead had helped out, too, on Strode's campaign for state senator, and when he had sat on the colony's board he had voted to authorize Priddy's previous, illegal sterilizations. Two months before Buck was institutionalized, the colony had named a new building after Whitehead. And just six days before Buck's trial, Strode put in a good word for Whitehead, who was applying for a government job. To make matters worse, Whitehead was a banking lawyer, not the best counsel to have in a reproductive rights case, but the board thought him adequate for his role in the "friendly" litigation, as they thought of it. He fit their purposes perfectly, for Whitehead would put up a show of defending Buck but wouldn't come close to the level of even competent counsel. From the outset, then, Carrie Buck's legal case was based on collusion, pure and simple.

Just two months later, on November 18, 1924, Carrie sat next to her newly assigned defense counsel in the Amherst, Virginia, Circuit Court, in a little white courthouse with a redbrick walkway and black shutters that dispensed justice for a rural area. Strode's case relied on three sets of witnesses, while Irving Whitehead was satisfied simply with tepid cross-examinations of these witnesses. Whitehead put no witnesses on the stand and submitted no evidence to contradict his friend's version of the facts.

The first set of Strode's witnesses was composed of locals who could bolster the image that Carrie and her family were socially inadequate, a technique that quickly became absurd. Many of them didn't know Carrie herself, or even her family members that well. One witness was the superintendent of the County Home, and had only seen Carrie's half brother Roy "passing through the place back and forth." Strode had to wring damning testimony against Roy out of the superintendent.

"You say you have seen him passing through the place: do you know anything about him?" Strode asked.

"I don't know anything particular about him. I think he is rather an unusual boy."

"In what way?"

"He struck me as being right peculiar."

"He is a peculiar boy?"

"I think so."

"Now, why can't you tell us what you know about him?"

The only thing the witness could dredge up was that he saw Roy once waiting for about twenty minutes for some friends who'd already come and gone.

"Is that the only time you saw him?"

"No, sir, I have seen him a number of times."

"But in your opinion he is mentally defective?"

"Yes, sir, but I can't recall any other specific instance that would cause me to think so—not any particular thing."

Strode tried to get the man to describe a couple of Carrie's cousins, but he got the same kinds of responses. Strode had more luck with a couple of Charlottesville nurses. One testified that Carrie's mother, Emma, was poor, lived in a bad neighborhood, was unable or unwilling to work, and the producer of illegitimate children. The way Strode and these nurses talked about the Buck family's intelligence also shows how disconnected people's concept of measuring intelligence had become since the cautious Binet method of twenty years before. They had abandoned testing altogether, leaving only the patina of scientific language in place.

"I would say that Emma [Carrie's mother] had the mentality of a child of twelve," one nurse concluded.

"That is the mother of these children?" Strode asked.

"Yes, sir, and the children less than that."

On cross-examination, while Whitehead managed to establish that the nurse didn't actually know Carrie Buck after age three, he didn't question her ability to assess the family's intelligence. He even allowed her to testify that Carrie had been born out of wedlock, which was irrelevant to her mental abilities and verifiably untrue through county records, had Whitehead bothered to check.

Strode put three schoolteachers on the stand who had taught some of the Buck children, and a superintendent of a local orphanage, and they bolstered the description that the family was feebleminded, poor, and sexually loose. Carrie Buck's sister Doris was still in the second grade after six years at school, a half brother hadn't done "passing work in the fourth grade," and a cousin was "normal dull."

Carrie Buck sat listening to her family being denigrated while, for his part, Whitehead called no teacher to the stand, an easily executed tactic that would have aided Buck's suit greatly. Paul Lombardo, the professor at the University of Virginia, has uncovered evidence that Carrie Buck had been a perfectly fine student.

"In the five years that she attended school, she was promoted to the sixth grade," Lombardo writes. "In fact, the year before she left school, her teacher entered the comment 'very good—deportment and lessons' and recommended her for promotion." Instead, thanks to Whitehead, the trial record concerning Buck's school years was reduced to a statement that she was "anti-social" and had written notes to boys.

Among the most damaging testimony was that from Caroline Wilhelm, the Red Cross social worker who had recently taken Carrie to the Lynchburg colony by train.

"From your experience as a social worker," Strode asked Wilhelm, "if Carrie were discharged from the colony still capable of child-bearing, is she likely to become the parent of deficient offspring?"

"I should judge so. I think a girl of her mentality is more or less at the mercy of other people, and this girl particularly, from her past record. Her mother had three illegitimate children, and I should say that Carrie would be very likely to have illegitimate children."

"So that the only way that she could be likely be kept from increasing her own kind would be by either segregation or something that would stop her power to propagate. Is she an asset or a liability to society?"

"A distinct liability, I should say."

"Did you have any personal dealings with Carrie?"

"Just in the few weeks between the time when the commission [institutionalizing Carrie] was held and when I brought her to Lynchburg."

"Was she obviously feebleminded?"

"I should say so, as a social worker."

To establish the feebleminded streak in the Bucks—from Emma to Carrie and then to Carrie's child Vivian—Strode then asked Wilhelm about the mental state of the baby.

"How old is the child?"

"It is not quite eight months old."

"Have you any impressions of the child?"

"It is difficult to judge probabilities of a child as young as that, but it seems to me not quite a normal baby. . . . In its appearance— I should say that perhaps my knowledge of the mother may prejudice me in that regard, but I saw the child at the same time as Mrs. Dobbs' daughter's baby, which is only three days older than this one, and there is a very decided difference in the development of the babies. . . . There is a look about it that is not quite normal, but just what it is, I can't tell."

An out-of-town eugenics expert Strode had called in for the trial had visited Vivian the day before the trial and a picture survives, showing the intelligence test they probably gave the infant. The apron-wearing Alice Dobbs sits with Vivian on her lap, holding a coin a couple of feet from the baby's eyes in her upheld hand. The baby appears to be looking at the camera rather than the coin, and her inattention to the proper object damned her as feebleminded.

The circularity of Strode's case was clear. Buck was feebleminded because she had a child out of wedlock and pregnant because she was feebleminded. The poor logic was too glaring for even Whitehead to ignore, and he picked up on it in his cross-examination, albeit briefly and to no effect. He asked one social worker if she based her diagnosis of Buck's feeblemindedness on the fact that she had borne an illegitimate baby.

"On that fact," the social worker said, "and that as a social worker I know that girls of that type—"

"Now, what is the type?"

"I should say, decidedly feeble-minded."

"But the question of pregnancy is not evidence of feeblemindedness, is it . . . ?"

"No, but a feeble-minded girl is much more likely to go wrong."

It was a crucial point, but it came and went as quickly as that. Whitehead moved on to other questions and never pointed out that Buck had actually been raped, which would have scuttled all moral arguments against her.

The testimony said more about the witnesses than it did about Carrie Buck. The case was based on gossip, class bias, and bad science: the idea that reputation equaled worth and that vague deficiencies could predictably be charted through a family. The sterilization case against Carrie was the legal manifestation of class warfare, bolstered by the application of intelligence testing. The colony wanted to make poor women's cheap labor available to the market, but still control them. They did this by sterilizing and releasing them, but reserving the right to reincarcerate them if they misbehaved. Dr. Albert Priddy and his lawyer, Aubrey Strode, discussed this openly at Carrie's trial.

"Now the demand for domestics in housework is so great that probably we could get rid of half of our young women of average intelligence, but I have had to abolish [the placement program]. They go out, and it is so common for them to come back pregnant that I have quit taking the risk. People don't care to take them when there is the constant chance of them becoming mothers," Priddy testified.

"Except for their liability to become pregnant, is there any insurmountable obstacle to their being put out in homes that way?" Strode asked.

"No, sir, none whatever."

For the defense, Aubrey Strode rested and Irving Whitehead put no witnesses on the stand: not Carrie Buck herself or other Buck family members, friends, or teachers.

Carrie's case climbed its way up to the Virginia Supreme Court, where Strode's well-researched forty-four-page argument vanquished Whitehead's flimsy eight-page document. And when the case went all the way to the U.S. Supreme Court, as if preordained, Justice Oliver Wendell Holmes's decision read as if Aubrey Strode had written it. Holmes, with no fact-finding ability of his own, relied readily on the facts as Strode had represented them and to which Whitehead had willfully acquiesced. To Holmes and the Court, Carrie Buck was an institutionalized "feeble minded white woman . . . the daughter of a feeble minded mother . . . and the mother of an illegitimate feeble minded child." If the facts in the lower courts claimed that it was possible to assess the mental ability of an eight-month-old child, then those were the facts. By now, the need to stop the Buck gene pool was self-evident and could be done, according to the Court, "without serious pain or substantial danger to life."

Fifteen years after it was published, and by now seriously questioned in academic psychology, Henry Goddard's Kallikak study offered scientific support for sterilizing Carrie Buck. During oral arguments, Holmes and his fellow justices listened to how "Old man John Callicac [sic] in 1775 had an illegitimate child by a feeble-minded woman" and burdened the world with hundreds of feeble-minded descendants. In the end, Holmes parroted the eugenics argument that feeblemindedness was genetic and caused crime.

"It is better for all the world," he wrote in his opinion, "if instead of waiting to execute degenerate offspring for crime, or to let them starve for their imbecility, society can prevent those who are manifestly unfit from continuing their kind. . . . Three generations of imbeciles [Emma, Carrie, and then Vivian] are enough." Seven other justices agreed with Holmes that Carrie Buck should therefore be sterilized. Only one justice dissented.

On the morning of October 19, 1927, Carrie Buck was taken to the Lynchburg colony's drab, two-story, redbrick building that housed its operating room. After years in the making, her sterilization was a remarkably quick and simple affair. A Dr. Bell administered anesthesia to Carrie and cut open her abdomen. He sliced out an inch of her Fallopian tubes and cauterized the loose ends with carbolic acid. Then he sewed her up. Three years of litigation were resolved in less than an hour, unceremoniously and without fanfare. Within two weeks, Carrie, healthy and young, was up and walking around again, aware only that she had undergone a surgery, but unclear of its exact nature. The colony hadn't seen fit to explain it to her.

"All they told me was that I had to get an operation on me," Carrie told reporters in 1980. "I never knew what it was for. Later on, a couple of the other girls told me what it was. They said they had it done on them."

Holmes was particularly proud of his opinion in *Buck v. Bell*. He wrote to a friend later in 1927, saying, "One decision that I wrote gave me pleasure, establishing the constitutionality of a law permitting the sterilization of imbeciles."

Legislators listen when the Supreme Court of the United States speaks, and such was the case with *Buck v Bell*. Indiana and North Dakota quickly passed eugenic sterilization laws in 1927, the same year as the Supreme Court decision. Mississippi followed the next year, as did nine other states in 1929, all using the Virginia law as a model. In 1920, twelve states had passed eugenic sterilization laws. By 1932, twenty-seven states had sterilization programs. As a result, forced sterilizations in the United States skyrocketed. In the 1930s, the brunt of these operations fell on poor white women like the Bucks, in particular; in some states, institutions operated on these women exclusively.

Once "the sterilization law was finally declared constitutional," one Virginia doctor put it, "there was a rush to sterilize as many patients as possible and as quickly as possible."

Even in their own terms, American eugenicists were overly inclusive in their operations. They ended up sterilizing many different types of people considered abnormal, and in the process managed to push other political agendas under the umbrella of eugenics. California, for instance, sterilized gays; how this fits into eugenics isn't obvious, given that it's a population that tends not to pass on its genes as frequently as others.

Buck v. Bell, malleable intelligence tests, and the vague eugenics and intelligence theory underpinning them led to the sterilization of 60,000 Americans in the twentieth century. California led the pack with more than 20,000 sterilizations, and Virginia followed with 8,300. In fact, the total figure of sterilizations in the United States is certainly higher, since many of the operations were done illegally and secretly, or speciously described as medical necessities. A 1931 Pennsylvania follow-up study of 270 patients who had been sterilized in that state hints at this truth. Pennsylvania is one of the few states that never legalized sterilization, but apparently doctors had performed the operation hundreds of times and even discussed them publicly without fear of reprisal. In other contemporary surveys of sterilization surgeries, too, state officials were often honest about not knowing the real number of surgeries performed by doctors within their borders

Paul Lombardo met Carrie in person just one time, in 1982, when she was seventy-six years old and he was in law school. He should have been studying, but when he found out where she was living he thought it was too exciting an opportunity to miss. "[She] was out in the country by Waynesboro in a state-run nursing home. I drove out there, met with her, talked with her. . . . And two weeks later she died. So I was probably the last person to interview her. And frankly it wasn't much of an interview. She was very tired, she was old and she was sick."

Carrie had remained in Virginia her whole life, living near the Blue Ridge Mountains and working odd jobs. She had worked as a farm laborer for a while and as a domestic in Front Royal, Virginia. She was married twice and, with her second husband in 1970, finally moved back to Charlottesville, the town of her youth. Just before Lombardo met her, she had been living in a "single-room cinderblock shed with no plumbing." But despite being diagnosed as feebleminded, she had led a crime-free and productive life. She liked to read and she sang in a church choir. Lombardo found that "even in her last weeks [she] was able to converse lucidly, recalling events from childhood."

Lombardo even tracked down school records for Vivian, Carrie's daughter, who had gone to elementary school for a few years in Charlottesville before she died at age eight from an unknown cause.

"The grade book I found showed her to be an 'honor roll' student, contradicting the impression of trial witnesses that as an infant she was 'peculiar,' 'not quite normal,' and probably 'feebleminded,'" Lombardo writes.

Lombardo had cracked one of the most famous Supreme Court cases of the twentieth century. Oliver Wendell Holmes had it wrong in the best phrase he had ever coined. Lombardo corrected him—"Three Generations, No Imbeciles"—in the title of one of his articles.

Carrie had been shy and reticent about the whole affair, but it couldn't have been easy being incorrectly and famously labeled a moron. Before she died, Carrie told reporters that "I tried helping everybody all my life, and I tried to be good to everybody. It just don't do no good to hold grudges."

Governments outside America pay attention to U.S. Supreme Court decisions, and *Buck v. Bell* served as a fount of rationalization for sterilization in Europe. The Germans had their own strong eugenics tradition that had picked up on Francis Galton's writings, so they weren't just following an American lead when it came to eugenic sterilization. But the Nazis used *Buck v. Bell* in their propaganda justifying sterilization, and when they wanted to whip up concern about the feebleminded they turned to Henry Herbert Goddard's *The Kallikak Family*. Thus the lives of two unwitting and undeserving young women from New Jersey and Virginia, Deborah Kallikak and Carrie Buck, truly did have a worldwide impact.

"Now that we know the laws of heredity," Adolf Hitler reportedly said, "it is possible to a large extent to prevent unhealthy and severely handicapped beings from coming into the world. I have studied with great interest the laws of several American states concerning prevention of reproduction by people whose progeny would, in all probability, be of no value or be injurious to the racial stock."

Chapter 9

Nazis and Intelligence Testing

Psychologists have shown that IQ test results correlate to some degree with certain important aspects of life, such as socioeconomic standing and even longevity. Intelligence remains, however, a trait that we struggle to define, let alone test. We do not really know what IQ tests tell us about individuals, and yet for a century we have relied on them to sort people in circumstances that are frequently life-defining and sometimes fearsomely dangerous.

Nowhere are the potential horrors of using IQ tests to make medical decisions made more manifest than in Nazi Germany, where to be too dumb (which the Nazis often defined as useless and burdensome) meant sterilization and then, as the years progressed, death. Soon after they took power in 1933, the Nazis enacted the Law for the Prevention of Offspring with Hereditary Diseases, which was modeled on an American statute. Back in 1914, Harry Laughlin, a biologist and America's most famous eugenicist, had drafted a model sterilization law for any U.S. state that was interested in copying it. American states did rely on it, and the Nazis followed suit. After the passage of the German sterilization law, Laughlin crowed, "To one versed in the history of eugenical sterilization in America, the text of the German statute reads almost like the 'American model sterilization law.'"

Laughlin had written his law to prevent all stripes of degenerates, including the feebleminded, from passing on their germplasm to subsequent generations. His list of "persons socially inadequate from defective inheritance" was impressively encompassing: the insane, the epileptic, blind, deaf, deformed, the "Inebriate," the diseased (that is, those with leprosy or tuberculosis), and the "Dependent (including the "orphans, ne'er-do-wells, the homeless, tramps and paupers.") All, according to Laughlin, ought to be sterilized. As a result, in addition to the feebleminded, the 1933 German law allowed for the sterilization of eight other hereditary ailments: schizophrenia, manic-depression, epilepsy, Huntington's chorea, blindness, deafness, physical deformities, and alcoholism.

The statute aside, in terms of actually practicing eugenics, the Nazis had one main thing going for them over their ideological brethren in the United States and other countries: dictatorial power. Considering that the Americans had a federalist republic, their states did a remarkably far-reaching job at segregating and then sterilizing many of their citizens, based in large part on IQ tests. Take away democracy, however, and there was perhaps only negative public opinion—the Catholic Church's in particular—to stop the Nazis from executing their plans. Sterilization and other eugenic policies could be dictated from Berlin to great effect.

The 1933 Nazi sterilization law, for instance, required public health service doctors and heads of mental institutions, prisons, and homes throughout the land to report any person afflicted with one or more of the nine "hereditary diseases." The law even required other medical professionals, such as midwives and dentists, to report degenerates as well, but in reality the "denouncements," as they were called, mainly came from doctors. Doctors denounced people in about 75 percent of all cases brought before tribunals, called hereditary health courts, which were specially created by the 1933 law to decide who should be sterilized.

The hereditary health courts consisted of three members: a jurist and two doctors (although the title "doctor" was interpreted broadly to include "race experts" of various kinds: medical doctors, population scientists, geneticists, psychiatrists, and others). By 1936 there were 205 of these courts, plus 18 appellate courts, throughout the Reich, deciding the reproductive fate of tens of thousands of people who rarely even appeared before them. Not surprisingly, the courts tended to agree with the petitioning doctors about who should be sterilized. In addition to shared ideological, professional, and class views, the courts' lightning, five-to-ten-minute review of each case didn't allow for much second guessing even were the judges so inclined. What the courts gained in efficiency they lost in justice and due process. In the years 1934 to 1936, they decided to sterilize subjects in 84 to 92 percent of the cases brought before them, leading to a mind-boggling total of 388,000 prosterilization decisions. This was easier decided than done, however; the courts' decisions left doctors scrambling to keep up, and they didn't get to all the subjects in any given year.

Of the nine potential hereditary ailments, most cases brought before the courts and two-thirds of all sterilization victims were diagnosed as feebleminded, which means that intelligence tests were of prime importance in most sterilization decisions. In cases of alleged feeblemindedness, the hereditary health courts reviewed intelligence tests specially created for them and included in everyone's medical file, which were presented at trial. As in the United States, feeblemindedness proved to be a handily vague catchall term that allowed the Germans to persecute people based on behavior, as well as test results. As a result, the courts often ordered sterilization for people they thought of as antisocial but labeled feebleminded: for example, poor prostitutes or political activists.

German intelligence tests were even less scientific than their American counterparts. They gave the impression that someone had sat down for an afternoon over a cup of coffee and scribbled out some questions he thought an average educated German should be able to answer. In the United States, Lewis Terman had at least spent ten years of painstaking research in the 1920s and 1930s reworking his Stanford-Binet exam, finally publishing a landmark revision in 1937. Regardless of whether or not he succeeded, Terman worked hard to make his tests objective. He tried out questions throughout the States to ensure that people of geographically diverse backgrounds and different socioeconomic statuses could be tested fairly.

By 1937, Terman was even willing to admit that intelligence testing wasn't an exact science. "The tools of psychology, particularly those dealing with the more complex mental processes, belong to an entirely different order of precision from those employed by the physical scientist. So far as one can now see, they always will," wrote Terman in 1937.

In the creation of their exams, let alone their uses, the Germans of the 1930s weren't inclined to worry about cultural, educational, or class biases. While Terman ended up with some dubious questions for all his efforts, it's hard to beat the German question "What does Christmas signify?" The answer, of course, depended upon what the occasion meant to the test taker: lots of presents, a day to mark the birth of Christ, or all the Christians finally at home and quiet. One can imagine that Romani and Jewish responses to this question would have differed significantly from Christians'.

Many other questions were also extremely culturally and educationally biased—"Who discovered America?" for example. Some questions were downright odd: "What would you do if you won the big lottery?" Somehow the German medical profession thought that these questions helped them diagnose feeblemindedness—a supposedly genetic disease.

People without formal education also might have had difficulty figuring out how much 300 Reichsmarks would grow in three years at 3 percent annual interest. And "General Life Knowledge" questions must have been odd for people who had been institutionalized for many years. Surely "How much does it cost to send something by mail?" and questions concerning the price of groceries would have unfairly stumped them.

Subjects' verbal ability was tested in ways similar to Terman's tests. Test takers were asked to form sentences when provided with three words, such as "Hunter-Rabbit-Field!" and "Soldier-War-Fatherland!" Could they distinguish between words such as "Error-Lie" and "Pond-Creek"? The German tests didn't assign an IQ

number. German doctors and psychiatrists instead simply categorized subjects into the three ubiquitous groups of feebleminded:
idiot, imbecile, and *débile* (the equivalent of the English term
"moron," the highest grade of feebleminded).

How test takers landed in their particular category of feebleminded was presumably left up to doctors' or psychiatrists' clinical
experience. They administered the tests orally and noted their subjective impressions at the end of the test, which provided a loop-
hole large enough to drive a Panzer tank through in case subjects
could actually answer the questions correctly. Tests required examiners to note *"Conduct during Interview*: Bearing, eyes, mimicry,
voice, pronunciation, word syntax, rapidity of answers, responsive-
ness, participation in the conversation."

A good example of how conduct influenced diagnosis is the case
of a twenty-one-year-old institutionalized Austrian by the name of
Erwin Ammann, who took an intelligence test in 1943. He knew
the capital of Germany and of France; he knew that Columbus discovered America and that Luther was "the founder of Protes-
tantism." He described Bismarck as "a Reich Chancellor" in about
1870 or 1880. Surprisingly correct and rapid responses, noted his
test administrator, but there was something about Ammann that
wasn't quite right: he had a "feebleminded appearance and behavior." Therefore the test administrator brought Ammann's case
before the area's hereditary health court and requested that he be
sterilized. Ammann didn't appear before the court to argue otherwise, and he was taken away and sterilized, an amazing choice considering that Germany's medical resources by 1943 were mainly
concentrated on supporting troops on the battlefield.

In rare instances, hereditary health courts rejected the request
for sterilization. For instance, courts were sometimes hesitant
when the subject was a member of the Nazi Party, although membership was not a guarantee of safe harbor. Take Hans Schmidt, for
instance, who had joined the Nazi Party in 1931, at age sixteen. By
1938 he was a postal worker, thanks to his party connections, but
also a schizophrenic, thanks to his genes. He was institutionalized

that year and his case brought before a hereditary health court in October. Despite Schmidt's party membership, the court ordered him sterilized; he appealed to a higher court, but the decision was affirmed. His legal recourse spent, Schmidt ran away, only to be caught by the police and returned to the state hospital. They sterilized him in December 1938, just two months after his initial "trial," reflecting the Nazi penchant for speed and efficiency. Since he was no longer a supposed threat to the gene pool, the hospital released him. Schmidt went back to his job at the post office and even remained a party member.

Cases of Nazis sterilizing Nazis aren't surprising, considering that the regime was purposefully overinclusive in its eugenics programs. An official 1936 memo worded the philosophy as follows: "Racial hygiene must always follow the principle that it is better to sterilize too many rather than too few."

One result of this overinclusion was that the Nazis often found everyday people who lived outside institutional walls to be feebleminded, and sterilized them. Extrainstitutional sterilizations were rare in the United States, by contrast, although they could garner news attention when they did occur. The most famous of these cases was the Ann Cooper Hewitt trial, now almost forgotten, but at the time a national sensation, with people following the San Francisco–based trial in their newspapers like installments of a soap opera.

Cooper Hewitt's father had been a millionaire and her mother a well-known socialite. When Cooper Hewitt was twenty, her dead father's will stated that she would inherit two-thirds of her father's millions only if she bore a child; but if she died without heirs, the fortune would pass to her mother. Luckily for her mother, Cooper Hewitt had to go to the hospital for an appendectomy. Before the operation, her mother persuaded the doctor to administer an intelligence test, resulting in the diagnosis of moron (again, the highest ranked of the feebleminded). As a result, and unknown to the patient, while the doctor removed her appendix he also cut her Fallopian tubes. When Cooper Hewitt discovered what had happened, she sued. Her mother claimed the sterilization was better for her daughter and society at large, and a media blitz followed.

Americans took sides with either mother or daughter and followed the story raptly. The trial court sided decidedly with Cooper Hewitt, but the mother won on appeal. Such was a relatively rare case for America, both in its provocative details and its extrainstitutional nature. But in Germany, two-thirds of all people sterilized lived outside institution walls.

In a dictatorial regime that controlled medicine and the law, the hereditary health courts were like quality control agents in an Upton Sinclair slaughterhouse. By the end of World War II, the Germans had sterilized four hundred thousand people within the Reich. This was 0.5 percent of all Germans and 1 percent of those between ages fifteen and fifty (more or less the reproductive years). The Germans managed to sterilize more people than all other countries with eugenic sterilization policies combined.

One of the main differences between the Americans and the Germans is that the Nazis took their eugenics thinking to the logical extreme: the top Nazis decided early on, before the war, to kill the genetically unworthy—the handicapped—although they couldn't execute as publicly as they could sterilize. The Germans had been debating killing institutionalized handicapped patients since World War I. At that time the issue seemed particularly acute, since resources for the handicapped—and even food for the doctors who cared for them—was in short supply, due in large part to a successful British naval blockade.

Years before the Nazis took power, German academics far more radical than their American counterparts consciously tied arguments for the killing of so-called degenerates (criminals and the like, including the feebleminded) to mercy killing of terminal patients in a great deal of pain (euthanasia). Further, if the best young Germans have sacrificed themselves on the fields of France, their thinking went, the severely mentally and physically handicapped, who consume many resources, also should sacrifice themselves for the good of the country.

The idea of fair sacrifice, however, was hardly exclusively German. In 1927, U.S. Supreme Court justice Oliver Wendell Holmes rationalized legalizing sterilization in *Buck v. Bell* in exactly the same way: "We have seen more than once that the public welfare may call upon the best citizens for their lives. It would be strange if it could not call upon those who already sap the strength of the State for these lesser sacrifices . . . in order to prevent our being swamped with incompetence." The Nazis took great solace from the fact that one of the world's greatest democracies shared their philosophy. Yes, there is a difference between the sterilization condoned by the U.S. Supreme Court and murder, but only in degree, not in eugenic logic.

The German euthanasia debates of the 1920s helped prepare professionals and members of the public for large-scale killing of "incurables" in the 1930s and 1940s. People often talked of "burdensome lives" and "useless eaters" when discussing institutionalized patients, whom they viewed as expensive millstones on the economy. Hitler picked up on the theme in a 1929 address to a Nuremberg party rally. "If Germany were to get a million [healthy] children a year and was to remove seven hundred to eight hundred thousand of the weakest people then the final result might even be an increase in strength. . . . Criminals have the opportunity of procreating, degenerates are raised artificially and with difficulty. And in this way we are gradually breeding the weak and killing off the strong." This is right out of the eugenics theory first promulgated by Francis Galton and underlay the use of German intelligence tests.

The adherents of eugenic killing needed only the right political circumstances, which, of course, were provided by the Nazis' assumption of power. Once in office, Hitler and his men made a concerted effort to prepare regular Germans for the murder of handicapped people. One poster showed a drawing of a healthy, blond everyman bearing a pole on his shoulders with a town behind him. The man's head is parallel to the ground, his sleeves are rolled up, and his knees are bent to carry his heavy burden, which consisted of a dark, simian-looking individual on one end and a cowering man in a hat on the other. "You Are Sharing the Load!" reads the caption. "A Genetically Ill Individual Costs Approximately 50,000 Reichsmarks by the Age of Sixty."

German students were indoctrinated even in their math problems, as one 1935–1936 high school textbook shows:

Problem 94

In one region of the German Reich there are 4,400 mentally ill in state institutions, 4,500 receiving state support, 1,600 in local hospitals, 200 in homes for the epileptic, and 1,500 in welfare homes. The state pays a minimum of 10 million RM/year for these institutions.

I.   What is the average cost to the state per inhabitant per year?
II. Using the result calculated from I, how much does it cost the state if:
     A. 868 patients stay longer than 10 years?
     B. 260 patients stay longer than 20 years?
     C. 112 patients stay longer than 25 years?

Problem 95

The construction of an insane asylum requires 6 million RM. How many housing units @ 15,000 RM could be built for the amount spent on insane asylums?

In 1936, a German ophthalmologist, of all people, wrote a very popular novel about a multiple sclerosis–suffering woman who asks her doctor husband to kill her. Out of love, he injects her with a lethal dose of morphine at home, while a friend tinkles out soothing tunes on their piano. The husband is arrested and boldly refuses to perjure himself by claiming an alibi concocted by his friends. At trial, he asks rhetorically, "Would you . . . if you were a cripple, want to vegetate forever?" Unsurprisingly, he is acquitted.

Gerhard Wagner, the Reich's chief physician, had the book made into a movie, *I Accuse*. The Nazis waited until the beginning of the war to release the movie, which was a big hit, and the following story might explain why they waited.

In 1935, the city of Nuremberg held a Nazi Party Congress. Wagner stood up to proclaim the "natural and God-given inequality of men." Over the previous seventy years, Wagner claimed, the number of mentally ill had grown by 450 percent, far outpacing population growth on the whole. "More than one billion reichsmarks is spent on the genetically disabled; contrast this with the 766 million spent on the police, or the 713 million spent on local administration, and one sees what a burden and unexcelled injustice this places on the normal, healthy members of the population." The time was now, he said, to discuss the disposal of "lives not worth living."

By the end of the war, the Nazis would kill well over two hundred thousand handicapped people, many of whom were diagnosed as feebleminded, which required the use of IQ tests to assess intellectual ability. When it came to killing, as it had with sterilization, the Germans thought it better to be overinclusive rather than underinclusive, and, as in many of their murderous programs, the Nazis went to surprising lengths to lend a perverse, in this case medical, legitimacy to their actions.

The example of a girl from Berlin named Ursula H. is illustrative of how the Germans used IQ tests and victims' behavior to condemn people to death. Her story reveals how dangerous it can be to believe that IQ tests reveal people's innate worth and that intelligence need not be defined beyond IQ results and personal behavior. The Germans created a hell for people they should have been comforting, and eugenic science and its integral tool, the intelligence test, provided a medical veneer.

Ursula H., a teenager with gentle features and fair skin, was born prematurely in 1923 when her mother fell off a ladder during her eighth month of pregnancy. She was the only child of a working-class Protestant family in the poor Kreuzberg district of Berlin, and falling and breaking seemed to be a family tradition. Ursula broke her femur on one of her father's birthdays, and on another occasion, her arm. As a young child she fell out of her stroller, hit her head, and suffered a concussion. According to her mother, Ursula was injured badly enough that she learned to walk and talk late, at the ages of two and four, respectively (Ursula herself, when she was eighteen, claimed the milestones came much later).

Ursula's education consisted of just three years of special education. After that, she lived at home, did household chores, and helped her mother sew fabric into coin purses to sell. Her mother found Ursula hard to control: she had temper tantrums as a kid and was frequently "naughty" and strong-willed. Worse, when she got older she talked to men in the street. Her parents sent her to a facilitated-living home for a year and a half, but she didn't get along with the other residents and had to leave.

After the Nazis came to power Ursula, at age fifteen in the late 1930s, was a perfect candidate for coerced sterilization. She was young (but old enough to reproduce), poor, ill educated, and female. Not surprisingly for someone who had only three years of formal education and had a head injury early in life, she performed horribly on intelligence tests. Despite Ursula's personal history, the Nazis considered her hereditarily feebleminded, but not in the severest degree. Like Carrie Buck, Deborah Kallikak, and Ann Cooper Hewitt before her, she wasn't an idiot: rather dangerously, from the Nazis' standpoint, she could function in society, attract a mate, and pass on her tainted genes.

As Americans often did, the Germans, too, defined intelligence by behavior in addition to (and sometimes in conflict with) test scores. Like the Americans, as well, their sterilization policy fell more heavily on women than men (60 percent of the people the Nazis sterilized for being feebleminded were women), and these women tended to be poor and powerless. Thus Ursula's penchant for chatting to men, and her poverty, led her to the operating table just as much as her poor intelligence test performance might have.

As with the Americans, the Germans didn't apply eugenics rationally and consistently. In Ursula's case this meant that within three years of her sterilization, and despite her severed Fallopian tubes that supposedly rendered her genetically harmless, a Berlin hospital doctor in February of 1942 diagnosed her with hereditary feeblemindedness and ordered her institutionalized. This diagnosis and incarceration would eventually lead to her death.

Despite her operation, which was supposed to mellow people, Ursula had broken a window at home and continued to talk to men on the street. She was strong-willed and difficult to control, her mother explained to the admitting doctor, whose name was Dr. Behrendt.

"[Ursula] only wanted to do what she wanted to do," the mother said.

In his initial notes about his new patient, Dr. Behrendt wrote that Ursula wasn't very useful. She couldn't knit or cook and she had been in and out of a halfway house. Ironically, though, Ursula had been sent to the asylum (referred to as "Wittenau," the Berlin neighborhood where it was located) alone via public transportation. Apparently, for someone who was implicitly deemed unable to take care of herself, Ursula was apparently capable and trustworthy enough to take a train or a bus unattended.

When she arrived at Wittenau, Ursula was a slender youth of 136 pounds. In her forward-facing institutional mug shot, she smiled slightly and looked directly into the camera's eye, which made her plain features appealing and just shy of pretty. Her light-colored hair was slicked back, perhaps with water or oil, and she wore a necklace of large, round, dark beads and a striped blouse with a wide, flat collar.

Her initial interview with Dr. Behrendt in February 1942 indicated that Ursula knew exactly where she was and what was happening. She told Dr. Behrendt that she was in the "loony bin or something like that." She knew the time of day, and when asked what season it was, she said with a shrug that it was winter. This ability to understand her surroundings would cause Ursula great mental and emotional pain in the next year and a half and put the lie to the German medical community's claim that the feebleminded deserved no pity because they lacked consciousness and awareness.

Beyond these questions about orientation, Dr. Behrendt's initial interview with Ursula revealed as much about what German doctors cared about as it did the mental state of a girl who had been little socialized or educated. Behrendt wanted to know if Ursula masturbated. She didn't. Nor was she pregnant, he noted, but he was curious about why Ursula talked to men.

"Because I would like to get married," she told him.

Dr. Behrendt also asked Ursula a few current-events questions of the type that appeared in German intelligence tests, as German doctors often did in a rough and ready way to gauge a person's mental abilities. He discovered that Ursula knew that Berlin was the capital, but didn't know how many people lived in it. She knew that the country was at war, but thought its enemies were Russia and Africa.

Ursula made "a very feebleminded impression," concluded Dr. Behrendt.

"Do you want to be here at Wittenau?" he asked. "Yes," she said, it was time to be with the "big girls"—away from her mother, with girls her own age.

At the beginning of her incarceration at Wittenau, Ursula didn't draw too much attention to herself, a good survival strategy in a German institution during the war, where bad behavior equaled low genetic worth. She was maintaining her weight, sleeping the night through, and working without burdening the staff (although she acted "stupid" sometimes and had to be prodded to work, the nurses claimed). Ursula could mend socks and sew on buttons, the staff noted. She could make rags, but not too quickly. On March 6, though, they decided that Ursula should join the cleaning crew "from today onward," a dangerous demotion in a medical culture where usefulness was paramount and useless people weren't worth caring for.

In the first few weeks, the staff moved Ursula from building to building, which must have been unsettling for her. During one of these moves, Ursula said, with a "silly laugh," according to Dr. Behrendt, that she had "already been in two homes." (Over the next year and more, the staff continually moved Ursula, and presumably the other patients, from building to building at Wittenau in what must have been a policy geared to producing anxiety in patients who already had a lot to be anxious about.)

Dr. Behrendt, however, ignored Ursula's nervous laughter to focus on his favorite topic: her sexual predation. He had recently had her checked out for syphilis and her blood tests had come back negative, but Behrendt was unwavering in his focus on sex.

"Why did you hit on men?" he demanded of the eighteen-year-old.

"Wanted to go out with them," Ursula responded.

"Not to sleep with them?"

Ursula was outraged at the question and claimed that she had not wanted to.

Behrendt followed up, though, unconvinced. "Did you have intercourse [with the men]?"

"No," she said indignantly. But when he persisted even more, Ursula, probably stressed, slipped into her working-class Berlin dialect and answered "Only one, that's all I had."

"Was he married?"

"Yes, he had a wife," but she insisted he was the only one, and she stuttered that she "didn't, didn't take any money for it."

Then, perhaps intimidated and angry, Ursula started to rant at the doctor, who continued to pepper her with questions. No, she didn't know his name and age. She only knew that he was a "conductor"—a man who took tickets for the train.

At the end of their conversation, the doctor summed up his meeting with the patient. "Feebleminded individual without judgment or criticism," Behrendt wrote in his notes. Rather mysteriously, he added, "To be monitored for start of menstruation."

Indeed, her medical file would indicate that her next period was April 23; and by the middle of the summer, the staff could report that Ursula was menstruating regularly. She was also working in the laundry room, operating the steam mangle, a machine with a series of rollers that dried and ironed clothes and was known on occasion to crush fingers. It was hot, sweaty, mindless, and menial work that the staff presumably thought Ursula could do without much supervision.

In July, after six months at Wittenau, Ursula, who was not overweight to begin with, had lost twenty-two pounds. At the end of the month, a woman named Dr. Conrad administered an intelligence test and discovered that Ursula knew very little about the outside world. Her answers were stranger now than when she had first arrived and talked to Dr. Behrendt.

"Who was Luther?" Dr. Conrad asked.

"Paulus," Ursula answered.

"When is Christmas?"

"On Christmas Eve twenty-fourth."

Ursula could say the days of the week forward but not backward. She could do only very basic math, such as 2 times 2. But when it came to "If 1½ lbs. cost 15 Pfennig, how much would 7 lbs. cost?" the girl who had hit her head and had just three years of special education was stumped.

"Where does the sun rise?" Dr. Conrad asked.

"Up in the sky," was Ursula's response.

Dr. Conrad asked her the difference between the words "error" and "lie," "lend" and "give," "stingy" and "thrifty." Ursula couldn't answer these questions. "Stairs-ladder?" elicited "You go up stairs and climb up a ladder."

She couldn't form good sentences out of three words provided, tell stories, or explain proverbs. "What does 'The apple never falls far from the trunk' mean?," Dr. Conrad asked.

"What kind of trunk?" was all Ursula could manage.

Dr. Conrad found Ursula to be "very feebleminded."

One of the last questions the doctor put to her was "How do you see your future?"

"I don't know yet," said Ursula, but she soon would. In addition to her perceived uselessness, her inability to answer these intelligence test questions would decide that future. Ursula would have enough intelligence to figure out that she was doomed to die, and long before the end this knowledge would cause her immense emotional suffering.

By the winter of 1942, ten months into her incarceration at Wittenau, the Berlin teenager Ursula H. was teetering dangerously toward becoming unproductive and had become listless. The staff had moved Ursula to other buildings a couple of more times recently and noted that she was no longer very alert. "Very much retarded. Behind her age group," her file read on December 19, defining intelligence by her fear-induced phlegmatic behavior.

Ursula was nevertheless surviving. She was not causing any disturbances or having behavioral problems, and she continued to work at the steam mangle. She had simply become quiet and lacked the spark of life. At the same time, however, Ursula began to deteriorate physically. She was complaining of headaches and "couldn't bend down."

Periodically, the staff asked her why she was at Wittenau.

"Because I talked to a man and smashed a window," she would reply.

Two months later, by February 9, 1943 (just shy of a year since she had delivered herself to Wittenau), Ursula was soiling herself and smearing the floor around her with feces. She was obsessed with her own death, frequently saying, "I'm afraid I have to die."

The staff again moved her to a new building in the institution. Just three days later, on February 12, the afternoon nurse noted that Ursula was "unclean, untidy. Needs help getting dressed," which must have been a burden to the staff—not a position any patient in Nazi Germany wanted to be in.

At this time, Ursula's stress and fear of death turned her nights into a living hell. She had problems sleeping and took to asking the nurses timidly, "Will I have to die soon?" In their night reports, the nurses repeatedly noted Ursula's verbalized fear of death and frequent need to visit the toilet. There is no indication that any measures were taken to alleviate this psychological and emotional pain, or that Ursula was comforted in any way. Still going through the vestigial motions of a normal medical regime, the nursing staff simply and dutifully noted the patient's behavior.

By the morning of February 18, Ursula was "crying intermittently" and asked to go outside in the sun, which she thought would be good for her. The nurses were now feeding her laxatives and seemed surprised when she continued to soil her bed.

On the night of the twentieth, Ursula got dressed and went into the corridor. In an apparent search for physical affection and warmth, she tried to get into bed with other patients. The next day, the staff moved her again.

Ursula remained dirty and still tried to slip into other patients' beds, the nurses noted. They embarrassed her by reading her previous reports of her bedwetting and incontinence. By March 4 the nurses noted that Ursula "was very unclean. Smears herself, the toilets and the floors with feces. Patient couldn't be kept in bed. Says she couldn't stay in bed, she would lose head and legs."

By June, Ursula was screaming all night and wasn't sleeping. Presumably because of her incontinence, the staff began to put her to bed in wood wool, the thin wood shavings used for packing materials. They sedated her, too, just to get her to be quiet and go to sleep. She began to hear voices that threatened to kill her. "Often sits upright," the night nurse noted on June 6, "with a fearful expression." Now she weighed just a hundred pounds, thirty-six pounds less than the young woman had been when she arrived.

Entries in Ursula's medical file are brief, and we can only guess what reality lay behind them. But of the morsels of facts scribbled out in the nurses' jotted notes, her progressively plummeting weight surely indicates not just a proper lack of medical care, but also mental stress caused by purposefully sadistic conditions. By July 1943, Ursula weighed seventy-nine pounds–fifty-seven pounds fewer than when she first arrived at Wittenau.

Surely one of the largest factors contributing to her stress was the large gray buses, formerly used by the Postal Service but now with their windows painted over so people couldn't see in or out, that arrived periodically at asylums and institutions for the handicapped in wartime Germany. The patients didn't know where the buses were headed. They showed up, certain patients were pushed on, and the remaining patients never heard from them again. Diagnosed as feebleminded or not, it wasn't hard for people to figure it out. Everywhere, rumors spread among inmates about the end result for those who rode the bus.

After the war, witnesses said that when the buses arrived at institutions they created a "sinister mood" and "raw fear" among patients. Even the dimmest *débiles* (morons) knew what was going on, and certainly merely physically deformed people, who were also incarcerated at places such as Wittenau, were unhindered in their awareness. Anecdotal evidence abounds that inmates knew what was happening. The mere fact that staff often had to tranquil-ize patients being transferred to ensure pliability is proof. Nurses at one institution "were astonished that the children [in their care] understood" what was happening and noted the kids played a "cof-fin game" that indicated the depth of their knowledge.

In addition to struggling physically, adult patients frequently voiced opposition to boarding the buses, even sometimes trying to chide their persecutors. "Is it my fault that I am born this way, that they do this to me?" one woman asked. One veteran put on his Iron Cross to shame the staff as he boarded the bus, while on a dif-ferent occasion a nun said, "All of us, who have been condemned to death, are now getting on the bus." Perhaps the pithiest summary of what was happening came from the patient who yelled out of her bus window, "Yes, we shall die, but that Hitler will go to hell."

How Ursula H. responded when her turn came to board the gray bus isn't known, but it is probable from her behavior and vocalized fears over the previous year that she knew what was in store for her. She had become a wreck of a human being, inconti-nent and wandering the halls at night, obsessed with death. As the conditions of her confinement created more anguish, her outward anxiety and perceived misbehavior made the staff all the more likely to have her killed; it was a nightmarish positive-feedback cycle. Eventually Wittenau turned Ursula into the unproductive, burdensome creature the Nazis wanted to kill.

On September 10, the staff at Wittenau sent the emaciated girl to Meseritz-Obrawalde, one of the most notorious killing centers during the war, about a hundred miles east of Berlin. From the bus, Ursula would have been put onto a train, which is how patients arrived at Meseritz-Obrawalde—in the middle of the night from at least twenty-six different German cities.

As postwar testimony revealed, nurses at Meseritz-Obrawalde, Ursula's final destination, were more likely to kill "patients who caused extra work for the nurses, those who were deaf-mute, ill, obstructive, or undisciplined, and anyone else who was simply annoying." Ursula, who had only been able to work a steam mangle, and who had been crying sleeplessly and smearing herself with her own feces for some months, must have been high on the nurses' kill list.

At Meseritz-Obrawalde, the patients weren't killed immediately upon arrival; their deaths were staggered and individual, sometimes occurring only after weeks or even months. Conditions at the hospital were abysmal and similar to those at concentration camps. Inmates were forced to work and answer to roll call, and the staff established a layer of "inmate trustees." Ursula did not endure these privations long, however, as she died just three days after her transfer, on September 13. The final entry in her medical file reads "Exitus Letalis," a bit of educated, medical frippery that surely doesn't describe the half of it.

The Meseritz-Obrawalde staff reported Ursula's cause of death as pneumonia, but there is a good chance that the nurses induced this condition by the use of drugs, which was a common Nazi killing method. When the Russians arrived at Meseritz-Obrawalde in 1945, they found a half-finished gas chamber, heaps of morphine-scopolamine, syringes, and a room full of clothes and shoes. After going through the institution's books, the Russians estimated that in the previous three years the staff had killed more than eighteen thousand patients. Survivors told them that they killed thirty to fifty patients a day. The vast majority of those transferred there died: 97 percent in 1944, for instance.

When it came to killing, as it had with sterilization, the Germans thought it better to be overinclusive rather than underinclusive.

By the end, the Germans were killing "asocials," bedwetters, regular citizens addled by Allied bombing runs, and forced foreign laborers who had fallen ill. They couldn't, or didn't want to, control themselves.

Historians are confident that the mentally retarded composed the largest group of handicapped people to be sexually sterilized by the Nazis, because the Germans publicized by disease the percentages of people operated on. They did not, however, publish breakdowns of who they killed during the so-called euthanasia programs for the simple reason that even in Nazi Germany such activities were illegal. Moreover, after the war, Germany's strict privacy laws concerning medical records have made it hard for historians to tally the losses case by case. Nevertheless, it is easy to imagine that most of the handicapped people murdered in Germany in the 1930s and 1940s were at least nominally mentally retarded, since feeblemindedness was such a malleable and handy catchall diagnosis. And to that end, intelligence tests allowed the Nazis to argue that they were scientifically discerning who was worthy and who was unworthy to live. The belief that IQ tests measured people's innate ability with laserlike precision, coupled with the lack of any real definition of intelligence, helped make this horrible sham possible.

Chapter 10

The Eleven-Plus in the United Kingdom

Not surprisingly, given its eugenic foundations, intelligence testing has often been concerned with both the smartest and the dimmest. Before World War II, there was often an obsession with the least gifted humans, manifested in the "menace of the feebleminded" and the sexual sterilization and killing of the feebleminded. On Ellis Island, Americans made efforts to keep the feebleminded out of the country, and psychologists tried to protect the U.S. Army from them. The various American states attempted to corral the feebleminded into institutions and to sterilize them. For their part, however, the British didn't go as far as the Americans (or the Germans, for sure): they only empowered local authorities to sequester, not sterilize, the feebleminded.

Nazi atrocities during World War II, however, put a damper on negative eugenics practices. They weren't stamped out entirely, as evidenced by the continued coerced sterilization practices in the United States, but they weren't nearly as popular. In their place, people began to focus on the other extreme, the most gifted and brightest: in a sense, there was a shift to positive eugenics. In postwar America, this was aided by the space and arms race with the Soviet Union. The launching of Sputnik did wonders for America's gifted programs, as it made people feel like the country was falling behind in a competition to produce scientists and technically capable citizens.

Each obsession, with the dumbest and the brightest, has its own drawbacks. The former can lead to negative eugenics and all its awful consequences. The latter can cause a country to ignore a vast majority of its people in the belief that only a slim minority, the very brightest, must be cultivated and cared for. In the decades after World War II, the English and Welsh school systems, aided by an exam called the eleven-plus and the intelligence theory underpinning it, is a perfect example.

The psychologist who did the most to provide the psychological theory that bolstered the eleven-plus was Cyril Burt. If T. H. Huxley was "Darwin's bulldog," arguing publicly for evolution in the nineteenth century, Burt was an entire team of dogs pulling Charles Spearman's message of general intelligence. In the early to midtwentieth century, Burt, an English psychologist, dedicated himself to proving the existence of g, its importance in life, its inheritability and testability. His ideas would lead to a failed effort to reshuffle all of English and Welsh society along lines defined by brainpower.

While belief in g can often lead to politically conservative positions—government intervention is pointless, for instance, if differences among people are mainly biological—it doesn't have to. In fact, in their day, Cyril Burt and many of his fellow psychologists were political radicals, often allied with the Labour Party. Their faith in intelligence was so great that they wanted to realign society based on how much g people had, a radical, not reactionary, point of view. Indeed, as early as 1926, Burt had testified before a government committee that a group intelligence test should be administered at age eleven to select and specially educate the top 2 percent, the most intellectually gifted, of children in the land. Like Lewis Terman working at Stanford across the Atlantic, Cyril Burt, at about the same time, created his own intelligence tests based on Alfred Binet's.

Burt was often interested in the distribution of intelligence among the different social classes, which is perhaps not surprising, given his country's obsession with social stratification. After administering his exams to students from different stations in life, and following their subsequent careers for years, he concluded that more than half of society occupied the correct position and should remain where it was. Working-class people, Burt discovered, tended to score lower on his tests than professionals. A considerable chunk of society, however, was out of whack. "It appears that well over 20 per cent of the male adults in this country have a higher intelligence than is requisite for the work they are doing and that about the same number have an intelligence which is inadequate." They either had too much g to work in the coal mines or sweep the streets, or they had too little to run a bank or be a surgeon. In a more just and efficient society, Burt thought, a person's smarts—his g—would dictate his position in life.

Burt's thinking, along with other forces in society, led to ten- and eleven-year-olds in England and Wales taking an exam called the eleven-plus, which sorted them into two different types of schools, the grammar and the secondary modern, which set them on two separate life paths. (There was a third alternative, called a technical school, which was sort of an intermediate level, but only about 4 percent of all students attended these due to a lack of resources in the post–World War II economy.) In the years between the world wars, Burt and other psychologists testified several times before a key government education committee, persuading its members, despite squabbling about what intelligence was exactly, that g existed and was testable and that students could be meaningfully ranked according to exam results.

"Intellectual development during childhood," the committee concluded, "appears to progress as if it were governed by a single central factor.... It appears to enter into everything which the child attempts to think, or say, or do and seems on the whole to be the most important factor in determining his work in the classroom. Our psychological witnesses assured us that it can be measured approximately by means of intelligence tests."

As a result of their efforts, group intelligence tests became thought of as "impervious to cramming" and particularly useful for "streaming" students into different ability groups, as well as for selecting who got scholarships. The British streamed their students early in life, just as the Americans were "tracking" theirs, but the British took it one step farther by sending students, usually at age twelve, to entirely different schools (and even streamed within those) based on performance on one exam. So great, they thought, was the chasm created by different amounts of g, and so powerful, too, they believed their tests to be.

Where Francis Galton a few generations before them had failed to devise "public examinations, conducted on established principles" to sort people, Cyril Burt and his fellow psychologists succeeded in persuading those in power that they had succeeded. In fact, so successful were they and the education reformers they persuaded, that for a couple of decades after World War II the British intelligence exam called the eleven-plus was equated with civic worth. Test results decided, in one day, the majority of children's educational and professional options upon leaving school.

Students who passed the eleven-plus attended grammar schools, which provided top-quality education in substantive academic subjects. These schools attracted the best teachers and the most gifted students (in theory), who liked to "learn for learning's sake," as was commonly intoned. Grammar schools groomed children for white-collar jobs and for business and government positions. They had institutional links to the colleges and universities of the nation and were supposed to cultivate Britain's future leaders (at least among students who didn't attend the fancy private schools, which, in the main, didn't require their students to take the eleven-plus).

The eleven-plus wasn't just one test created and administered by the central Ministry of Education, but rather each Local Education Authority (LEA), of which there were roughly 150 throughout England and Wales, used its own exam to decide where children would be educated at the secondary level. (Scotland didn't use the eleven-plus, but had its own sorting test.) Some LEAs used multiple-choice exams, while others didn't; LEAs would try one thing for a while and then move on to something else. They would often have mental arithmetic questions, which had to be computed without the use of pencil and paper, reading comprehension, vocabulary tests, and perhaps an essay.

For instance, in 1955, the Glamorgan Education Authority (a district in South Wales) had teachers read out mental arithmetic problems such as "In a box of oranges there are eighty-four more good ones than bad ones. If the number of bad ones is two-ninths of the number of good ones, how many oranges are in the box?" The same year the students had half an hour to write an essay, choosing among subjects such as "Dressing a doll," "Camping," or "A winter storm." There was also a reading comprehension section, after which students answered questions such as "(1) How often had Juan visited Palma?" And "Explain the meaning of . . . *horse-shoe bay; tanned by the sun to a glowing bronze; tourists; drag-net.*" There was also a punctuation test and the IQ test classic, analogies. "(10) Sorrow is to tears as joy is to _____."

In short, British intelligence tests were like those elsewhere: they measured and compared students' knowledge of words, language, and mathematics, under the assumption that the exam offered unfettered insight into innate ability and could distinguish among students accordingly.

The pressures on the ten- and eleven-year-olds taking the eleven-plus were immense, especially since everyone (teachers, administrators, peers, and parents) seemed to make up their minds early on who was supposed to pass and who was not even worthy to take the exam. There was a sense of claustrophobia, that everyone was watching, and adults didn't mince words when speaking to young children about it. "'If you don't buck your ideas up, my girl, you will end up in the clothing factory,'" Patricia Morgan, a Welsh woman who took the exam in 1948, recalled people telling her before the exam. In working-class South Wales, that was a very palpable threat.

After the exam, in the tight-knit coal-mining villages where Morgan grew up, adults would stop children in the street and ask them if they had passed. "I can remember coming home from school and people saying, 'How have you done? How have you done? Have you passed?' And when you said you had passed, they usually gave you sixpence. I mean people you didn't know," said Morgan.

Most embarrassingly (for those who failed, at least), lists of those who passed were printed in the local papers for all to read. Proof of how important the exam was is evidenced by the fact that many people today in their sixties and seventies still have newspaper clippings with their names listed in them as well as grammar school acceptance letters—all stimulated by a one-day exam taken fifty and sixty years ago. When asked if they remembered exam day the most frequent response is "vividly." They remember what the exam looked like, what was on it, where they took it, and how they felt. One woman described her exam papers as follows:

"I can see the paper; I can smell the paper. The paper was a little bit slinky. It was measured. If you folded an eight-and-a-half-by-eleven standard paper and folded it so that it became eight and a half vertically by five and a half, so it opened up like a little book. And the typeface was small and I can see [in my mind's eye] sort of a header on the front page."

She later dug out the exam from a box in her garage to discover that her description was absolutely correct.

The grammar schools, attended by passers of the eleven-plus, were renowned for providing top-class education. "It was pretty grim," said Morgan of her grammar school in Porth, South Wales, in the late forties and early fifties. "It was very hard and there were hundreds of rules that you could break, but it was only when I left school that I realized that we had very highly qualified teachers in the school. You know, people who had been to Oxford and Cambridge and got first-class degrees."

Even physically, grammar schools were often superior to "secondary modern" schools, where eleven-plus failures were sent. Morgan's school had parquet floors, a central corridor with statuary and pictures, and groomed grounds. It was a real step up from her dingy elementary school. And when asked what the secondary modern most of her classmates had gone to was like, Morgan just laughed and said, "Not as nice. Nothing like it."

Separate but equal education along race lines didn't work in the United States, and at about the same time separate and expressly unequal education didn't work in England and Wales. There was a general impression that LEA administrators desperately needed adult bodies, any bodies, at the heads of secondary modern classrooms after World War II. Recently demobilized men and women coming out of the military services who needed jobs could find them in secondary modern schools, even if they had no background in teaching.

"The teachers were not [university] graduates, they were people who had been to teacher-training college. Many of them had been on intensive courses after their war service. You know, they were young people who came out of the army and the air force. . . . I'm not saying they weren't good, some of them were, but there was definitely a divide between [the secondary modern and grammar school teachers]," Morgan said.

Their quality can be summed up by the historian A. J. P. Taylor's advice to children who didn't pass the eleven-plus to "run away to sea rather than go to a secondary modern." At their worst, the schools were almost human holding tanks, designed to baby-sit children until the universal education age was met (fifteen after World War II, sixteen after 1972) and then release them to "dead-end jobs," if anything at all. They could stamp out even the most inquisitive student's curiosity. Take Mike Clements, for instance, a restless boy who grew up in Cardiff, the capital of Wales, in the 1950s and 1960s. Mike's family had been in the working-class neighborhood of Ely for generations; his parents had been raised there, and a grandfather had fought and died in a nearby pub. A photo of Mike and his pals shows a ragtag crew with uneven, home-cut bangs and various and assorted hand-me-down sweater-vests and jackets.

Ely circumscribed their world. Clements and his friends played under close gray Welsh skies in the sprawling development of row after row of tiny, attached, small-windowed brick houses built for workers and their families. Their parents and grandparents worked in the Ely Paper Mill or in shops and other factories. To an American eye, the group of pictured kids looks at once familiar but exotic, as if they were being groomed to form yet another British rock band. But for every Beatle there are countless coal miners and factory workers, which is how most of Clements's cohort spent their working lives.

Clements was initially successful at school. When he was about nine, he was gobbling up Anna Sewell, Charles Dickens, and Robert Louis Stevenson. He says his teachers thought he had a reading and spelling age well in advance of his years and they put him in the A stream throughout his years at school.

Outside of school, Clements was imbued early with an entrepreneurial spirit. Before age ten he started making little carnival-like games for other kids on the street out of cardboard shoeboxes. He'd base them on real games, such as bagatelle, and charge them a coin or two to play. Like all good betting houses, Clements designed the games in his favor, and more often than not, he says, his friends would be "relieve[d] of their pocket money." He also delivered groceries and newspapers, washed cars, gardened, and chopped wood for money.

"So I knew that I would support myself," he says now, at fifty-six. "I knew that at ten, twelve years old."

But Clements's junior school failed to prepare him and his schoolmates for an exam that mattered more than entrepreneurial spirit: an exam that, despite its billing, could quite obviously be prepped for. Clements also lacked that critical support at home, so in 1960, although his mother knew that the eleven-plus mattered, all she gave her son in the way of preparation was a one-inch-tall plastic black cat on exam day. It was an odd, ambiguous gesture, for the significance of a black cat crossing your path can portend good or bad, depending on your point of view. But Clements put it in his shirt pocket and walked the couple of miles to school, just as he did every morning.

"It used to be that if a black cat crossed your path some said that it meant good luck, others that it used to be bad. In my case it meant bad, probably," Clements said. Then, in a reversal that sums up how many of us feel about critical junctures in life, he paused for a moment and said, "Having said that, probably good."

When his teacher passed out the exam, his spirits plummeted; he had no idea what was going on. The questions on his exam were so odd it was almost as if they were written in another language. He looked about the room and realized, from the bemused looks on all the other boys' faces, that everyone else was having the same reaction.

After the exam, Clements walked outside and pulled the little black cat out of his pocket. A lot of bloody good this did, he thought, and flicked it away. Clements could remember only a few students out of about a hundred at his elementary school making the grammar school cut. It was his luck to have grown up with parents who didn't pay attention and teachers who had decided that the boys of Ely, en masse, were not worth prepping for a test that would influence the rest of their lives. Other schools in South Wales and the rest of the country focused single-mindedly on the exam.

Exam results were hand-delivered, and on the appointed day people stood out on their "doorsteps to see who would enjoy something of a future career," Clements said. Before the fateful day, a friend of his advised him that if the brown delivery envelope is "thick, you're not thick." (Grammar school enrollment papers would fatten it.) A child—and all his neighbors—didn't have to open an envelope so thin it had seemingly nothing in it to know he was destined to be a laborer. Despite his reading and spelling ability, Clements received a thin one.

What happened in Ely on results day in 1960 is precisely what the eleven-plus was intended to do, although not expressly or publicly. Group intelligence tests are most often meant to sort large numbers of people into binary groups: worthy and unworthy, whatever the context, whether it be on Ellis Island, in Nazi asylums, or in schools. The need often arises when there is an overabundance of bodies for positions, and British schools after the war were prime candidates for the use of intelligence tests. The U.K. population was booming, and Parliament had recently passed a law raising the age of universal education to fifteen, which resulted in the over-stuffing of schools. In particular, council housing estates such as Mike Clements's in Ely, which were springing up everywhere after the war, were producing an overabundance of children. In 1947, the government needed to provide 1.15 million new school places to keep up with the growing population, but it failed to then and for years thereafter, and when human systems are stressed, the need for efficiency overrides care for individuals.

By design, most students failed the eleven-plus, although differences in the pass rate were due to geography rather than in the innate ability of different groups. In certain areas there were spaces in grammar school for only 8 percent of the local students, whereas in other areas up to 60 percent could be accommodated. In Britain after World War II, geography mattered more than brains, and the families who could afford it moved into areas with more grammar school spots. Passing the eleven-plus became a national hysteria, causing even a cereal company to place sample test questions in its boxes.

Many of the families who couldn't afford to move to a school area with abundant grammar school seats pressured their kids to study hard and lobbied their local schools to teach to the exam, resulting in a warping of school curricula throughout the land. Nowhere was this more apparent than in South Wales, where there were higher proportions of semiskilled and unskilled laborers than anywhere else in the country. For those families who cared, passing the eleven-plus was a ticket out of the coal mines and factories, and the consequences of failure were stark. The boys did well at school or they were down the mine at age fifteen or sixteen. Going to a grammar school could mean avoiding black lung, tunnel collapse, deadly coal-dust explosions, losing a finger or getting a hand crushed in a machine, no respect, a dull job, and poor pay. For the girls, failing the eleven-plus could mean ending up in a shop or a factory, if they worked at all.

As a result, parental anxiety over the exam caused many schools to become simply eleven-plus training grounds, which was better than not prepping their kids at all (as in Mike Clements's case) but which defeated the purpose of the exam. Students spent years before the eleven-plus practicing math in their heads, reading passages from books, and answering questions about them—if that's what was likely to be on their local eleven-plus. The effect of the exam on schools caused one member of Parliament to claim, "Some headmasters have moulded the whole of their curriculum around the grammar school entrance examination. From the time the child comes into the primary school at the age of seven, his attention is directed towards [this] examination. The whole of the primary school curriculum is distorted and warped . . . and this warping . . . is a very evil thing."

Good teachers taught unabashedly to the test. While in theory British psychologists had thought intelligence tests would promote a "childcentric" education by placing each student in an appropriate academic environment, in practice schools focused on institutional efficiency and high-exam-passage rates. Teachers had to decide, usually when the children were five to seven years old, who was, and was not, mentally capable of passing the exam. Schools thus spent years preparing only the students they thought were capable of passing the exam.

Schools divided these young students into A, B, and C streams (with A being the brightest), but large schools also might have had a D stream. Once in the lower streams it was very difficult for a child to get out, and as the years passed, it became progressively harder because the substantive gaps in what was being taught in the various streams grew to uncrossable chasms. Everyone in the A stream would be prepped for the eleven-plus, and to some extent students in the B stream, as well, although their chances of passing were greatly diminished. C and D stream children often were not even allowed to take the exam, let alone prepped for it. Late bloomers were obviously at a disadvantage.

Thus, the eleven-plus didn't really select for the best and brightest on a scientific basis at age ten or eleven, as the psychologists had hoped. The selection process happened much earlier and it turned out that grooming, manners, presentation, parental expectation, and cultural stimulation at home and a whole host of other environmental factors influenced teachers' choices of who to place in what stream. As a result, more middle-class than working-class children filled the A streams.

Even a child's birth date affected his chances of getting into the A stream. According to Adrian Wooldridge, a journalist for the *Economist* magazine who's written a terrific history of English education and psychology, "Children born between September and December had a one-in-two chance of being placed in an A-stream, whereas those born during the rest of the year had only a one-in-three or a one-in-four chance. In schools with four streams, almost twice as many summer-born as winter-born children entered the D-stream."

The British affinity for hierarchy and stratification manifested itself not only in the gulf between grammar and secondary modern schools, but also in the continued division of classes within those schools. The eleven-plus was a mere crossroads to yet more streaming to come. At Mike Clements's Cyntwell Secondary Modern, in Cardiff, the different classes in each year were called T, O, and P (instead of A, B, and C). The T stood for technical and implied that the boys in this stream were capable of doing skilled jobs once they graduated. Clements was placed in this group—in fact, the highest stream (T1) of three within the technical stream. The O meant ordinary—"road sweeper material," as Clements put it. And the final, subterranean level at the secondary modern was P, but Clements couldn't recall what this stood for. "Peasant, if you like," he joked.

As Cyril Burt put it in 1923, "it is the duty of the community, first, to ascertain what is the mental level of each individual child;

then to give him the education most appropriate to his level; and lastly, before it leaves him, to guide him into the career for which his measure of intelligence has marked him out." Mike Clements's secondary school was the reality of this supposedly "child-centered" education psychologists had advocated between the world wars. While it didn't provide good, individualized attention, it certainly did sort children for future jobs and, more broadly, standing in society.

When Clements visited his secondary modern's careers officer, he told him he wanted to be a farm laborer—not a farmer, but a farmhand, and the man was dumbfounded. "Are you sure that's really what you want to do?" the careers man asked. Clements was a good student in the highest stream.

Eventually, the desire to work on a farm faded, and at age fifteen, Clements graduated. He took no exams to graduate; he had simply reached the end of the carpet. He could have sought "certificates of merit" in activities such as woodwork or metalwork, but he wasn't interested, and even now he doesn't know if they meant anything in the outside world.

"We were just bunged into . . . this sausage machine and out the other end ready to go into the factories and that's what happened to me," Clements said. "I went into a factory that my father was working in and my brother. My mother had worked in [it], my grandfather and my grandmother; everyone had worked in this particular paper mill in the area that we lived in. We were fodder for the mill, if you like."

It's what happened to most secondary modern graduates. In the 1950s, one critic concluded that only one in twenty-two thousand students who did not attend grammar schools went on to a university.

This is not to say that attending grammar school guaranteed the life of a mandarin. For starters, only 10 percent of grammar school students made it to a university, and it was these students— primarily the A stream grammar school kids—who were the ultimate focus of all the English and Welsh systems' winnowing and sorting. This tiny minority of all students were the prized gems of the system countrywide; they were groomed for university, offered the most challenging classes and best teachers. The A stream grammar students might be offered Latin, for instance, while B and C streams were offered French.

The educational system and the eleven-plus failed because they were too clumsy and rigid. Educators and psychologists, ironically, didn't take into account the psychology of young children. They simply assumed each child would try his or her best. But talk to people who took the eleven-plus, and anecdotal evidence abounds that all children weren't motivated to try their best. One research neurologist in London cites a colleague, "one of the best medical researchers in the country," who had purposefully failed the exam as a kid because his local grammar school's uniforms were "naff." It's an attitude easily conceivable for a ten- or eleven-year-old boy that calls for a more flexible system with individualized attention: not a do-or-die sorting process resolved in one day and that rests on dubious theory.

Just passing the exam, too, was no guarantee that the student would be motivated in grammar school. "The friends that I had," a former Welsh coal miner explained, "none of them had passed the eleven-plus, so I stood out like a sore thumb." His friends made fun of him, and while it was "pure jealousy because I had made the grade and they hadn't," he was still young and impressionable and ended up not studying hard enough to continue his education beyond a few years at the local grammar school. There was no mechanism in the schools for increasing motivation. As a result, he worked down the pit, as they called the coal mines, alongside his friends who had gone to the secondary modern.

Socioeconomic class also had a profound affect on how children performed on IQ tests in England and Wales at the time. IQ scores of lower-working-class kids, researchers discovered, decreased as they grew to eleven, whereas it increased among middle-class students—a strange pattern for tests purporting to measure innate ability. It's not surprising, then, that IQ tests at age eight couldn't predict how a child would do on the eleven-plus exam.

In short, the eleven-plus wasn't good at sifting through human chaff looking for hitherto unnoticed talent, as it was supposed to. Fifteen years after World War II, the same ratio of working-class to middle-class children attended university as had between the years 1928 and 1947. The concept of objective intelligence testing may have been a threat to the status quo, but not its practice.

By the 1960s, many researchers in Britain began to believe that the eleven-plus and IQ tests that schools had been using weren't precise and reliable enough to be used for such draconian sorting of children. People became particularly concerned with "borderline" students who scored well—say, the 110 to 120 IQ range—but might or might not have been admitted to grammar school, depending on locale. For these students in particular they discovered that environment mattered a great deal. In the words of Adrian Wooldridge, author of *Measuring the Mind*, researchers found that "The condition of the home, the degree of parental encouragement, the academic record of the primary school (measured by the proportion of its pupils regularly going to grammar schools), and the 'streams' into which children were initially divided—all these environmental factors sharply distorted the allocation of places, improving the chances of middle-class children and damaging those of their working-class contemporaries."

A system that sent kids to a good school or a bad school based on a one-day exam simply didn't take into account the effects of poverty, which becomes apparent within moments of talking to people who grew up in impoverished South Wales after World War II. Some students had to decline a grammar school position because of even nominal costs. One woman who could have attended the Garw Grammar School in 1948 didn't because her parents couldn't afford the uniform. "The children who did go were usually an only child or [their] fathers were officials in the colleries [sic]," she wrote. "I often wonder how many [potential] future PRIMEMINISTERS went to work underground because they were too poor to pay for a uniform."

Once in grammar school, middle-class children were again much more likely to succeed than poor kids were. Of middle-class children with IQs in the range of 115 to 129, 34 percent continued their education beyond grammar school. Of working-class children in the same IQ range, only 15 percent did so. Working-class kids often dropped out of grammar school for financial reasons.

"If you went on to the grammar school you had . . . to rely on the simple pocket money that you were getting off your parents. Whereas if you went to the mines at least you were earning your own wage, even though [you] probably gave 80 percent of it to your parents. But that 20 percent would be more than you'd get through pocket money," explained a former Welsh coal miner.

Schools can't compensate for all social inequities, but why not simply provide good education throughout the system, which is at least within the purview of schools?

By the mid-1960s, the grammar school system, the eleven-plus, and IQ tests in general fell out of political and educational favor in Britain. Psychologists had made promises too bold. Their exams were oversold and overrelied on, and they were much poorer predictors of success than was claimed. One government report concluded that "if the IQ had been made the single criterion at nine or ten for sorting the children into sheep and goats, and if the same criterion had been used again at nineteen, it would have been found that a mistake had been made in 20 percent of the cases." Psychologists began to admit that prepping and the quality of education could significantly affect scores on IQ tests and on English and math exams. Like short kids barred from physical education who later grew to over six feet tall, the eleven-plus punished late developers in particular, and these were offered no second chance.

Based even on intelligence theory, the practical use of the eleven-plus made little sense. Intelligence experts since Francis Galton in the Victorian era have argued that intelligence is distributed among the general population along a continuum with no clear points of demarcation, but the English and Welsh school systems were binary. You either went to a good school or a bad school, and there was little to no hope of transfer between the two, no matter how brilliantly you performed in your studies after the exam.

By the mid-1960s in the United Kingdom, the political winds turned in favor of an environmentalist interpretation of IQ. By this time, working-class political movements opposed what they perceived as an elitist, bipartite educational system and applied pressure for change. Just as important, middle-class parents were tired of worrying that their children might not be accepted to grammar schools—and of having to shell out for private schools if their children failed the eleven-plus. Thus, in 1965, when Anthony Crosland became minister of education and science, he vowed to put an end to grammar schools. "'If it's the last thing I do,' he told his wife, 'I'm going to destroy every fucking grammar school in England. And Wales. And Northern Ireland.'" He wouldn't prove to be entirely successful, although most of the United Kingdom did move away from the grammar school model.

The entire time the eleven-plus was in use, the true elites in the fancy upper-class "public" schools (as these private schools are called in the United Kingdom) were unaffected by the eleven-plus. As one vociferous eleven-plus critic put it, when Winston Churchill was a boy he produced nothing more than "a large blob of ink" on his entrance exam to Harrow, one of the most venerable and esteemed public schools, and yet was admitted because of family connections. The eleven-plus did nothing to upset these upper-class entitlements. More broadly, the education system didn't radically reengineer society based on smarts, but merely dictated who was worthy to be in the middle-class professions (and, unsurprisingly, the answer was most often the children of the existing middle class).

Failing the eleven-plus was not an absolute bar to professional success in life. Those successes came, however, despite people's exam results. Eleven-plus failures often made it in the arts, technical professions such as engineering and manufacturing, or business, where stringent educational backgrounds weren't often required.

Indeed, failing the eleven-plus imposed a certain scrappiness on people who wanted to improve their lot in life, as evidenced by Mike Clements's career. After graduating at fifteen from his secondary modern in Cardiff in the mid-1960s, Clements worked in the Ely Paper Mill for a few years and then embarked on a dizzying array of entrepreneurial efforts until the mid-1990s. He was a bus conductor and a car mechanic, he rented out halls to stage dance parties, he bought and sold property, ran a scrap metal business, had a printing company, and managed a truck company. He started a detective agency with his brother and even drove a cab for a while.

Amazingly, when he had some free time, Mike would go to the Cardiff central library to read. He became fascinated by the British common law system, because it was "so volatile and dynamic." He loved the way "judges can steer this law for betterment usually, the way they want to steer it." He began to notice that one judge's opinions in particular—Lord Alfred Denning's—struck his fancy.

"I used to thirst for his cases," Clements said.

Mike thought Denning was "a benefit to the planet," and in April 1995 he wrote to his lordship telling him so. At the time, Lord Denning was master of the rolls, the third-highest judge in the United Kingdom and the highest civil judge on the court of appeals for England and Wales. He had been a towering figure in British law for years and had been influencing contract law and other areas since the late 1940s. For a working-class man from Cardiff, it was a bold move.

The two struck up a correspondence that lasted until Lord Denning's death in 1999. Before he died, Denning encouraged Clements to go to law school. For a long time now, white-collar professions have required certain educational backgrounds, and law is among the most hidebound and hierarchy-conscious. Leaving school at fifteen without a decent education doesn't usually lead to hanging up a shingle these days.

Four decades after taking the eleven-plus, however, Clements talked about it by phone from his house in the Dominican Republic, where he spends part of each year. He's now a practicing solicitor, in Cardiff, with various businesses on the side. Oddly enough, he's not bitter.

"My firm belief, more so now, but for a very long time has been that the [educational] system had to be streamlined," Mike Clements said recently. "We can't have a world full of physicians and lawyers and nobody to clean the sewers, so the streamlining kicks in obviously at a very early age. And we were part of that system. They didn't want us all in grammar school."

Chapter 11

Intelligence Testing and the Death Penalty in the United States

IQ tests provide probabilistic predictions. A person with an IQ of 120 is more likely to have a white-collar job, and be successful at it, than someone with a 90 IQ. Poor people, welfare recipients, criminals behind bars, high school dropouts, the unemployed, and single mothers tend, to varying degrees, to have low IQs. High scorers, on the other hand, tend to be healthier and live longer than their low-scoring counterparts. The predictive rates are never great, but they exist.

In terms of understanding what an individual can and can't do, however, it's not clear what IQ scores tell us. What IQ must a student have to be able to learn calculus, for instance? IQ scores do not tell us with any certainty what someone is capable of understanding, although they are used as if they do all the time. The most extreme example is death penalty cases in the United States. In 2002, the U.S. Supreme Court decided, despite having ruled the opposite about a dozen years earlier, that states could no longer execute the mentally retarded, believing that their lack of intelligence affects how they behave, think, talk, and understand the world around them. The mentally retarded often might know the difference between right and wrong, the Supreme Court acknowledged, but they have "diminished capacities to understand and process information, to communicate, to abstract from mistakes

159

and learn from experience, to engage in logical reasoning, to control impulses, and to understand the reactions of others. There is no evidence that they are more likely to engage in criminal conduct than others, but there is abundant evidence that they often act on impulse rather than pursuant to a premeditated plan, and that in group settings they are followers rather than leaders."

In *Atkins v. Virginia*, the Court presciently realized that the main problem with its ruling would be figuring out which defendants were and which weren't mentally retarded. "To the extent there is serious disagreement about the execution of mentally retarded offenders, it is in determining which offenders are in fact retarded." The Court decided to leave the thorny issue of defining mental retardation up to each individual state. Many states after *Atkins* defined it as an IQ score of 70 or less and problems coping in life that manifested before age eighteen.

The main question here is whether the WAIS-III, the predominant IQ test in America and indeed the world and the one used in *Atkins v. Virginia*, offers sufficient insight into how capital defendants think to warrant relying on it in a life-or-death matter. Before coming to this question, however, it's better to review the facts of *Atkins*, which show how slippery and difficult the definition of mental retardation is. The defendant, Daryl Atkins, scored (at least initially) below the IQ threshold and showed considerable problems functioning at a young age, but he also seemed to plan and take charge during the murder he and a friend committed.

Just a few months before the night of the murder, which happened in the early hours of August 17, 1996, Atkins, age eighteen, had left high school without properly graduating. He says he finished school through the eleventh grade, but he was so behind his age group he was difficult to categorize; his high school had sometimes called him a senior, at other times a sophomore. From early elementary school, his teachers hadn't quite known what to do with him but pass him along to the next grade. He seemed to do okay up to the first grade, but after that he couldn't cope, and the system let him slip through. They held him back for second grade and he then performed satisfactorily. But by the fourth grade he was failing again, receiving three Ds and four Fs; his teachers moved him right along anyway.

"And the [school] transcript says placed in fifth," says Dr. Evan Nelson, a psychologist who later analyzed Daryl and testified at his murder trial. "In other words, this was a social promotion to keep him up. This wasn't because they believed that he necessarily passed fourth grade. And in fifth grade indeed, he doesn't do so well either, two satisfactories, six Ds and two Fs."

Teachers kept promoting Atkins, and by the eighth grade his grades had plummeted to Fs across the board. Despite failing a statewide literacy test required for entering high school, Atkins was moved on to high school, where he took tenth grade twice and finally was put into a special education program for the first time.

Since leaving high school Atkins had been getting drunk and high and committing violent robberies. At the end of April 1996, Atkins and a couple of friends had robbed four men on the street at gunpoint. A few weeks later he took a knife into an auto parts shop and made away with thousands of dollars from the safe. In early June he broke into a house in the middle of the night and managed to haul away a TV, some jewelry, a leather coat, and more. A couple of weeks after that, Atkins and an accomplice abducted a pizza delivery man in his car and threatened to kill him unless he swam away through a swamp. Finally, just the week before the night of the murder, Daryl shot a woman in her front yard.

"I went and lay on my front porch," she reported. "I wanted to keep my daughter from running out of the house because I didn't know if he would shoot her."

On August 16, 1996, Atkins and his friend William Jones, who was twenty-six, had been partying all day and night. "We was drinking and smoking weed," said Jones at trial. He remembered drinking half a dozen thirty-two- and forty-ounce cans of beer and two bottles of premixed gin and juice and smoking a bunch of weed. They didn't eat anything all day that Jones could remember; they just got addled.

A couple of other friends who liked to party occasionally came and went like supporting actors on a very hazy stage. When the liquor ran low, whoever had money to put in the kitty did so and they'd muster a sortie to the ABC Store for mixed drinks or for beer at the 7-Eleven in the strip mall a short walk away.

At about ten thirty or eleven that night, Daryl borrowed a brown-handled, black semiautomatic handgun from one of his friends. He tucked the gun, movie style, behind his big belt buckle and, a little while later, walked out the door with Jones to get some more liquor from the 7-Eleven. From their ugly redbrick, two-story apartment buildings they drunkenly wandered through a little park and passed an elementary school en route to the strip mall down the street.

Hampton, Virginia, just next door to the larger Newport News, can be particularly rough at night. The town's thuggish youth element emerges to loiter around the 7-Eleven, despite a sign admonishing them not to. Lifelong Hampton resident and 7-Eleven manager Carol Owens says that "We have a great clientele, we serve many of the military personnel . . . [but] it all changes when the sun goes down." At night, "old people won't come in by themselves. They at least want to be watched by somebody" while they're in the store.

With the gun tucked away unobtrusively, Atkins and his buddy Jones didn't stand out in such a milieu at about midnight. "I had brought my dollar and fifty," Jones says. "I was going to get me one [beer], and [Daryl] said wait, he was going to panhandle and get some change up."

Jones got his big beer and then walked two shops down to the corner and stood in front of the Soaps-and-Suds Laundromat to watch Atkins ask for money. Atkins stood in front of the 7-Eleven and got lucky with a couple of people, but he wanted more. His opportunity came in a 1995 purple Nissan pickup truck, driven by a tall, redheaded twenty-one-year-old airman named Eric Nesbitt.

Nesbitt had had a full day by the time he reached the 7-Eleven. He was a mechanic at Langley Air Force Base, and he had started his job at seven that morning, as he did most days. He had attended a squadron barbecue, looked at an apartment he was interested in, and worked a part-time job at an auto parts store to supplement his low military wages. On his way home to the air base he got $60 in cash from his bank's ATM and pulled in front of the 7-Eleven just before midnight.

According to Jones, who, unlike Atkins, had a consistent, believable story, Atkins approached Nesbitt in his truck, and the two men talked for a little while. Jones walked over to find out what was going on and saw that Atkins was pointing the gun at Nesbitt.

"Move over, let my friend drive," Atkins said, and Nesbitt complied by scooting over. Jones got behind the wheel while Atkins, gun still drawn, was on the passenger side, sandwiching Nesbitt in the middle. They were robbing Nesbitt, but of what and in what manner wasn't yet clear to the criminals' drug- and alcohol-fogged brains. Jones pulled the truck around the corner behind the 7-Eleven, and Atkins asked Nesbitt if he had any money. Eric pulled the money out of his pocket and handed it over, but it wasn't enough to satisfy Atkins, so Nesbitt produced an ATM card and offered to get them more. Now they had a plan, so Jones pulled out onto the main road again while Atkins kept the gun on Nesbitt. At trial, Jones recounted Nesbitt as saying, "Take it [the money], that he didn't care just as long as we didn't hurt him."

Jones drove back in the same direction Eric had come from his auto parts job, back past Baptist churches, a private Christian high school, and a cemetery. They pulled up at the drive-through ATM and Nesbitt silently withdrew $200. The crooks' impromptu planning, however, took them no farther than this, and they made their way back to their apartment buildings, parked outside, and tried to figure out what to do. They worried that Nesbitt could identify them, and Jones came up with the idea of tying him to a tree in some remote place.

"Yes, yes," Jones recalled Nesbitt saying, "just tie me up as long as you just don't hurt me. "

Now the only problem was finding a tree remote enough to tie Nesbitt to.

"We couldn't think of nowhere in Hampton," Jones said of his densely populated town, which lies at the end of a peninsula surrounded by the Chesapeake Bay and the James River. Only to the north, beyond Newport News and toward the more rural York County, was there the possibility of seclusion, and Atkins thought he knew where. He had a grandfather who was a farmer and lived in a wooded region, although he had only visited him once a few years earlier. Atkins remembered the way and that near his grandfather's house was a stretch of road uncommonly traveled.

For the second time that night the three men retraced Nesbitt's route back toward his work and bank, but this time they got onto Interstate 64 and drove northward. For about half an hour the wide highway had commercial strips or large, noise-reducing cinderblock walls on both sides. There was enough time to talk, and Jones filled it by asking Nesbitt where he worked and what his romantic setup was and learned that he had a girlfriend. Atkins, still sitting on the passenger side, didn't say anything, but occupied himself by failing to remove the radio from the dashboard.

After a while trees appeared along the highway, and Jones exited and headed east. Atkins directed him to a spot where a slim dirt road met up with the single-lane, macadamized Crafford. It had only recently stopped raining, a mist was hanging in the air, and it was still hot, never dipping below seventy all night long, and muggy in that cloying, energy-depleting way it is on the East Coast throughout August.

Jones parked the truck and Atkins got out, ordering Nesbitt to do the same. Atkins had picked his spot well. Towering trees surrounded them, and it was pitch black. Gone were the streetlights of Hampton and Newport News; the only light was from the truck's cab, illuminated by the open door. The nearest houses were a clump of five in a hamlet called Newport News Park, about half a mile away. Nesbitt got out of the truck and took two steps on the muddy, unpaved road, but then Atkins opened up with the semi-automatic handgun at close range. He shot Nesbitt, quickly putting eighteen holes in his body; some bullets passed through

Nesbitt's arms to his abdomen, while others entered his body first and his arms on the way out. All but two of the .380-caliber full-metal jacket bullets passed through him entirely.

The murderers left Nesbitt lying curled up in "a fetal position" a few feet away from the truck on the ground, and he would die in a few minutes. A few hours after the murder, an early morning commuter would find Nesbitt's body and report it to the police. It didn't take them long to track down the video of Nesbitt taking money out of the ATM at gunpoint, the faces of his two assailants clearly in view. The police distributed pictures from the video to the news media, and within a few days people had called in to identify William Jones and his friend Daryl Atkins. It took a few days to find William Jones, who had hidden in a series of motels in the area. Atkins, however, was easy to find: he had simply returned home after the crime.

Atkins first went on trial in February 1998, and the court assigned Dr. Evan Nelson, a forensic psychologist, to analyze Atkins's mental abilities. Nelson looked at Daryl's grades in school and court records of previous crimes; he talked to family members and interviewed deputies at the jail where Atkins was being held. Nelson also administered an IQ test called the Wechsler Adult Intelligence Scale III, or the WAIS-III, which should take about an hour and a half, but because Atkins performed so poorly and couldn't answer a lot of the questions, the exam lasted under an hour.

As Nelson said at trial, the WAIS-III is "the standard IQ test for adults here in the United States." There are Wechsler tests for children as well, from age two and a half on up, and their reach is global. Harcourt Assessment, which publishes the tests, won't reveal how much money they make from the exams, but they say they are licensed for use in thirty countries around the world, and by all accounts the company makes many millions off the tests.

The Wechsler tests are used in any number of contexts, not just criminal trials. The largest use today is diagnosing students' learning disabilities, and many private schools also rely on them heavily in their school admissions. Neuropsychologists use them to assess brain functioning in head injury and Alzheimer's patients. Social Security mental health benefits are often tied to WAIS-III and other IQ test results, and industrial psychologists help businesses decide who to hire and promote based on them. IQ tests are everywhere, and the Wechsler tests have been the most prevalent of the individual, one-on-one intelligence tests from the middle of the twentieth century to today. Many psychologists refer to them as the "gold standard" by which to measure all other intelligence tests.

In Daryl Atkins's case, Nelson calculated with the WAIS-III that his IQ was 59, with the range of possible scores being from 45 to 155 and the average being 100. "That means that he falls in the range of being mildly mentally retarded," Nelson said at trial. He explained that mentally retarded people find it "harder to reason. . . . On the whole, people who are mentally retarded are not leaders."

In the end, though, the jury either wasn't convinced that Atkins was mentally retarded, or they thought he was but still deserved to be executed. From what they heard, Atkins didn't seem so stupid that he followed Jones around sheeplike; quite the opposite. Atkins seemed intelligent enough to come up with a plan, even if not a very good one, and follow it through. Despite his IQ of 59, Daryl was capable of deciding to borrow a gun; kidnap Eric in front of the 7-Eleven; pick a remote location; and, of course, kill him. They found him guilty of capital murder, an offense punished by death.

Atkins appealed to the Virginia Supreme Court and won another sentencing hearing by successfully arguing that his jury had been given a misleading verdict form. Back in the same Yorktown courthouse in 1999, Dr. Evan Nelson testified again and reiterated that the defendant was mildly mentally retarded, but this time the prosecution rolled out its own psychologist (one, not surprisingly, known for finding defendants mentally capable). Dr. Stanton Samenow administered only bits of the WAIS-III, which some psychologists consider bad form, a Wechsler memory test, and a smattering of other questions to gauge Atkins's intelligence. Based on these tests, on the way the defendant spoke, on "his vocabulary and syntax," and on his awareness of current events, Samenow thought he had "average intelligence, at least."

"I asked him on the twenty-third of July, 'Who died last week?' He said, 'Kennedy.' I said, 'How?' 'His plane crashed.' I said, 'Well, did anyone else die?' And he said, 'I think his wife and a friend.' I asked him where the plane was flying to. He did not know the answer to that. . . . I said, 'Well, who was Mr. Kennedy's father?' And he said, 'JFK.' I said, 'Who was that?' He said, 'He was president.' And I said, 'About when?' And he said, '1961.'"

It's not so different from German doctors during World War II asking people who Bismarck was or what Christmas signified. All claims of expertise aside, psychologists often get a rough sense for how smart a person is just as a layperson does—how aware of the world he is, and what his language is like. Samenow concluded that other than the IQ score of 59 elicited by Dr. Nelson, there was no indication that Atkins was mentally retarded. This second jury also sentenced him to death.

His lawyers appealed to the Virginia Supreme Court again, this time arguing that he shouldn't be executed because he was mentally retarded. The highest court in Virginia rejected the argument, saying it was "not willing to commute Atkins' sentence of death to life imprisonment merely because of his IQ score." This comported with U.S. Supreme Court precedent at the time, which held that states could constitutionally execute mentally retarded defendants.

In 2000, Atkins's attorneys appealed this decision, believing that they could persuade the U.S. Supreme Court to overturn its previous decision. In a 6–3 decision, the Court agreed, barring execution of the mentally retarded (and sending Atkins's case back to Yorktown for yet another jury to decide if he actually was retarded). The Court left it up to each state to decide how it would determine mental retardation and, not surprisingly, a tangle of laws has ensued, at least among the states that have bothered to legislate on the matter since *Atkins v. Virginia*.

The Virginia legislature responded to Atkins's Supreme Court case by passing a law requiring defendants to prove that they have an IQ of less than 70—not at the time of the crime, but presently— and a history of impaired life functioning since before age eighteen. In January 2005, seven years after Atkins's first trial, Dr. Evan

Nelson tested Atkins again, and he fully expected him to score
below a 70. Previously, during the second sentencing hearing at
Yorktown, in 1999, Nelson had explained to the jury that Daryl
might be able to score slightly higher than his original 59, but not
much.

"When I saw him [for the first time]," the psychologist said,
"he was mildly depressed. So the chances are he could have scored
two or three points higher if he had been in slightly better condition. But there's nothing to suggest that he was so impaired that he
could have scored, say, 21 points higher to get into the 80-point
range. That would just be an astounding difference."

Indeed, this time, in 2005, Atkins scored a 64, still well under
the death penalty wire and within the range that Nelson expected.
But two days later, the prosecution's expert witness, Dr. Stanton
Samenow, showed up at the jail to test Atkins, and the results made
the defense panic. Atkins scored a 76, significantly higher than the
70 cutoff for execution.

How could Atkins's score have risen seventeen points? Was he
now no longer mentally retarded? One possibility is that Atkins
had learned a lot over the past seven years of litigation, which
affected his score on what is essentially an achievement test. Much
of the WAIS-III tests language, and Atkins's vocabulary had been
involuntarily improved; he probably received a better education
during his trials than in all his years at school combined. In 1999,
for instance, a psychiatrist had asked him what "perjury" meant,
and Atkins responded with "lying."

"He stated that 'oath' meant a promise to tell the truth and that
when people testify they, 'tell their story—their side of it,'" this
psychiatrist reported to the court.

Researchers estimate that children whose parents are on welfare are exposed to one-fifth the number of words at home compared to children in white-collar homes. It's unlikely, given Atkins's
impoverished background, that words such as "voir dire,"
"peremptory strike," and "venire" were bandied about his father's
apartment, but he had been exposed to them and more in the
American legal system since his arrest in 1996.

Atkins learned more than just words at the defendant's table. The psychiatrist who had interviewed him in 1999 discovered that he had picked up on how the legal system operated; Atkins knew, for instance, that he could represent himself in court but thought it was better to have lawyers, and he understood that it was the judge's role to instruct the jury on how to reach its conclusions.

Another possible explanation for Atkins's improved scores in 2005 might just be that he took two tests so close together—the prosecution tested Atkins two days after the defense did. Practice makes perfect, or at least, in Atkins's case, a 76. One reason why psychologists keep their tests under lock and key is to ensure that questions are new to test takers: otherwise you end up with an arms-race-like SAT situation. Psychologists aptly call improved scores through multiple administrations of a test the "practice effect." It's highly likely that the prosecution knew about the practice effect when it sent in Dr. Samenow to test Atkins so soon after the defense's testing. It was a wily tactic; in February 2005, they even filed a motion with the judge to keep the jury from learning about the practice effect.

This third time around, it was the jury's job solely to decide if Atkins was mentally retarded. After listening to seven days of testimony about IQ scores and Atkins's capacity to function in daily life, the jury deliberated for almost thirteen hours before deciding that he was not mentally retarded. They were the third jury to decide against Atkins, despite the swinging IQ scores. In June 2006, however, the Virginia Supreme Court decided yet again that Daryl Atkins deserved another trial to determine whether he is mentally retarded. His IQ scores, and the psychologists who administer and interpret them, will be the foci of attention for the fourth time.

Before the U.S. Supreme Court case *Atkins v. Virginia*, prosecutors often used a defendant's low IQ scores to argue that a defendant in a capital murder trial was incorrigible—he was so dumb he was permanently dangerous—to obtain execution. Now, after *Atkins v. Virginia*, prosecutors want to show the reverse: that a defendant's scores are high enough that he can be executed. The defense view of IQ scores, too, has flip-flopped. Defense lawyers want their clients to have low IQs. The result is a battle of experts and competing IQ scores.

Truth (or at least the resolution of legal problems) in common law systems, as in America, is arrived at through an adversarial system, so the fact that defense lawyers and prosecutors battle over IQ test results in this way is not enough to condemn the practice. Moreover, it's not that the rationale behind the Supreme Court decision in *Atkins* is incorrect; mentally retarded people have an impaired understanding of the world. The problem is with the test itself, which will lead to more intolerable arbitrariness in a legal area rife with it.

Judges and juries should not take WAIS-III results as reliable indicators of mental retardation. IQ tests, including the WAIS-III, are reliable in the sense that adults' scores tend not to vary much. People who score a 115 tend to score thereabouts consistently, unless they take the test repeatedly, become better educated, develop an avid reading or drinking habit late in life, or suffer a head injury. These are fairly rare occurrences unless the person happens to be a defendant in a capital murder trial. These defendants are in uncommon circumstances wherein people with educationally and culturally bereft backgrounds are exposed to ideas, language, and repeated testing.

More disturbingly (and with broader application beyond just the legal sphere), IQ tests don't measure intelligence, despite what psychologists tell us. The next question is, If not intelligence, what do they measure?

Chapter 12

What Do IQ Tests Really Measure?

Most psychologists believe they can test intelligence and that the measured entity is extremely important. "Human differences have enormous social and political implications, intelligence is one of the most important human differences, and tests reveal them," e-mailed one leading academic psychologist. Psychologists have struggled to define intelligence, and they differ vigorously over what it is, but ever since Charles Spearman and his naming of general intelligence, the majority definition boils down to "brainpower."

At Daryl Atkins's first trial, Dr. Evan Nelson defined intelligence as "some innate ability to think and reason and understand. In the ideal world, intelligence would have nothing to do with level of education, it refers to essentially brainpower and not necessarily knowledge, although it's often hard to separate the two." Nelson thought that Atkins's score of 59 was a reliable indication of his "current intellectual functioning."

What, though, does Atkins's score of 59 really mean? Looking at the basic structure of intelligence tests helps to answer that question. IQ tests, like the WAIS-III that Nelson administered to Atkins, are often made up of "verbal" and "nonverbal" questions because American psychologists at the beginning of the century had literate, illiterate, and non-English-speaking people to test.

(The term *verbal* can include mathematics questions.) This verbal/nonverbal structure did not arise from intelligence theory or a sophisticated model of how the brain works; it arose from historical circumstance. The doctors on Ellis Island and psychologists in the U.S. Army during World War I had many people who couldn't read English, so they had to use nonverbal "performance" questions—such as putting together a picture of a ship with puzzle pieces—to measure intelligence. These questions ended up in the army Beta test, and then finally in the WAIS and other Wechsler exams. The verbal section of the WAIS, too, is based in large part on the army Alpha, the tests for literates that in turn came from previous sources, such as Alfred Binet via Lewis Terman.

So when psychologists administer the WAIS today they are traveling on a well-worn track, based not on theory but on practical precedents. Well before World War I, Alfred Binet asked, "When someone has offended you and asks you to excuse him, what ought you to do?" The army Alpha exam tested common sense, too, as in the following example:

> Freezing water bursts pipes because
>
> ☐ cold makes the pipes weaker
> ☐ water expands when it freezes
> ☐ the ice stops the flow of water

An example that Nelson gave of a WAIS commonsense question at Atkins's first trial was remarkably similar: "What is the thing to do if a water pipe breaks in your house?"

Questions like these, from the "comprehension" subtest, are obviously and unabashedly tests of knowledge and schooling, and more broadly the test taker's general life experiences. If you're an uneducated farmhand in the Mississippi Delta, you are less likely to know that Shakespeare was the author of *Hamlet*, another of Nelson's examples, than if you got a Ph.D. in literature from Harvard.

The rest of the WAIS-III subtests, not just the comprehension subtest, have changed remarkably little from their inception in

1939. Today, only two of the WAIS-III's fourteen subtests are based on question types devised from the 1960s onward. One subtest is from the 1930s, and the remaining eleven are pre-World War I technology. In the 1880s, for instance, Francis Galton used digit-span, the ability to parrot back a series of numbers (backward and forward), and it remains a WAIS subtest today.

The bulk of verbal questions, however, originate from Alfred Binet's tests. Binet had no construct of what intelligence was, but he figured out that distinctions could be made among children of different ages if he tested their language and reasoning ability. In the 1930s, David Wechsler, the original creator of the WAIS exam, similarly had no or little theory behind his tests, and the exam questions remain remarkably similar throughout the century. In short, we test without theory, but rather on the ability to distinguish among people in a rough-and-ready way.

Binet's insight was that intelligence testers should be measuring higher reasoning, such as abstract thinking, so he asked French schoolchildren what the similarities were between "a fly and an ant; a poppy and blood; or a newspaper, a label and a picture." The same test of "similarities" exists today on the WAIS-III, an exam for American adults.

"Degree of abstractness should be evaluated," a popular psychologists' guide for WAIS-III administration reads today. "[R]esponses may be *abstract* (*table* and *chair* are "furniture"), *concrete* (*pants* and *tie* are "made of cloth"), or *functional* (*map* and *compass* "tell you where you are going"). Similarly, in the "comprehension" subtest, abstract explanations for proverbs such as "The grass is always greener on the other side" result in higher scores than more concrete answers.

Of the seven verbal subtests on the WAIS-III, six are based on Lewis Terman's Stanford-Binet, first published in 1916, and/or the World War I army Alpha. Similarly, four of seven nonverbal subtests are from the army exams. The "picture completion" subtest—pointing out that a rabbit lacks an ear, or a tennis match a net—was used during World War I and before, as were the "picture arrangement" and "digit symbol-coding" subtests. The block toy task that Ellis Island doctors devised, in which immigrants put together pictures, remains codified in the Wechsler exams. The same is true of the jigsaw puzzles the doctors figured everyone would recognize, such as a ship or the profile of a face.

Thus IQ test technology, which grew out of practical and historical necessity (not from knowledge of or agreement about what intelligence actually is), hasn't changed much in the hundred years since Alfred Binet published his first test, in 1905. Change has occurred, but often in formalistic ways, such as the use of multiple-choice questions for group tests and cultural adaptation of the questions to America and elsewhere. The decades-long structure of verbal and performance questions in the Wechsler tests and other IQ exams does not come from intelligence or cognitive theory but from historical legacy, statistical relationships between how people score on tests and subtests, and some power to predict future behavior. Psychology's resistance to change is what keeps this structure alive.

David Wechsler was one of the army's young test administrators during World War I, having just completed a master's degree at Columbia University. As a student before and after the war, and even when he was in the army, Wechsler was able to study and work with almost every famous psychologist of his day, and in the process he was exposed to the gamut of psychology's thinking on intelligence. At Columbia University he studied under James McKeen Cattell, the man discussed in chapter 2 who discovered that his anthropometric tests didn't correlate with grades or each other, and with Edward Thorndike, a psychologist who believed that intelligence was composed of independent and specific abilities—that is, not just one thing. But Wechsler also spent a few months in England studying with Charles Spearman, who had famously named general intelligence, and in France with yet more psychologists.

In the face of all these varied and contradictory opinions about what intelligence was, Wechsler, who was hugely practical, concluded that his more senior psychologists "were all right." It wasn't a particularly theoretically grounded point of view, but it made him extremely flexible and open-minded when it came to creating tests. Eventually, in the 1930s, Wechsler took the tests he was familiar with from World War I, and other testing methods known to psychologists at the time, and just jammed them all together into a usable and multifaceted exam. Psychologists liked it so much it overshadowed Lewis Terman's Stanford-Binet.

The origin of David Wechsler's tests can surprise even practicing psychologists who administer them. Jack Naglieri, an academic psychologist at George Mason University, often gives talks around the country and in the process shows his audience questions from the World War I U.S. Army exams. When they see them, "people go, that looks just like a Wechsler item and I say, Yeah, it is because Wechsler stole all of them. . . . What Wechsler did was that he took a group-administered test [from World War I] and made it into an individual test. That was really what he did . . . his real contribution was providing a test that clinical psychologists could use."

What was most radical about Wechsler's first test, the Wechsler-Bellevue Intelligence Scale (1939), was that psychologists would now administer both the verbal and the nonverbal tests together to subjects. Putting the two types of test questions together made no sense to many psychologists at the time. Why give the performance, nonverbal questions—playing with blocks, working with pictures—to people who could read and speak English? Like Alfred Binet and Charles Spearman before him, Wechsler thought psychologists should be measuring many different types of mental abilities, and the performance questions, in particular, he thought, offered examiners insights into people's personalities, not just their measurable intelligence. Wechsler also knew that most of the subtests correlated well with each other. That is, people who did well on vocabulary and arithmetic subtests, for instance, also tended to do well on the various performance subtests, so these activities were mentally related in some way.

Ultimately, Wechsler was modest about what he thought his exam tested. His tests resulted in one number, such as Daryl Atkins's 59, which he thought represented a person's ability to do intellectual work. But he didn't think IQ tests could measure intelligence so straightforwardly. Whatever they test, he wrote, "certainly it is not something which can be expressed by one single factor alone, say "g," whether you define it in its most general terms as mental energy, the ability to educe relations or merely as the intellectual factor. Intelligence is this and yet something more."

The ability to do intellectual work was important, but Wechsler didn't think this was "the only important or paramount factor." He called the "something more" of intelligence, such as enthusiasm, persistence, and the ability to plan, "nonintellective factors." Wechsler even wanted to test these nonintellective factors, but he never successfully created an exam to do so. We are left with tests claiming to be of general intelligence. Despite the lack of theory underlying them, and Wechsler's own misgivings about their narrowness, we still use them as if they answer much or all about a person's cognitive abilities. Talk to psychologists who administer Wechsler tests for private school admissions, for instance, and they will tell you that the WISC and WPPSI (the kids' tests) are heavily relied on as a measure for how well a child will learn in the future, without measuring his nonintellective factors.

Do Wechsler's various and old subtests, lashed together like logs to make a raft, usefully reveal how well people think? It's easy to see that someone of decent mental ability, but uneducated, might score poorly on verbal questions. That conclusion, however, is not as intuitive when it comes to nonverbal performance questions. On the WAIS Matrix Reasoning subtest, for instance, subjects are asked to figure out nonverbal patterns as represented by a series of pictures. At the easiest level—and they get progressively harder—the psychologist might show the test taker an image of an empty box; then an image of a colored-in box; then an empty arrow, and the test taker is to infer that the final step is a colored-in arrow.

"These questions are very important because they don't rely at all on schooling," Dr. Nelson said at Atkins's trial. "It really doesn't matter if you've been to school or not. None of us ever did this sort of thing as part of our traditional education."

This is one of the myths that psychologists keep alive; schooling and personal experience, however, influence all IQ tests and question types. Depending on something as arbitrary as a birth date, some nine-year-olds will be in the third grade, while others will be in the fourth. On average, the fourth-grade nine-year-olds have higher IQs than the third-grade nine-year-olds. This holds true even for nonverbal tests of abstract reasoning, such as the matrix questions on the Wechsler tests.

Rather counterintuitively, it turns out that nonverbal tests are more affected by people's environment than straightforward tests of knowledge, such as vocabulary and arithmetic. In the 1980s, a New Zealand political scientist named James Flynn discovered that throughout the developed world IQ scores were rising every year, creating vast point spreads between one generation and the next. Flynn put out an all-points bulletin to fellow academics in various countries to send him large numbers of people's scores from as far back as possible to the present. Initially he was able to gather scores from fourteen countries that had been testing men, often in the military, since the 1940s and 1950s with the same intelligence tests. By the late 1990s, Flynn had data from twenty countries. Since the subjects, despite the passage of time, had taken the same tests, Flynn could quite easily compare the scores of two or more generations.

Flynn was particularly interested in a test called Ravens Progressive Matrices, upon which the WAIS-III Matrix subtest is based. Ravens, created in the 1930s, has pretty much kept to the same sixty questions over the years, making it ideal for comparing IQ scores of different generations. As Flynn puts it, the content of Ravens is "culture reduced," avoiding words or symbols one would find in schools, in the workplace, or anywhere else in the culture. Psychologists believe the matrices test "fluid" intelligence—that is, on-the-spot reasoning and problem-solving—as opposed to the acquired knowledge of "crystallized" intelligence that, for instance, a vocabulary test measures. Many psychologists also believe that Ravens are the purest measure of g, so many experts, before Flynn's studies, assumed that Ravens scores would remain constant between generations. A generation can't become radically innately smarter than the immediately preceding one, can it?

They couldn't have been more wrong. Every year, Ravens scores are increasing worldwide. As an illustration, the Dutch military had been giving all of its eighteen-year-old recruits the same reduced Ravens, just forty of sixty questions, since 1945. Over the years, the percentage of men who were able to answer more than twenty-four of the forty questions correctly increased staggeringly. In 1952, just 31 percent of men did so, but by 1962 it was up to 46 percent. In 1972, 63 percent of the men could answer more than twenty-four correctly, and by 1981–1982, 82 percent got them right, representing an average gain of more than 20 IQ points over thirty years. These findings were corroborated to varying degrees in every other country from which Flynn collected data.

Understandably, Flynn's studies have caused considerable consternation and debate within psychology. Ever since the tool was invented, psychologists have believed that they can explain people's ability to understand the world around them by administering IQ tests. Arthur Jensen, a famous University of California psychologist, has said that someone with an IQ of 75 can enjoy baseball, but not properly understand the game's rules, the details of how the league works, or even how many players are on a team. But Flynn's findings make it difficult to extrapolate from what an IQ score tells you about people's mental abilities.

"Take a woman with an IQ of 110 who taught for 30 years in the Netherlands," Flynn wrote. "In 1952 she was brighter than 75% of her senior students; by 1967, they were her equals; by 1982, 75% of them were brighter than she was. Has that really been the career experience of Dutch teachers?"

The results of two other studies involving Ravens have allowed researchers to compare how well people born in 1877 performed to adults' scores today. In 1942, British adults ranging from ages twenty-five to sixty-five took Ravens, and a study of the same age group, on the same test, was conducted in 1992. The more recent generations scored significantly higher than the preceding generations, with the result that twenty-five-year-olds in 1992 appear to be surprisingly smarter than their Victorian counterparts. Flynn calculated that by today's standards, at least 70 percent of late-nineteenth-century Britons would have an IQ of less than 75. If IQ tests measure intelligence in absolute terms, how did anybody get anything done in the nineteenth century?

"How reasonable is it to assume that 70% of late-nineteenth-century Britons could not, even if it were their chief interest, understand the rules of cricket?" Flynn asked. "The military data, which are of impeccable quality, pose the same question. Can we assume that in 1952, almost 40% of Dutch men lacked the capacity to understand soccer, their most favored national sport?"

Interestingly, scores from education-reliant tests such as the Stanford-Binet and Wechsler exams also have risen throughout the world, to the tune of about 9 to 18 points per generation depending on the country. But in general, the more education-dependent an exam or subtest, the less it has risen, if at all. For instance, people do not appear to be improving on the Wechsler subtests of arithmetic and vocabulary. (Germans, for some reason, are an exception to this; they are busy learning new words at a surprising rate.)

No one knows for sure why IQ scores are going up. Is it universal education, the advent of video games, test-taking savvy, improved diets, or some combination of factors? The debates rage in academia. One thing is clear, though: it's not a quick and radical change to the gene pool.

"Massive IQ gains cannot be due to genetic factors," Flynn wrote. "Reproductive differentials between social classes would have to be impossibly large to raise the mean IQ even 1 point in a single generation."

Large intergenerational IQ gains are a pretty serious blow to psychologists who believe that their tests measure intelligence, innate or not. Is the present batch of thirty-year-olds that much smarter than their parents? There has been no great surge in the number of patents registered or in academic achievement, Flynn has noted; people are pretty much plodding along—efficiently, inefficiently, as smart or as dumb as they used to be. Rising IQ scores provide strong evidence that despite many psychologists' claims, IQ tests measure knowledge and "abstract problem-solving abilities."

As Flynn remarked, "psychologists should stop saying that IQ tests measure intelligence. They should say that IQ tests measure abstract problem-solving ability (APSA), a term that accurately conveys our ignorance. We know people solve problems on IQ tests; we suspect those problems are so detached, or so abstracted from reality, that the ability to solve them can diverge over time from the real-world problem-solving ability called intelligence; thus far we know little else."

Where people come down on what IQ tests measure matters a great deal in the practical world. If Daryl Atkins has a small vocabulary, doesn't know what to do when a pipe bursts in his apartment, and isn't good at arithmetic, we either know he lacks knowledge or has extremely low g. In the former, he still might be smart enough to plan a murder and understand legal proceedings; in the latter he's biologically too stupid to be executed in good conscience.

Chapter 13

Alternatives to IQ

Intuitively, *g* both does and doesn't make sense. That good test takers do well on most tests is undeniably true (and that they tend somewhat to do better in life than bad testers is unsurprising), but this doesn't establish that intelligence is singular, no matter how strong the tendencies. Examples of very smart students who are remarkably dim in other areas of their life abound. Howard Marks, for instance, is Britain's most famous drug smuggler. In the 1970s and 1980s he smuggled many, many tons of marijuana into the United Kingdom and the United States, orchestrating it from his family home in Majorca.

In 1956, the eleven-plus correctly identified Marks as a student who could learn at the highest levels. Despite his working-class background in South Wales, Marks became one of the most brilliant students of his generation. He scored remarkably high grades on his A levels, the university entrance exams taken at age seventeen, went to Oxford University, and studied physics. Becoming a physicist or anything else mainstream, for that matter, seemed too dull for Marks, and after graduating he quickly turned to driving large amounts of marijuana across borders.

British and American law enforcement tracked him for years and eventually, in the 1990s, the DEA caught up to him, landing him in Terre Haute Federal Penitentiary for seven years. Looking back, he frames his career in terms of intelligence and personality. When asked if he would have imported marijuana had it been legal, as a merchant would wine, Marks didn't have to think long.

"No, I don't think so. No. I don't particularly like that kind of trade," he said.

The very illegality of dope drew him to the business. A degree in physics from Oxford did give Marks options other than drug smuggling, but his attitude toward the mainstream made him see only a few. He could have been "a nuclear scientist letting off bombs. I was qualified in nuclear physics; perhaps it was an ethical decision not to be a nuclear scientist." In Marks's mind, drug smuggling was the only career for him.

Many of his contemporaries in the 1970s claimed to be smuggling marijuana for ideological reasons—sticking it to supposedly "fascist" governments—but Marks didn't even pay lip service to such sentiments.

"There was a frustration with the law against marijuana and I certainly felt that I could break it without breaking any ethical code I had. But I wouldn't go so far as to say I did it just because of [the unjustness of its illegality], it just wouldn't be true," Marks said.

As he put it, Marks became a smuggler for two reasons: "an exciting profession and a lot of product loyalty."

There isn't a psychologist around who would deny that motivation and interests shape life path in addition to smarts. What's interesting about Marks, however, is his analysis of what makes a good smuggler. He was caught, he points out, and the best smugglers get away with it.

"You don't have to be smart businesswise," Marks said, "because you are catering for a demand that is never satisfied." Nor does a smuggler need academic smarts, which he chalked up to "a memory and handwriting speed test."

What smugglers need, Marks said, is social intelligence, which Marks said he also had in abundance. "Social intelligence is nothing more than just being charming and polite." In Britain, Marks is famous for this, and for being a stellar student. For years, he charmed his way into deals—in the shipping business, customs offices, and at docks—and out of legal predicaments.

According to Marks, what he lacked, though, were street smarts—"stuff that isn't taught." "Street intelligence I don't have," said Marks with a laugh. "I was never any good at figuring out whether I was being followed or anything. And I made terrible choices of partners to work with."

Some of his partners ratted on him when they were arrested, and for years, off and on, he teamed up with an Irish gun-running sociopath who had a tendency to get in the news. Also, if you love being around your family, choosing a profession that may result in seven years in the Terre Haute penitentiary might not be the smartest choice.

Academic psychologists hate hokey journalistic accounts of intelligence like the one above. It isn't science, they point out, and they're right: talking to someone who famously smoked twenty joints a day about what he thinks intelligence is doesn't prove a thing. At the same time, Marks may not be wrong to view intelligence as multifaceted.

While there have always been psychologists who didn't buy into *g*, in the 1980s there began a new proliferation of ideas among intelligence experts, some of which entered public awareness; others, however, remain outside mainstream consciousness. The most famous alternative theory is Howard Gardner's multiple intelligences, which he propounded in his 1983 book *Frames of Mind* and has since elaborated on in many subsequent publications.

Gardner's theory of multiple intelligences was radical from its very methodological start. Unlike his fellow psychologists over the previous eighty years of intelligence work, Gardner did not construct his view of intelligence from statistical analyses of test results. Instead, when deciding whether a mental ability was a distinct "intelligence," he used eight criteria based on findings from various disciplines. He looked, for example, for mental abilities that had been isolated in brain-damaged patients, emphasized in idiot savants, distinguished in our evolutionary history and psychological development, and that required identifiable clusters of subabilities.

This approach allowed Gardner to evaluate many mental abilities and throw out those that didn't fit the criteria. He was provisionally left with seven intelligences, which he discussed in *Frames of Mind.* These included linguistic, logical-mathematical, musical, bodily-kinesthetic, spatial, interpersonal, and intrapersonal intelligences. As the years progressed, Gardner has considered other candidates for this list, such as naturalist, spiritual, and existential intelligences.

While many academic psychologists personally admire Gardner, not surprisingly, the majority reject his work and conclusions. One psychologist, who didn't wish his name attached to his comment, likened Gardner to Freud: he is one of the best writers around, he said, but his work doesn't stand up to close scientific scrutiny. Academics also critically point out that Gardner hasn't written a test, but he probably considers this a strength.

"Intelligences are not things that can be seen or counted," he has written. "Instead, they are potentials—presumably, neural ones—that will or will not be activated, depending upon the values of a particular culture, the opportunities available in that culture, and the personal decisions made by individuals and/or their families, schoolteachers, and others."

With this view of intelligences, it's hard to imagine that Gardner would bother devising tests. It also means it is difficult to compare Gardner's theory of multiple intelligences with the more traditional approach of testing *g*. There are mountains of studies, after all, that calculate how predictive IQ scores are in various contexts, such as the workplace, for instance. Employers can be told how much to rely on IQ tests when hiring people, but in the hard-nosed world of business it is much harder to grasp how important it is to consider applicants' multiple and various intelligences.

Despite this lack of measurability, however, teachers and educators have been very receptive to Gardner's work. This makes sense, for education is a field that at least should be concerned with understanding the various ways people learn and operate. Unlike the theory of *g*, Gardner has offered teachers a window into viewing students holistically and helping them.

Ultimately, testing a singular, rankable intelligence is about institutional efficiency, and Howard Gardner's multiple intelli-

gences is not. Teachers in classrooms are not as worried about efficiency; they are more concerned about understanding their students as best they can to help them learn. Institutional pressures,
however, tend to push school admissions and business human
resource officers to focus on efficiency, rather than dealing holistically with people. Single numbers, facilitated by social science that
indicates they are helpful to varying degrees depending on context,
are the easiest, if not the best, ways to make sorting decisions.

One of the effects of *Frames of Mind* and Gardner's theories was
to wrest the word "intelligence" from mainstream psychologists
and elasticize the concept. Thus, in 1995, Daniel Goleman could
write a book called *Emotional Intelligence*, arguing that knowing
yourself, understanding others, and attributes such as empathy and
persistence mean more in life than IQ-measured intelligence. The
trend has done nothing but continue, leading to books bearing
titles such as *Raise Your Child's Social IQ: Stepping Stones to People
Skills for Kids*, which surely results in a derisive snort from psychology's old guard.

Unlike Howard Gardner and Daniel Goleman, however, some
researchers in the past quarter century have staunchly believed in the
usefulness of psychological testing, although they, too, became tired
of the old line that "Intelligence is what the tests test," as one expert
famously defined intelligence in the early 1920s. These intelligence
testers have moved significantly from the verbal-nonverbal model
enshrined in IQ tests during World War I. Seventy-five years after
the publication of the first modern intelligence test, researchers
now create exams based on actual theories of intelligence. If people
need to be tested, this is a move in the right direction.

The most prominent advocate of theory-based testing is Yale
University psychologist Robert Sternberg, who was himself an
extremely bad intelligence test taker when he was between ages six
to eight, which almost paradoxically created his lifelong fascination
with testing (and not so contradictorily made him open to the problems of testing, but without disavowing the field). Sternberg grew
up in New Jersey in the 1950s and attended a public elementary

school. "At least where I grew up, they [had] group IQ tests every year or two. So it was stressful and I didn't handle the stress well," he said. What the school did with the test results "beats the hell out of me," but the teachers probably used them, he thought, to track their students within their classes and relied on them when deciding how best to teach each student.

Robert Sternberg's teachers never revealed his IQ test results, but he said he didn't need to see them to know how badly he did. "If time is called on a subtest and you are on the second or third item of maybe twenty, then you didn't do well. I didn't answer them, I just froze . . . seeing words on a page but not being able, quite, to read them," he said.

"It's a little like the male role in sex: if you worry about failing, you do. The anxiety creates the situation where the thing you're worried about comes true."

Sternberg was the kind of kid who couldn't stand being judged, and he lacked confidence. "If I was in a school play and had to memorize lines I had the same reaction." When he used to practice the cello Sternberg could play well; when he auditioned he was "terrible." "It was the anxiety of having three judges sitting there and being evaluated," he said.

These childhood experiences allowed Sternberg, more than most academic psychologists, who presumably scored well, in the main, to empathize with how people feel when taking tests. "We tend often to underestimate the effects of state of mind. The score is presented as an ability score and people don't talk about your state of mind when you took it," Sternberg said. It's the myth of objective tests: they're objective only in the sense that they are graded uniformly; they're not objective to write or to take.

Sternberg's fourth-grade teacher, a Mrs. Alexa, believed in him despite the bad test results. He can't remember anything she said in particular; it was more the confidence she conveyed to him. Mrs. Alexa's influence was such that Sternberg dedicated his book *Successful Intelligence* to her, thanking her "for turning my life around.

"You know, it's like when you're in a relationship with someone as an adult. Often the distinction between a good relationship and a bad relationship is not exactly in the words. It's in the stuff, the nonverbals, that pass between you." As he got older, Sternberg gained in confidence, did well on the SATs, and attended Yale.

Sternberg has coined the term "successful intelligence," which is broader than general intelligence and is defined as "the ability to achieve success in life in terms of one's personal standards within one's sociocultural context." He believes that there are three components to successful intelligence: analytic, creative, and practical. "The analytical aspect is used to solve problems, the creative aspect to decide what problems to solve, and the practical aspect to make solutions effective," he wrote.

Sternberg conveys these ideas extremely well to the general public. As in the story about his childhood, he personalizes his theory and isn't caught in a narrow ideological box. He also publishes copiously, having published more than six hundred articles and books, which makes many other psychologists in his field jealous. But critics within psychology believe that Sternberg has problems operationalizing his ideas, and it is true that there is no generally available test of successful intelligence for psychologists or institutions to use. At this point successful intelligence is mainly just a theory, although a compelling one.

Since 1983, with the publication of Alan and Nadeen Kaufman's Kaufman Assessment Battery for Children (the K-ABC), researchers in the area of cognitive processing have been more successful than Sternberg at producing tests and taking them to market, although they have by no means broken the general intelligence test stranglehold. Like Sternberg, they, too, created theory before writing their exams and for these researchers it was based on advances made over the past several decades in cognitive science. In 1997, for instance, George Mason University psychologist Jack Naglieri based his test of cognition, the Cognitive Assessment System (CAS), on four distinct brain-based mental functions. His test was mainly based on the work of a Soviet scientist who, in the 1960s and 1970s, studied war veterans suffering from injuries to specific parts of the brain. The research revealed that different parts of the brain contributed to four distinct mental processes: attention, the ability to process stimuli simultaneously and order them appropriately, and planning.

During an interview in his large second-story corner office at George Mason University, Naglieri stated repeatedly that his CAS exam is more meaningful and helpful than traditional IQ tests. Take the assessment and treatment of a learning disability, for example, he said. The traditional and still widely used definition of a learning disability is a discrepancy between ability, as defined by IQ, and achievement. Say a student has an IQ of 125 but can't read very well. How does that knowledge help his teachers?

The ability-achievement discrepancy "is a stupid concept if you think about it," said Naglieri. "What does that mean? You don't know what's wrong with that kid. If you don't know what's wrong, how can you tell the teacher what to do?"

In the end, the child is simply stuck into special education classes with no road map for getting him out. IQ tests can't point to any particular psychological process that a child is having problems with, but Naglieri believes that his theories and tests can. For example, his CAS test might show that a student who can't read very well also has difficulty simultaneously processing multiple stimuli. Therefore, teachers can work on simultaneous processing within the context of reading by breaking stories down into related parts, for example, or asking students to summarize a story they've just read.

When practicing psychologists use the Wechsler and other traditional IQ tests, on the other hand, they are forced to read into the exam conclusions about the subject's intelligence that aren't necessarily right.

"I think that we as psychologists have done a huge disservice to our profession by making practitioners have to decide what tests measure," said Naglieri. "That doesn't make any sense. I mean, if

[David] Wechsler couldn't tell you what each of the subtests measure, why should you have to figure it out?"

Take the picture arrangement subtest in the WAIS-III. Psychologists give subjects a series of cards with pictures on them and tell them to put them in proper story order. Psychologists have been doing this for a long time, and they've often assumed that people with more social knowledge and intelligence will do better on these tests, but this has turned out to be empirically unprovable, said Naglieri. Ordering pictures into their proper place isn't related to anything we can measure about people's social abilities or understanding.

Naglieri thinks practicing psychologists need to know about people's intelligence, so they read into Wechsler subtests conclusions that aren't necessarily there. "But that's what we do in this field, we make this stuff up. I'm being truthful; we essentially make it up," Naglieri said. "My argument is the reason that they are trying to pull [interpretations] out of the test is because they didn't get an answer that they needed [from the main single score]. So they looked deeper into the test itself to try to find an answer. My argument is that you should look at a different test."

The problem is that the Wechsler tests, along with the Stanford-Binet to some degree, are so dominant that psychologists don't have many other tests to turn to, even if they're interested. Psychologists consider the Wechsler tests and the Stanford-Binet the "gold standard" of intelligence testing, so it's going to be hard to get psychology to shift away from them, despite their questionable usefulness in many contexts. They've been around a long time and are firmly entrenched.

"How many years did it take us to move from the horse to the automobile?" Naglieri asked. "A long time and they coexisted for like fifty years. . . . I remember my own experience from moving from a typewriter to a computer and how so many people resisted that. I mean people are hard to change. Everyplace you go talking about intelligence, what do you see? Wechsler and Binet. It's everywhere; it's in every book and every magazine and everyplace you look. Everybody thinks that's what intelligence is and they refer to it as the gold standard and it's not made of gold as far as I'm concerned, but it's so well entrenched."

One of the pitfalls of often politically liberal criticism of intelligence testing over the years is that it rejects the entire field. The history of measuring intelligence is full of abuses, catastrophically terrible policy ideas, and prickly intelligence testers who have been too hostile to change and outside criticism. But it would be a mistake to dismiss all intelligence research and tests. Institutions and individuals are allowed to pick and choose which experts they believe and what tests to use. Outright rejection of these tests has often been based on the untenable claim that everyone is the same, that all differences in ability are the product of environment. Albert Einstein was a better physicist than the average bartender, and it would be surprising if some chunk of this weren't due to inborn ability. Is it so impossible that a test could have ascertained Einstein's abilities before he revolutionized the field?

At present that test is a physics achievement test rather than an intelligence test. The latter hasn't crawled far enough away from the primordial sludge for us to rely on it heavily and singularly to sort people.

The problem is that IQ tests don't offer insight into how people actually think. If we want to replace these old exams, rather than simply eliminate them, listening to psychologists with alternative tests and theories of intelligence is a good place to start.

Chapter 14

The SAT

In 1954, twenty-five hundred white students boycotted Anacostia High School, in Washington, D.C., to protest against court-ordered desegregation of public schools. After four days, administrators persuaded them to return by threatening the students' extracurricular activities: no more football or theater productions unless they came back to school. The students returned, but only for a little while. Gradually the whites voted with their feet by moving out of the neighborhood, to the suburbs or the white-dominated northwest of the city.

Fifty years after the boycott, all the students who attend Anacostia High School are black and destined, it seems, to form the left-hand rise of the bell curve. Seventy-three percent are considered "economically disadvantaged." They've grown up in a neighborhood that has the highest murder rate in a city famous for homicide, in a place where killings are so frequent that the local news media often don't bother reporting on them. The Environmental Protection Agency calculates that the Anacostia River, which burbles near the high school and, choked with tires and other urban detritus, gathers two billion gallons of raw sewage every year.

Anacostia students enter their school through three plain concrete Doric columns and four sets of red double doors. The first person they see in the darkened foyer is an unformidable, uniformed security guard sitting on a stool at a wooden podium waiting for either of two metal detectors to sound off. Administrative offices are down the main hall, through the jostling teenagers and on the left.

To speak to Wensworth E. Lovell, one of the school's guidance counselors, visitors have to knock on locked double glass and wood doors and wait for a student to open them and usher them in, as if to see an old-time party boss tucked away in a back room. Lovell has close-cropped gray hair and a goatee, and he has an easy rapport with the students who like to congregate in his small, cluttered office. Lovell smiles a lot, kidding his charges gently in a voice that still hints at his Trinidadian roots. Despite the two-o'clock hour on a cold day in January, Lovell hadn't eaten since breakfast, and he gulped soup from a large plastic cup that sits on his desk next to an urn labeled "Ex-wife's ashes." He's worked in public schools for twenty-seven years, ten of them as a guidance counselor.

In preparation for an interview about the SAT, Lovell asked the students to leave, and they retreated to the foyer. Once they're outside, Lovell said he thinks worsening social, economic, and family circumstances have changed today's students. "Their morals, values are disheartening," he said. "It's a different generation now. Bill Cosby was right. I know some disagree, but I don't." The kids outside need some discipline, Lovell said. Many don't have parents, or their homes are full of drugs and violence, or they are raised by grandparents who can't control them. The students lack role models, and Lovell said he provides one. "I could have dealt drugs, become a pipehead," he tells his students, but he didn't.

On particularly rough days, Lovell looks up at a picture hanging on his wall of a house he owns in Trinidad. It's large enough that he's considering running a bed-and-breakfast in it when he leaves D.C. "Give me two more years and I'll be able to retire," he said, gazing at it.

When asked what he thinks about the famous college entrance exam, the SAT, Lovell sighed.

"We need mental health tests here," not standardized tests, he said. For the students or teachers? "Both," he said, and laughed. But Lovell seemed more composed than exhausted, as if he'd seen it all before and then a few more times. "If I weren't calm I'd be up in St. Elizabeth's," he said, gesturing with a turned head and raised eyebrows toward D.C.'s famous Victorian-era mental hospital that still houses John Hinckley, somewhere out the window behind him in Anacostia, out over the snow.

"We get tired of tests," Lovell said. He thinks the kids in Anacostia have it bad enough without getting measured by some yardstick concocted in a faraway place. They should be tested on what they've learned at their school, he said, not dictated by someone else on a national level. Whatever's going on in the students' lives, they're not learning what's on the national tests. "The vocabulary on the SAT is not what they are exposed to," either in their classes or at home, he said.

When it comes to the national debate over exams, Lovell is an outlier. Although everyone appears to be concerned with children at schools such as Anacostia, especially in light of President George W. Bush's No Child Left Behind policy, the trend is far away from considering individualized exams for each school; quite the opposite.

Roughly 40 percent of Lovell's students tell him that they plan on going to college, which for most of them means a community or junior college. Many of them won't even make it that far, he said, but if college is on their minds, Anacostia High has to make it possible. For these students, a dynamic young teacher, up the concrete stairs from Lovell's office and down a windowless hallway, has recently established an elective SAT class.

Talking to the teacher, Jimmy D'Andrea, who arrived four years ago to teach biology, is like listening to a friend who has just come back from Afghanistan, where tales of hardship are mixed with stories of overcoming long odds. Earlier that year, D'Andrea had noticed that one senior boy's grades had plummeted rapidly. After some inquiries, D'Andrea learned that the boy's parents had died, that his grandparents were no longer living, and that he was bouncing from one home to another, sleeping on couches and on the verge of homelessness. D'Andrea, a registered foster parent, took him in.

Half of D'Andrea's classroom is filled with typical high school metal chair and desk units, and he has put up hortatory slogans on his walls, such as "Respect yourself," "Respect your teacher." The other half is a science lab with sinks and science equipment. Instead of teaching just science, the SAT has turned D'Andrea, a twenty-six-year-old from small-town Alabama, into a jack-of-all-subjects. Every year, Anacostia students score the worst, or within whispering distance of the bottom, on the SAT in the District of Columbia. In 2003, their average math score was 336 and their average verbal score was 345 (average scores nationwide in the same year were 519 and 507, respectively). D'Andrea thought he could change this, and he already had, to the tune of 100 points on the combined score average, when he talked about it in early 2005.

"I'm definitely not one to just teach to the test, but I guess I've modified my viewpoint because the SAT can compensate [for a low GPA]," said D'Andrea, who was a study in brown on a winter's day, wearing a brown striped sweater and light brown slacks to complement his brown eyes and short brown hair. Two years before, D'Andrea decided that his students needed encouragement applying to college, and extra help preparing for the SAT. He looked about for nonprofits to fund an elective class to motivate tenth-graders and give them a running start at least one and a half years before the big test. He thought it would be easy to find funding, or at least volunteers to help out in the class, since D.C. has nonprofits like Geneva has banks. But he was surprised by how hard it was. "Sometimes, when you say the name of the area [Anacostia], you don't get a lot of positive response," he said.

Ideally, D'Andrea said, he needs $20,000 to cover his SAT class materials, such as scientific calculators, and his biggest expense, a college-visiting trip in the spring. D'Andrea has ended up cobbling together about $7,000 a year and some in-kind donations from a handful of sources, requiring him and his students to operate on the cheap. He piles his students into borrowed vans, takes them to eat at college campus cafeterias, which cost only 3 or 4 dollars per student and are all you can eat, and they stay in inexpensive motels. Over one week, his class visits mainly historically black institutions in the Mid-Atlantic states and the Southeast, such as Virginia State, North Carolina A & T, North Carolina Central, Spelman, Morehouse, and Clark in Atlanta.

The rest of the time is spent in D'Andrea's long classroom on the second floor of Anacostia High. To convince his students that they can go to college, D'Andrea has them read *A Hope in the Unseen*, a book by former *Wall Street Journal* reporter Ron Suskind about a boy from Anacostia who made it to Brown University despite a combined SAT score of 980 (out of a possible 1,600, and he had to take it a number of times to get even that mediocre scores). The book "can be a little tedious at times," D'Andrea said, "but the students generally find it very motivational." They can relate to the hurdles the student faced. "One winter the characters didn't have heat, [one] of the things that our students face either short-term or -long."

D'Andrea's biggest battle is with his students' lack of motivation. "All my students are incredible," he said, "You'd like them." But getting them to class—even keeping them in school—is tough. The freshman class at Anacostia High usually starts out with about 250 students. By the time they're seniors, the class shrinks to about 100.

"In some cases there may be legitimate reasons [for not coming to school]. They may be at home taking care of younger brothers and sisters," or somebody in the family might be sick. But there are some illegitimate reasons as well. "The call of the streets, if you want to call it that," D'Andrea said. The girls get pregnant and drop out of school, and "little hoods" in the neighborhood recruit students to join their gangs. And if the students join a gang, coming to school isn't part of the daily agenda.

Ultimately, support for attending school must come from the home. "If you don't have support at home, why bother to go to school?" asked D'Andrea.

Jimmy D'Andrea is positive and hopeful. He sees kids every day coming to school despite the odds, motivating themselves to achieve. "We've got a whole lot more potential to go up than some schools in [suburban] Montgomery County."

When he first arrived in Washington, D'Andrea was stunned at his students' skill level. "Many of the students have the basic decoding skills from first, second, and third grades," he said, but it doesn't go much further. Ask them to read out loud and although they may stumble over words occasionally everything pretty much seems fine. "Then when you start asking questions, everything is really not fine. . . . [They can] recognize and say the word, but may not be able to read the sentence and comprehend its meaning."

Where this problem comes from is difficult to pinpoint, he said. Something has gone wrong in elementary and middle schools. "By the time most students get here they are reading at upper elementary school levels. On average fifth-, sixth-grade level," and it's the same for the students' mathematics abilities. The implications for an SAT class are obvious: much of his time is teaching basics in a game of catch-up.

"We spent a week just reviewing the operation of positive and negative numbers," D'Andrea said. "Just eight times negative three, kind of thing. . . . We'll spend a couple weeks reviewing fractions and decimals, just all the basic math skills that we need."

The manner of teaching that the SAT requires makes him chafe. "I think the grammar is crazy," D'Andrea said, pointing out that nobody teaches the rules in a vacuum anymore, but teaching to the test requires him to. Teachers today prefer to teach grammar through "holistic writing," by making their students draft and redraft papers. "And now we're going back to finding the error in the sentence. Some cases are very reasonable things—double negatives, subject-verb agreement. But [sometimes] they're trying to trick you: the pronoun doesn't agree with the antecedent. They're trying to put a phrase in the middle you won't see." In the SAT, students are asked to identify the underlined phrase, if any, that is incorrect:

<u>As</u> we rely more and more on the Internet, <u>your</u> need for
A   B

effective security planning and design <u>to safeguard</u> data
                                                  C

<u>has increased.</u> <u>No error</u>
        D   E

As this question involving the Internet illustrates, the SAT can seem otherworldly to D'Andrea's students. "I think it's very hard to have an understanding of what students here have been exposed to. Now, when you take into account that students here haven't really traveled that much, or really haven't been out of Southeast [D.C.] that much," you begin to understand the problems they might face on a national standardized test, said D'Andrea. In the sample SAT reading section that tests sentence "correctness and effectiveness of expression," one question stem provided by the College Board reads,

The Portuguese musical tradition known as *fado*, or "fate," has been called the Portuguese blues because <u>of their songs that bemoan someone's</u> misfortune, especially the loss of romantic love.

It's easy to see how the subject matter of such a question is off-putting to poor students who haven't traveled, with little experience of the outside world. D'Andrea believes that the SAT creators don't know "what is common knowledge" in a place like Anacostia, a community that lacks a lot of middle-class institutions such as recreational centers. Until the mid-1990s, the students shopped mainly at corner markets because the community lacked a supermarket, and the students are a lot less mobile than their middle-class counterparts.

In contrast to most American high schools, visitors can have their pick of prime parking spots in front of Anacostia High, because not one of its more than 600 students has a car. They can't afford them. When asked if he was sure that none has a car, D'Andrea thought for a moment and said, "I'm sure I would know if there was somebody who did." It would be big news.

Compare this to Walt Whitman High School in suburban Maryland, roughly ten miles away on the white side of town, where 272 parking spaces for students are nowhere near enough to cover the 450 students who drive themselves to school. To cope, the school established a lottery system, leaving those who didn't get spots to park scattered throughout the neighborhood.

D'Andrea pointed out that most Anacostia students didn't even have a driver's license. "One, you've got to go and get your learner's [permit] and all that stuff. . . . But then you've got to go and take a test to get your license; you got to go with somebody who is a licensed driver who has a car with [an emergency] brake in the middle." And that person has to be over twenty-one. These seemingly minor hurdles are enough to prevent most students at Anacostia High from getting their license.

The lack of high school drivers and middle-class infrastructure and amenities isn't just an economic indicator; it also has surprising ramifications for taking the SAT. No cars means the students take the SAT only when it's administered in Anacostia or very close by. Public transportation isn't good in and out of Anacostia, so getting to the exam early on a Saturday morning across town or in the suburbs is prohibitively hard.

Even if they could get there, the new essay portion of the exam has bumped the test price to more than $40, up from $28. If you're poor, you get to take the exam free twice, but many middle-class students take it more times if they're unhappy with their scores. D'Andrea has given out his credit card number on occasion to students who need it for the exam. "That's the thing about teaching in a situation here as opposed to others. Unless you have no heart or no passion for what you do, you can't just stay completely separate," he said.

There are two things underpinning this description of Anacostia, both of which make Americans tense: poverty and race, although the effects of socioeconomics on test performance are far less inflammatory than race. It's easier to understand the economic differences between Anacostia and better-appointed schools that cater to affluent communities than it is to analyze the effects of race and test taking. Many students at Anacostia can't afford to take the SAT more than twice or hire fancy tutors because they're poor, not because they're black.

In Washington, you don't have to go far for both economic and ethnic contrasts to Anacostia High School. Washington's private schools are some of the best in the country, and they are predominantly white, although they all make efforts to diversify their student body. The private schools are less open to writers wandering in and reporting on their activities; they're like the best corporate attorneys, with nothing to gain from publicity, and a blue-chip reputation to lose by exposure. They are able to choose outstanding students, and their teachers are top-notch. When in town, the Harvard rep is far more likely to stop by Sidwell Friends School than he is Anacostia. About half a dozen Washington area private schools are among the top fifty high schools in the country in terms of sending their graduates to Harvard, Yale, and Princeton. Many parents have this in mind when choosing which schools their three- and four-year-olds will apply to, and the competition to get in is fierce. For some of these schools the SAT is almost an afterthought; their students take prep classes and do extremely well.

The top-quality suburban public schools have to swing a little harder for their students. Parents scrutinize schools' standardized test scores, which are public knowledge, and they often provide elective SAT prep classes, as Anacostia does. Walt Whitman High School is among the best public high schools in the country. With its expansive parking lot, stadium, and gleaming glass-fronted building, it's physically different from Anacostia and looks more like a corporate campus than a high school. But more importantly, its student body is more sophisticated. Almost 80 percent are white, and only about 2 percent are considered economically disadvantaged.

The median household income is greater than \$100,000 a year, and the parents are professionals working at the nearby National Institutes of Health and other high-powered organizations such as the World Bank, the *Washington Post*, or embassies from around the world. The school is so that good people believe it explains the higher housing prices in its catchment area.

Suzanne Coker, head of the English Department at Whitman, said that even among the kids it's "cool to be smart," a pretty remarkable teen culture for America, and students and parents say the pressures to excel are enormous. The school recently opened up its advanced placement classes (that is, special college prep classes that culminate in a nationwide achievement test) to any student who wanted to attend. Seven sections of the advanced placement English classes for the eleventh and twelfth grades quickly filled up.

"That's huge, huge," said Coker, gesticulating and emphasizing the second "huge."

Coker said people worried that the high school's averages on the advanced placement exam would plummet, but they haven't at all. The kids have consistently scored far above the national averages.

Dr. Alan Goodwin, Walt Whitman's principal, said there's only one drawback to such a school. "When you have such good kids and test scores you have to be careful not to be complacent. You can only go down; it's a danger," he said. Ever since middle school, he explains, the present class taking the SAT, in 2004–2005, had been particularly bright. The students just might achieve the highest SAT averages in the school's history. In December they had an average of 1,266, while in January it was 1,256, but there were a lot of first-time takers.

On a clear, brisk February day in 2005, Goodwin wore a charcoal gray suit, blue tie, and blue and white striped shirt; he has wavy hair, which is graying slightly, and glasses. Like Wensworth Lovell at Anacostia, Goodwin has an easy, open manner with his students, who periodically popped in his office during a conversation about the SAT. At one point a boy and a girl came through a door behind Goodwin's desk. The girl told him that "the trial run of the robot" is going on right now in the auditorium. Goodwin was too busy to come out to see it, but he asked if "you have decided not to do it in the halls."

"No," the boy said, "doing it in the auditorium," and they beat a retreat back through the door.

A few minutes later, while Goodwin was sitting at his computer responding to e-mails, a teacher knocked on the door, called him "Doc," and told him he had the gymnast with him. Goodwin got up from behind his desk, welcomed a petite girl to his office, and introduced her to a visitor as "the number one junior gymnast in America." Goodwin wanted to make sure she could fit in all her schoolwork as she jetted around the globe, competing.

"Where are you going next?" Goodwin asked her.

"I'm going to France in two weeks," she said. "Then I'm going to Portugal after that."

"Does your mother travel with you?" Goodwin wanted to know, and he nodded as the girl told him she's coming to France but can't make it to Portugal.

He talked to her about the 2008 Olympics. "It's good to have goals," he said. "How's it going in your classes?"

"Good," she said, but didn't elaborate.

After she left, Goodwin emphasized that he couldn't take credit for his students' high test scores. "We have teachers who teach well, supportive parents of their children's education, [and] our teachers push their kids."

The following month, in March 2005, high school students nationwide would take a much-touted new version of the SAT, but Goodwin didn't think the changes were going to be a problem for his kids. "It won't actually affect this school," he said. "The written [portion] is actually basic. The only problem that I see is that the students may try to write too much."

There's something special about how the SAT is perceived in America. Fast runners cover forty yards quickly, and smart people do well on their SATs. No matter how many years ago people took the exam, they remember their scores—and how they felt when they received them. For the top scorers it's a source of pride, a reassuring number that proves they are intelligent. For many other people their scores bring frustration and shame, a fear that the number reveals their innate mediocrity or stupidity. The SAT is intimidating not only because it affects which college people get into—and, at least in perception, their future—but also because of its history. Until very recently, the College Board claimed the SAT measured aptitude, another way of saying natural intelligence, and this historic puffery leaves a decided aftertaste.

Like the Wechsler exams, the SAT arose directly out of World War I. In the 1920s, the army testers fanned out to their various institutions and introduced group IQ tests based on the army tests. Carl Brigham, a young officer during the war, subsequently became a psychology professor at Princeton University and one of the twentieth century's most important test creators. At Princeton he tried out the Alpha test (the one for literates) on freshmen and discovered he had to make it a lot harder. After ratcheting it up, he turned the army Alpha into the SAT in 1926. Similar to the psychologists during the war, Brigham claimed the questions tested aptitude without defining the word or thinking about it much.

Today, there is no consensus on whether the SAT is a group intelligence test, but at the very least it is fair to say that it derives from the granddaddy of group IQ tests—the World War I U.S. Army tests—and that vestiges remain. The modern SAT is like an IQ test without the performance "nonverbal" problems; thus high school students have been saved from playing with blocks and arranging pictures in their proper story order. And the SAT's structure remains similar to the army Alpha's in its reliance on verbal and mathematics abilities and its use of a series of mainly discrete, independent multiple-choice questions. Also, like many other group IQ tests, it's used to determine who is worthy and who is unworthy to enter institutions.

Over the past few years the debate about how useful the SAT is in university admissions has intensified. Much of the discussion turns on the exam's surprisingly low predictive rates. On the old 1,600-point SAT scale it turns out that spreads as large 300 points don't mean much when it comes to predicting who will get good or bad grades in college. After extensive study of its student body, the University of California (UC) found that the SAT (before the 2005 changes) explains about 13 percent of the variance in university freshman year grades. That is, there's a little, but not much overlap between what contributes to both freshman year grades and SAT scores, although what those common contributing factors are isn't clear: math and verbal knowledge, obviously, but to some extent also confidence, test strategy training, ability to focus, booze consumption, desire to achieve, and God knows what else. The SAT's powers to predict college grades gets worse as students go through their sophomore, junior, and senior years. UC also discovered that high school grades and achievement test scores are slightly better predictors than the SAT, although there is no agreement with this conclusion in some other studies. Suffice it to say that nothing predicts college performance, even just freshman year grades, particularly well.

One of the main arguments for intelligence tests over the past century is that they are the best tools for identifying bright but poor students; but on this point in particular the SAT fails. The exam doesn't predict college grades any better than students' socioeconomic background and their parents' education level. After visiting schools such as Anacostia and Walt Whitman, it's easy to see how differences in culture, economics, and opportunities matter more than the SAT when it comes to predicting college grades. Rather than requiring SAT scores, university admissions officers might as well simply ask applicants what kind of money they come from and how many degrees—if any—their parents have piled up.

In recent years, colleges and universities have begun to take a hard look at the SAT. By 2005, more than seven hundred colleges and universities had either disregarded or significantly downplayed the SAT. Most of these are small-name schools that do not attract many applicants, so perhaps it's easier for them to throw the test overboard. But a number of the skeptical institutions do get large numbers of applicants—for example, Bates and Bowdoin colleges in Maine, Hamilton College in New York, and the University of Texas.

The most significant school to question the SAT is the University of California. In 2000, Richard Atkinson, then president of that university, visited a fancy private school and was shocked to find "a class of twelve-year-old students studying verbal analogies in anticipation of the SAT. I learned that they spend hours each month—directly and indirectly—preparing for the SAT, studying long lists of analogies such as 'untruthful is to mendaciousness' as 'circumspection is to caution.' The time involved was not aimed at developing the students' reading and writing abilities but rather their test-taking skills."

A year after this visit, in February 2001, Atkinson traveled to Washington, D.C., to deliver a speech that was so controversial it made headlines before he even opened his mouth. The day before his speech he picked up a copy of the *Washington Post* outside his hotel room door and was floored to read a headline above the fold, "Key SAT Test under Fire in Calif.: University President Proposes New Admissions Criteria." The article included excerpts from the speech, which had been leaked to the press beforehand. Similar articles appeared on the front pages of the *Los Angeles Times*, the *Chicago Tribune*, and the *New York Times* the same day.

In his speech the next day, Atkinson announced that he had recommended that the University of California drop the SAT, and any other intelligence test, and use only "standardized tests that assess mastery of specific subject areas" in its admissions process. This was big news for the College Board, the nonprofit that owns the SAT, and businesses such as the Education Testing Service and test prep companies that make tens of millions of dollars a year from the exam. In 2001, students in California represented more than 12 percent of SAT takers, and if UC were to stop accepting SAT results, many other schools would follow. Not only was his position as president of the University of California important, but also Atkinson himself cut a formidable figure. While not an intelligence expert per se, he's a cognitive psychologist by training and comfortable analyzing the arcane, wizard-behind-the-curtain world of psychometrics.

But what's also interesting about Atkinson's recommendation that UC dump the SAT is that it was counterhistorical. The population in California is booming, applications to UC are way up, and administrators know the trend will continue. In addition, the university system has promised the youth of California that if they end up in the top 12.5 percent of their graduating classes there will be a place for them somewhere in the university system. Historically, such a crunch of new bodies waiting to be sorted into bins labeled "worthy" and "unworthy" would lead an institution to turn to IQ tests. Knowing full well that the numbers of applicants were about to jump, Atkinson recommended the opposite: an expensive, slower, "comprehensive" admissions approach that eschewed IQ tests of any kind.

For Richard Atkinson, this meant achievement tests of some nature. In his 2001 speech in Washington, D.C., he argued that achievement tests would "help strengthen high school curricula and pedagogy, create a stronger connection between what students accomplish in high school and their likelihood of being admitted to UC, and focus student attention on mastery of subject matter rather than test preparation."

Atkinson based his opinion on studies of UC students that indicated that grades and SAT II test scores (which are subject-specific achievement tests) are slightly better predictors of college performance than is the regular SAT, known as the SAT I. According to Atkinson, "the UC data show that high school grades plus the SAT II account for about 21 percent of the explained variance in first-year college grades. When the SAT I is added to high school grades and the SAT II, the explained variance increases from 21 percent to 21.1 percent, a trivial increment."

Before Atkinson delivered his speech in Washington, D.C., the College Board had already backed away from its claim that it was testing innate ability. In 1990 it had changed the name from the Scholastic Aptitude Test to the Scholastic Assessment Test. Tests of aptitude are intelligence tests; assessment implies something less innate. In 1996, it pushed the nominal changes even further, giving up entirely on the claim that the SAT was an acronym at all. The SAT became just the SAT; rather fittingly, the three letters stood for nothing at all.

Atkinson's recommendation to UC to drop the SAT pushed the College Board to make more than nominal changes, although it did do another name change (to the "New SAT"). In fact, Atkinson's decision came at the right time, for Gaston Caperton III, who had been in charge of the College Board since 1999, seemed receptive to change and was passionate about education. Even to himself, Caperton at first seemed like an odd choice to be president of the College Board.

"I was certainly not chosen for [the job] because of my SAT scores, though, perhaps, despite them," he wrote.

What Caperton did have was blue-chip executive experience. He was governor of West Virginia in the late 1980s and 1990s, and education had been a top priority for him. During his tenure, dramatically more West Virginia high school students took advance placement classes and exams than had in the past. Nevertheless, when a headhunter contacted him about the top job at the College Board, Caperton was taken aback. He knew very little about the College Board and thought, "Why would I be interested in being president of a testing company?"

But when the headhunter showed Caperton some materials on what the College Board actually does, he was floored.

"I was amazed to discover the depth and breadth of the organization and, more importantly, the potential it had for playing a crucial role in helping to meet the United States' most important challenge: seamlessly combining equity with excellence in American education." Gaston Caperton took the job as president of the College Board because he is a crusader for education, which may at first seem counterintuitive, but it's not necessarily so considering that institution's history.

In the late 1930s, Harvard began using the SAT to give people outside the "right" circles—wealthy New England WASP ones—

scholarships based on merit. In part because the scholarship students ended up performing well, the Ivy League began teetering toward considering intelligence to be more important in its students than character traits idealized by old blue-blood families. It was the beginning of a sea change in how elite American educational institutions viewed their societal roles and the makeup of their student bodies. By 1942, all universities that belonged to the College Board, including those in the Ivy League, were using the SAT for admissions and not just for scholarship applicants. At this point the numbers weren't huge—only about ten thousand college applicants—but it did lend credence to the exam.

Again, it took a world war to promote a test. During World War II, an assistant dean at Harvard got the U.S. military to use the SAT as an officer selection tool. The military tested three hundred thousand men across the country with it, which made it immediately apparent that the SAT could sort graduating high school students everywhere. After the war, a Harvard official established the Educational Testing Service, and soon most colleges and universities were requiring the SAT.

As Nicholas Lemann, the dean of the Columbia School of Journalism who has written extensively on the SAT, has said, "It's worth noting that what is in effect a national personnel system was set up without any legislative sanction, or press coverage, or public debate—that's why the debate [over the usefulness of the SAT] is taking place now, long after the fact."

Once the SAT was established, every applicant took the same test regardless of ethnicity, pedigree, education, or geography. For elite schools such as the Ivies, it certainly beat the previous system of elite WASPy entitlement, but other universities throughout the country didn't necessarily use it to level the playing field. As late as 1979, the UC system, for instance, considered applicants' SAT scores not because they were great measurements of ability or prediction but simply to keep people out. They had too many applicants.

According to former UC president Richard Atkinson, "The decision to include SAT scores in the [UC's] Eligibility Index was based not on an analysis of the SAT's predictive power but on its ability to serve as a screen that would reduce the pool of eligible students."

Regardless of the universities' particular rationale for using the SAT, the College Board retains lofty, meritocratic goals, and most Americans underappreciate its impact on education. It is not a testing company; it's a nonprofit that seeks to provide colleges with tools (mainly the SAT, of course) for selecting the best candidates and to ensure that students have fair and equal access to these colleges, based on personal merit. It's easy to see why Caperton took the job as College Board president, and why the University of California's threat to walk away from the SAT presented his organization with an opportunity to revamp the most important test in America. Caperton believes that they have.

"This [new] test is really going to create a revolution in the schools," Caperton said in 2003.

Whether this is true is open to debate. It's certainly true that UC has affected, to some extent, the test's content and the way the College Board markets the SAT. In part, the board now says it's a way of influencing high school curricula, like an achievement test would, which is a decided break from the rationale underlying IQ tests. While the desire to affect positively what's taught in America's classrooms might be noble, it's a little unsettling to think that an organization unaccountable to millions of students and their parents has such influence. At least local boards of education can be voted out of office if they're not doing a good job. Why would the country want to cede revolutionary change in our classrooms to the College Board?

The changes the College Board wrought stretched the exam to a three and three-quarter-hour ordeal, up forty-five minutes from the previous SAT. The changes included bringing the math up to an Algebra II level and, in an effort to bolster the teaching of reading, they lengthened the reading comprehension portion and dropped the analogies section. Most famously, the College Board, in March 2005, added a twenty-five-minute essay to the "New SAT," believing it would promote writing across the country.

Many teachers say the exam's new essay has simply added the burden of teaching a very limited style of composition to already tightly packed curricula. Students and their parents panicked about the essay, which turned into cash-register music to the test prep companies' ears. No one knew exactly what the essays would look like before the first exam, but some of the companies recommended that students simply memorize a response and shoehorn it into whatever subject ETS threw at them. This approach made educators groan and would surely defeat the purpose of the writing exam, which was meant to be a sort of first-draft test to see how students thought and made arguments on the spur of the moment. In the end, there was evidence that students who simply wrote longer got higher grades, regardless of writing style, analytical ability, or factual errors. After looking at graded essays from the "New SAT," the director of MIT's writing program wrote, "I discovered that I could guess an essay's prescribed score just by looking at its length—even from across a room."

What's interesting is that Richard Atkinson thinks that the changes to the New SAT are revolutionary. "I believe this is an ideal solution that reflects the changes called for in my ACE speech. In a brief time, college admissions will have undergone a revolutionary change—a change that will affect millions of young people."

Atkinson believes that Gaston Caperton, the head of the College Board, deserves most of the credit for persuading his organization to change its test. Apparently many of the College Board higher-ups didn't want to, despite considerable evidence that the old SAT I wasn't that useful. "I admire Caperton greatly," Atkinson wrote. "He showed courage and leadership, and change in the SAT I would not have occurred without his involvement."

Nevertheless, it's probably too much to ask for the changes in the New SAT to cause a revolution in our schools. Richard Atkinson believes the New SAT is more aligned with school curricula, but schools do not appear to be dropping their SAT prep classes, which would indicate that they thought their regular classes alone would prepare their students. These elective SAT-prep classes take time, resources, and teachers from other possible subjects. Enrollment at prep companies such as Stanley Kaplan, too, is up after the introduction of the new exam. Surely this wouldn't be the case if parents and students thought the test was satisfactorily covered in school.

Parents, students, and test prep companies are like thieves constantly adapting to new safe technology. They'll work like mad to crack the code of new tests, and it's a question of when they'll do it, not if. The amount that test prep companies help is debatable, but despite the fact that for decades the ETS tried to deny that prepping improved SAT performance, Kaplan and Princeton Review and other companies have been raising students' scores since the 1950s. The same was true for the eleven-plus in Great Britain.

Some test prep is probably ineffectual and wacky, such as test questions in cereal boxes and old Singer Sewing machine ad copy that promised consumers that using its machines improved general intelligence. A more modern-day example is in Montgomery County, Maryland, where the public schools have special magnet schools for the gifted. There, in recent years, parents have made a rush on LEGO blocks in the belief that the little toys might improve their second-graders' scores on the Ravens Progressive Matrices. These questionable test prep strategies aside, it's been an open secret for decades, especially for the middle class, that IQ tests can and should be prepped for.

Test prep in and out of school will continue for the New SAT, and lower-class kids will, like always, suffer an unfair disadvantage. Despite Jimmy D'Andrea's herculean and laudable efforts in his SAT class, on average Anacostia students scored a 1042 (352 on the critical reading section, 331 on the math, and 359 on the new essay section) on the New SAT in 2006. Out of a possible 2400 this was considerably below the average score in Washington, D.C., public schools (at 1441) and far below the national average of 1518. Given Anacostia students' level of education by the time they start studying for the SAT, and the economic hurdles they face in their daily lives, it is almost inconceivable that the New SAT will change how they perform or the teaching in their school.

Not surprisingly, Walt Whitman High School students continue to test at the highest levels. In May 2006, Goodwin, Whitman's principal, expected his students' scores to be the highest in the county. "I have been told that based on earlier results so far that our scores on the two original sections are as good as last year . . . a record." When the scores came out, Goodwin learned he was right. On average in 2006, his students scored 1884 on the New SAT (622 on the critical reading section, 639 on the math, and 623 on the new essay section), well above the national average. In fact, Walt Whitman was the highest scoring school in Montgomery County, Maryland, by more than 50 points.

It's not easy to decide what to do with the SAT: scrap it or improve it? Some psychologists believe the latter, and urge for even more radical changes. Robert Sternberg, the Yale psychologist discussed in the previous chapter, believes he has an exam based on "successful intelligence" that will be fairer and more predictive of college GPA than the current SAT. Sternberg thinks the SAT is too narrow, so he and fellow researchers created a multiple-choice, essay, and performance exam that tests creativity and practicality in addition to analytical abilities (which he says the SAT already tests).

Some of Sternberg's multiple-choice questions feel very old-school IQ. For instance, Sternberg's test asks students to figure out a numeric pattern in a series of numbers and do problems of "everyday math." But he also goes far beyond this. To test their practical skills, test takers would have to figure out a map and plot paths through it. Examinees also watch a short movie that presents potentially real everyday problems, which they have to solve. For example, they watch a student asking a professor for a letter of recommendation when, through nonverbal cues, it is apparent that the professor doesn't recognize him. Sternberg tests creativity by requiring test takers to do calculations wherein the numbers operate in novel ways, and to write a short story from a selection of titles, such as "The Octopus's Sneakers," and put captions to cartoons.

After trying out their test on students nationwide, Sternberg and his colleagues discovered that it predicted college GPA nearly twice as well as the SAT I (the study was done before the New

SAT). It also greatly reduced mean score differences among ethnic groups, one of Sternberg's express goals. Sternberg's test is worth exploring, especially if it's as predictive as he says, but the problem remains that it still wouldn't bolster schools' core curricula. Schools would still have elective classes on Sternberg's test, with kids practicing storytelling, map reading, and number sequences. Stanley Kaplan would probably make even more money.

Instead, why not simply stop using the SAT? Proponents of the SAT argue that colleges need one standard metric with which to compare students around the country. They say it's hard to know exactly what grades mean at each high school: an A might be harder to achieve in one school than in another, and grade inflation makes the problem worse. More and more students (at least in the wealthy suburbs) seem to be getting As. In addition, standardized test scores reduce the likelihood that admissions officers' prejudices come into play. These are fine meritocratic arguments in favor of standardized tests, and it's true that in the past they've helped the country come closer to achieving these goals. After World War II the LSAT, for instance, helped open some law school doors that had previously barred Catholics and Jews.

But beyond the level-playing-field argument, the SAT doesn't appear to be very useful. It certainly doesn't predict college grades very well. The main problem with the SAT, however, is that, like the eleven-plus exam, it can warp and burden schools' curricula. Jimmy D'Andrea and his fellow teachers at Anacostia High School need to be focusing on their core classes rather than teaching test-taking skills and SAT prep in a game of catch-up. The question is whether there is an alternative to the SAT that is still a common measuring stick, yet won't warp schools' curricula and create additional burdens.

The best alternative is subject-specific achievement tests that would test students directly on what they've learned in English, math, art, the humanities, and the sciences. Such tests would bolster what students learned in class and satisfy the level-playing-field requirement that everyone take the same entrance exam. Moreover, unlike the SAT, achievement tests are predictive regardless of the student's social and economic background.

"After controlling for family income and parents' education, the predictive power of the SAT II [which are achievement tests] is undiminished, whereas the relationship between SAT I scores and UC freshman grades virtually disappears," wrote Richard Atkinson.

Unfortunately, there are problems with achievement tests, too. In essence, the country would almost be establishing a national curriculum, something Americans are hesitant to do in their decentralized education system. If the country is going to have a nationally standardized test for literature, for instance, who would decide which books students should read? Who has the authority to say that Milton is out but Shakespeare is in? Some researchers, as well, believe that students at places like Anacostia High School may even do worse on achievement tests than they do on the SAT.

"There's a danger that making [admissions tests] too curriculum-dependent will actually increase overall score gaps for some minority groups. . . . Because we have such huge disparities in the quality of schooling in the country, kids who go to crummy schools may be disadvantaged," wrote Rebecca Zwick, a professor in UC Santa Barbara's Department of Education.

The answer to that problem is not to stick with the same test, or to choose new entrance exams based on how ethnic groups perform compared to one another, but to persuade all communities to support their children's education and to provide high-quality public schools everywhere. Using achievement tests rather than the SAT won't reduce black-white differences in test scores or solve the larger socioeconomic problems. But they might allow Jimmy D'Andrea to teach what he originally intended—biology—rather than have to scrape together an SAT class. Anacostia High School's real problem isn't the SAT, but the poverty its students live in and a culture that doesn't emphasize education enough. These are bigger problems and are harder to crack, but it's where society's energy should be focused. Countries should not look to tests, no matter how well devised, to create revolutions in education.

Chapter 15

Black and White IQ

In the United States, whenever IQ is discussed, race is the six-ton woolly mammoth standing in the corner of the room. It's always there, even if the speakers choose not to acknowledge it. It doesn't have to be this way—in fact, it shouldn't even be an issue—but for some reason, American psychology is obsessed with the subject. In the main, studying different "races'" IQs is not considered a worthwhile scientific endeavor beyond U.S. borders. Given the history discussed in the previous fourteen chapters, as well as the evidence that IQ tests measure knowledge and difficult-to-define abstract problem-solving abilities rather than innate intelligence, it's hard to believe that the study of racial differences is taken seriously. In the early twentieth century, American psychologists such as Henry Goddard used to report on the varying intelligence of European "races" and nationalities arriving on Ellis Island. People eventually viewed these studies as bogus, but for some reason many American psychologists think the study of black-white differences remains scientifically viable (as well as reports, collaterally, on Asian and Jewish populations' intelligence).

Even assuming that one buys into the existence of biologically distinct "races," the roughness of IQ tests ought to lead, at a minimum, to agnosticism on the subject. Until people live in equal conditions in terms of education, income, and health, and there exist far more exact mental measurement tools than IQ tests, there should be a collective shrugging of shoulders. Even then, it's not clear why the subject would be particularly interesting or useful.

Psychologists continue to pursue this nauseating inquiry, however, often becoming defensive when asked why it's important to study, but not coming up with satisfying answers to the question. Academic freedom is important, and if they choose to make a study of the issue, no one should stop them. But the obsession is strange and, at times, harmful. The author of this book once had a conversation with a U.S. congressman who had just read an interesting article about "cold-weather Jews" being smarter than their warm-weather counterparts. The explanation, he said, was that it took more smarts for the chilly Jews' ancestors to survive in adverse weather. Psychologists' denials notwithstanding, so-called dispassionate research has a way of trickling out into the mainstream; one can only hope it's not used in policymaking.

To witness the work and opinions on the subject of race differences, a December 2004 conference in New Orleans is illustrative. There, intelligence researchers from the United States and Europe gathered for the Fifth Annual Conference of the International Society for Intelligence Research (ISIR), which was held in the ballroom up the wide staircase of the Bourbon Hotel. For much of their time the attendees listened to talks about how general intelligence might differ in men and women, blacks, whites, and Asians. Outside the high-ceilinged, chandeliered conference room, beyond the gray curtains covering tall windows and all traces of natural light, revelers engaged in decidedly low-g activity on Bourbon Street. While young ladies from around the country lifted their shirts for plastic beads thrown by men chugging beer from gigantic plastic boots, the mood inside the ballroom was decidedly more somber.

Earl Hunt, a psychologist from the University of Washington, said that the ISIR "is the conservative wing [of intelligence research], if you will." Hunt doesn't mean this in the political sense, but rather that the social scientists—mainly psychologists—by and large believe wholeheartedly in g. For many ISIR members, as opposed to most Americans, it's easier to talk about how blacks and whites might differ in intelligence than it is to question the existence of g (and it might have helped that there were no African Americans in the ballroom). As a result, intelligence researchers are often wary of writers and journalists because many opinions that often (but that are not required to) flow from believing in *g* are out of step with mainstream political thought.

Many intelligence researchers believe that studies of twins indicate, for instance, that by adulthood our genes determine 80 percent of our intelligence, as measured by IQ tests. Nonpsychologist experts (notably geneticists) often believe the percentage is much less. In contrast to what the psychologists think, however, the interesting issue is not what percentage of IQ is inherited, for surely every human ability is some combination of inherited and learned. The ability to lawn-bowl, for example, is surely some mixture, but how interesting is it to know the exact balance? The important question is what IQ tests measure. Once it becomes clear that IQ tests don't measure intelligence, but knowledge and a hard-to-define abstract problem-solving ability, the issue of resolving the exact percentage of heredity versus environment doesn't shed light on black-white differences in intelligence.

Nevertheless, whatever the IQ balance between nature and nurture is, for many laypeople the very thought that heredity might play a large role sounds fatalistic, and indeed it is, to hear many psychologists talk about it. When extrapolated as an explanation of the traditional fifteen-point difference between average black and white test scores—which has held fairly constant over almost a century—the topic, and its cancerous fatalism, becomes incendiary. Researchers who attend the ISIR conference are more willing than the average citizen to consider and state publicly that this racial gap may be due at least in part to genetic differences. Not all researchers at the ISIR conference believe this, but they unanimously think that they should be honest about whatever science digs up.

"Look, there is a perfectly legitimate discussion of race as a genetic concept," said Hunt. "People say there is no such thing as race or it isn't a biological concept. If we don't use the term 'race' we would have to invent another term for nonrandom clustering of trait markers." He paused for a moment to let that sink in with his interviewer. It's such an emotional and important subject that he was choosing his words very carefully. "Be careful how I said that and think very carefully what nonrandom clustering means. Genes are not distributed randomly over the human species. There are clusters of genes."

As the lawyers say, this statement is not offered for the truth of the matter asserted, but simply to reveal psychologists' mind-set. There is ample opposition, perhaps overwhelmingly, to the concept of race in population genetics, anthropology, and other fields. Whatever one's conclusion, everyone agrees, even the psychologists, that nobody has isolated human "intelligence genes" (or even "IQ genes") and figured out how they differ among the various ethnicities. We are left with IQ test results alone. One would imagine, since the subject is potentially so damaging, that this reality alone would cause people to beg off, but America's obsession with race has guaranteed that the inquiry into race differences will remain with the tenacity of foot fungus: impossible to eradicate, with occasional flare-ups.

Due to the lack of genetic data, discussions of race differences must rely on metaphor and analogy. Hunt is fair-skinned, bald, and suffers from skin cancer, and he used these facts to illustrate that clusters of genes interact with the environment. His doctor once said to him, "'You're a Celt.'" Celts are more likely than other groups to get skin cancer. "'The Celts were doing just fine,'" his doctor pointed out, "'so long as they stayed in England and Ireland, but when they went out and conquered India they got into trouble.'"

Hunt's skin color metaphor illustrates the field's just-the-facts-ma'am professional pride. But what Hunt doesn't share with some of his colleagues is an unfounded fatalism about race and human potential in general that has been endemic in intelligence research since Francis Galton. In off-the-cuff remarks between presentations, Hunt commented that he thought the average fifteen-point difference between blacks and whites is probably the result of environmental differences. He also said that "g is no excuse" in life. In other words, if someone's IQ isn't so high, he's got to work harder—

implying that, within reason, he can probably get to where he wants to go educationally and professionally. Just half an hour earlier another academic, not such a kindly, gnomic fellow as Hunt, said that he asks his son whether he wants to work so hard in his math classes, because the son's IQ scores reveal that he doesn't have much *g*. IQ results are often like Rorschach blots, to compare them to another antiquated psychological tool; it's not clear what they mean, but people's interpretation of them reflects more about their perspective than it does about the ink on the page.

This IQ fatalism often extends dangerously beyond unhealthy advice to family members. In America, the biggest Rorschach blot moment comes when people discuss this average fifteen-point differential between African Americans and whites—the mean black score being lower, of course. For some the fifteen points indicate that on average blacks are genetically not as smart as whites; for others the point spread means that the tests are biased in favor of whites, or that it reflects differences in each group's environment. To say the least, the different positions lead to heated debates, in large part because nobody comes to these discussions without personal biases, assumptions, or ideological predispositions. And yet at the same time, the discourse is limited to the language of science, lending it the veneer of objectivity. Given that there is internal debate even within psychology regarding what IQ tests measure, as well as admissions all around that no direct tests of biological mental ability exist, in order to take a stand one way or another on the reasons behind the point spread one must make intellectual leaps and inferences. Even Hans Eysenck, one of the most famous hereditarians of the twentieth century, conceded that science has no test of pure genetic ability: "There is no direct biological test of possible biological differentiation," he wrote, "all the evidence must be circumstantial."

Circumstantial evidence is awfully appealing, however, if one tends to agree with it. Strangely, there appears to be little prudent agnosticism among academic psychologists, or at least among the most vocal ones on the issue of black-white differences. Perhaps the most famous lines about race in the field of intelligence were penned by Arthur Jensen, a professor emeritus of educational psychology at Berkeley. (Now in his eighties, Jensen sat in the front row of the 2004 ISIR conference.) Back in 1969, just four years after the first Head Start program and fifteen years after *Brown v. Board of Education*, Jensen caused a brouhaha when he wrote, "Compensatory education has been tried and apparently it has failed." That blacks still lagged behind whites in academic performance and IQ scores led him to state that "we are left with various lines of evidence, no one of which is definitive alone, but which, viewed all together, make it a not unreasonable hypothesis that genetic factors are strongly implicated in the average Negro-white intelligence difference."

Tortured writing, yes, as well as a remarkable statement that led to uproar throughout the nation. The idea that education policy—dismantling programs such as Head Start—might be influenced by ultimately inconclusive, IQ-fatalistic positions is sickening. While the environmental differences between Anacostia and Walt Whitman high schools don't prove that their average SAT score differences aren't due to genetics, they do make the hereditarian position an uphill battle.

There are intelligence researchers who look at the same black-white point spread and conclude that the differences are due to the environment. Joseph Fagan, a professor of psychology at Case Western Reserve University, who spoke at the 2004 ISIR Conference, is one of them. When it comes to taking IQ tests, he believes, African Americans are like foreigners in that they grow up speaking a language other than standard English.

"Blacks and whites differ in IQ by 15 points total, there is no debate about that," Fagan said, perhaps the only statement on intelligence and race everyone in the room would agree upon. Fagan's own studies corroborate this finding. In the early 2000s, he gave three groups of students (whites; blacks; and foreign, nonnative English-speaking whites) an IQ test of vocabulary called the Peabody Revised. Sure enough, native English-speaking whites scored the best—sixteen points higher than the African Americans and eighteen points higher than the non-native speakers, keeping roughly to the historical trend.

IQ tests involve word knowledge, Fagan argued, and he wanted to know whether the linguistic playing field could be leveled among his three groups. Fagan first sought to determine whether the black students "spoke another language" (other than standard English) by giving all three groups a test of "black" English. On this test, African Americans answered 85 to 90 percent of the questions correctly while whites, both native and non-native English speakers, could only answer 40 percent of the questions correctly. From this, Fagan inferred that whites speak standard English while African Americans have to speak both standard English and black English, hampering their traditional IQ scores, just like non-native white English speakers' scores are affected.

Fagan then leveled the playing field by providing his subjects with a list of obscure and old words to study—words he presumed they didn't know already, such as "venter," which means belly—and then gave them a vocabulary test. On average, whites, blacks, and non-native English speakers performed the same. Of course, there was still a range of scores, but it couldn't be explained by race or native language. What explained why some people scored better than others, then? Fagan believed that at least part of the answer must be individuals' ability to process information.

To test this information-processing hypothesis, Fagan asked subjects in another experiment to rate a series of pictures of faces they had never seen before for attractiveness. He wasn't actually interested in which faces they thought were attractive, he just wanted to see, without letting on, how well the subjects could remember the faces later in the day, and whether there were black-white differences in this ability. After rating the faces, the subjects took the Peabody IQ test, and then Fagan tested how well they could pick the pictures they had seen previously out of a lineup of new faces. On average blacks, whites, and non-native speakers could recognize faces equally well. Just as important, a subject's ability to remember a novel face also predicted IQ score on the Peabody, supporting Fagan's hypothesis that information processing is more important than race or native language.

"Aside from the social importance of the finding," Fagan said, his studies also indicate that IQ has "multiple determinants. ... One is information processing ability and the second is the information provided by the culture for processing."

Fagan was very careful how he couched his results. "Let me say something very quickly," Fagan was sure to add at the end of his presentation. "I'm not saying there are multiple intelligences. That's not what I'm saying." Multiple intelligences would not have gone over well with the ISIR crowd. What he was saying was that "you can take all sorts of standard tests, give new information and ... erase the black-white differences."

Other researchers have found that once test creators move away from the traditional verbal-nonverbal IQ test model, black-white differences look substantially different. They have discovered that blacks and whites of similar background ("e.g., age, sex, parent education, community setting, and region") score much closer together on some nonverbal tests. On Jack Naglieri's Cognitive Assessment System, for example, blacks were shown to have an average score of 95.3 while whites had a 98.8. On Naglieri's Nonverbal Performance Test, however, blacks outscored whites on average, 99.3 to 95.1. Psychologist Robert Sternberg, at Yale, has similarly found that he can reduce differences among ethnic groups on the SAT and GMAT (the business school entrance exam) by devising questions that augment those exams' narrow content.

During the question-and-answer time after Joseph Fagan's talk at the ISIR conference, only one or two hands went up, and people asked small, technical questions. Fagan's argument that IQ tests measure knowledge and cultural differences, like much of intelligence research, has been around a while, so people probably thought it was unsurprising. His paper was, however, a direct rebuttal to the work of Arthur Jensen, the retired UC Berkeley professor who sat, sometimes with a small smile on his face, throughout Fagan's talk but said not a word. In the past he has told an interviewer that "insufficient familiarity with standard English and the use of 'Black English' was a popular claim in the 1960s and '70s." In contrast to the evidence presented in Naglieri's CAS and Nonverbal Performance Test, Jensen said, "Black-White IQ differences are as large or larger on a variety of non-verbal tests that make no use of alphanumeric symbols as on verbal tests."

He further argues that cultural explanations (differences in diet, education, home environment, and many others) for the lower average African American scores are not sufficient to explain the consistent differences between blacks and whites. But why should there be a burden to prove that the differences are environmental rather than biological? Given that tools acute enough to answer these questions do not exist, surely the wisest position is to operate as if groups of people are innately equal. Individuals, not groups, can then succeed or fail in any given endeavor as they may.

Cloak themselves in science as they may, when psychologists make claims such as "Compensatory education has been tried and apparently it has failed," they are entering the realm of policy. Ever since Francis Galton in the Victorian era, intelligence researchers have been addicted to making sweeping pronouncements about policy and the structure of society—who's at the top, who's at the bottom, and why—a subject well beyond their ken. The issue has existed since Galton first drew up bell curve charts putatively showing that Africans' average innate abilities were lower than Europeans'. Today in America, Galton's intellectual heirs argue that civil rights era legislation should be dismantled because IQ is largely hereditary. As one author put it in the early 1990s, "Failure has plagued the many programs based on 'reverse discrimination' set in place since the 1950s, and scientific research now reveals the reason why this is the case: differences in intelligence are around 70% dependent upon heredity, with other human qualities being rated variably between 50% up to as much as 90 to 95% dependent on heredity. This being the case, the failure of remedial programs based solely on environmental adjustment is easily understandable."

It's not just "scientific research now" that informs some psychologists about the futility of charity, welfare, or affirmative action. Intelligence experts have always relied on the science of the day to argue for cutting social programs. Compare the quotation in the previous paragraph to what Lewis Terman wrote in 1916: "It hardly needs to be emphasized that when charity organizations help the feeble-minded to float along in a social and industrial world, and to produce and rear children after their kind, a doubtful service is rendered. A little psychological research would aid the united charities of any city to direct their expenditures into more profitable channels than would otherwise be possible." The terminology has changed but the message is the same.

When hereditarians take ideological positions, they shouldn't be surprised when people of different political persuasions attack their ideas, but many hereditarians feel particularly battered and abused by the Marxist and left-wing critics of the 1960s and 1970s. They also view modern-day political correctness as anathema to the spirit of free inquiry. Ever since the 1980s, however, the political pendulum has started to swing back in their favor, making them feel akin to the Irish monks who spent the Dark Ages copying the Bible in caves on barren, rocky, westerly isles. While the invaders were tearing down stone churches and aqueducts (in the modern case, erecting social and economic programs on the misguided belief that we're all genetically equal), they managed to keep the flame of civilization alive through their research. But, they feel, often at great personal cost.

Intelligence researchers with a hereditarian bent have been treated poorly over the years, which only contributes to their wound-licking state of mind. Their tenured faculty jobs have been threatened and even on occasion their physical persons, simply for stating professional beliefs, which is, after all, what they're paid to do. In the late 1960s, Arthur Jensen's last name was turned into an "ism" synonymous with racism: "Jensenism." The University of California had to provide him with a bodyguard after he had received numerous death threats and after radical students interfered with his classes and speeches.

At the ISIR Conference in 2004, however, there was no need for security at the Bourbon Hotel. Only a few journalists who cover the intelligence beat showed up, and there were no protesters in sight, either. The youth of this generation—at least the ones around the hotel—seemed more focused on inebriation and bartering beads for breasts. Times have changed.

While intelligence researchers find it's safer to occupy the towns again, some ISIR members are still hesitant to talk to journalists, whom they believe often don't understand science or bury it in politically correct reporting. They've also been purposefully burned by reporters in the past. Linda Gottfredson, a controversial sociologist in the Department of Education at the University of Delaware who has had her share of flack, gave large amounts of time to a *GQ* journalist in 1994, even inviting him home to eat dinner with her family. The magazine sent out a photographer to shoot her and, after the photos were developed, asked her to pick the best one. She did, but she was shocked with the results when the article came out. Retelling the story during a break in the conference, the acrid memory of the article was still evident in her face. She blanched and said *GQ* made her look like "some kind of devil" in the photograph.

In the article's picture of Gottfredson, her shimmering, fuzzy sepia head floats bodiless, like the image of a wicked witch eerily conjured up in the lake of a fantasy novel. Her tight smile looks menacing, her nose and two moles accentuated, and her gray, full-bodied hair looks like the Heat Mizer from the children's TV Christmas special. All the other photos in the article were edited in the same way, including that of another researcher from Toronto, Canada, who also was in attendance. Taken together, the photos had a rogues' gallery, Khmer Rouge war criminals look about them.

Such treatment makes intelligence researchers wary. The ISIR keynote speaker, Ian Deary, from Edinborough University, only grants interviews by e-mail so he can have complete control over his quotes. And a psychologist from Virginia who became progressively more aggressive during an interview about employment and race said, "You can quote me as saying I wear a I Hate the Red

States T-shirt." In short, the academics are tired of being personally attacked rather than having their ideas addressed.

The problem is, though, that IQ testing and intelligence research have scientifically justified some remarkably god-awful policies in the past hundred years; in the case of the Nazis, nothing short of murder. So when psychologists start talking about social policies and the structure of society, they should tread wearily in light of their field's sketchy past. Moreover, some ISIR members just come across as wacky, giving a handy hook to journalists who might be looking for it. It's still possible to meet people who use the terms "Negroid" and "Mongoloid" at ISIR meetings. One researcher there argues that "Orientals" have higher IQs than whites and blacks today because during the Ice Age, Asian weather selected for the smartest, who could survive more often than their stupid counterparts by hunting big animals, creating fire, and making tools. Another professor presented a paper showing that the various skin colors of the world actually predict IQ better than race (the lighter the epidermis, the higher the score), rather oddly basing his research solely on a 1966 Italian-language geography textbook. The field of intelligence research contains more cranks than most.

Academics should have wide latitude to debate and research, and not be dragged around behind the proverbial pickup truck for their ideas, but society better be frightfully confident of their positions if it's going to make policy based on them. Just because intelligence researchers are supposed to be scientists doesn't mean they are any better than the rest of us at coming up with sound policies for our countries. In fact, they might be worse.

In real life, Linda Gottfredson, who was pictured unfairly in *GQ*, is not an evil witch. She tilts her head to one side during conversation and listens intently. She's a nice-looking woman who wore flats, stockings, and long, one-color dresses, either red or blue, to the conference. Her Heat Mizer hair turns out simply to be full-bodied. And for some reason, quite refreshingly, she's still trusting enough to talk to journalists. But although Gottfredson's thoughtful and open, we shouldn't necessarily start drafting or repealing laws after talking to her.

Gottfredson came to intelligence research through the sociology of personnel selection. Early in her career she believed in multiple intelligences, but she "kept rummaging around" for aptitudes that could be useful to assess in personnel decisions—aptitudes that would predict who would be a good worker and who wouldn't. By the mid-1980s she discovered psychologists' g and thought it sounded promising. It wasn't long before she began to think about the connections among IQ, employment, race, and crime.

By 1985, Gottfredson was arguing that society's occupational ladder has evolved over time along the lines of people's intelligence. That is, people are brain surgeons because they are smarter than truck drivers are—and that genetics placed a scalpel in the surgeon's hands and a wheel in the driver's. In other words, she believes as Cyril Burt thought in the midtwentieth century that many people's IQs have sorted them into their natural positions. Society's structure "wasn't ordained by God," she said, "it grew" from differences in intelligence.

Believing that IQ tests measure, in large part, an innate ability called intelligence can lead to positions that exist only through the looking glass. Gottfredson argues that because African Americans on average score 15 points lower than whites do, one in six blacks (the number who score below 75) are at risk for being genetically unable "to master the elementary school curriculum or function independently in adulthood in modern societies."

By about 1980, however, the average black IQ score in America was the same as or higher than the white average in the 1930s, due to the inevitable rise of scores in every population. Are blacks today biologically smarter than whites in the 1930s, but not as innately smart as whites today? Human evolution doesn't happen that quickly.

And during the same interview, Gottfredson talked about how her own two daughters had tested poorly when they transferred to a new school in the second grade because their previous one, a Waldorf school, began to teach reading at an older age.

"They were put in a special education class for reading, and that reading teacher was very happy. It was probably the only time she had kids that learned to read immediately. In two months they were readers and they have read night and day since," she said.

It's impossible to know what has produced a person's or a group's measurable ability—it's some compounding of both environment and genetics, but this doesn't seem to dissuade the hereditarians from making bold statements about people, policy, and the country at large.

"When you have good tests," Gottfredson said, "and *g*-loaded tests [that is, exams psychologists believe test general intelligence the best] turn out to be the most useful overall and you have big racial differences, then you have set up a real democratic dilemma."

Electing corrupt politicians, killing journalists for what they write, and not properly educating people create a democratic dilemma. IQ test results, given what they test, do not. Even conceding, for the sake of argument only, that IQ tests primarily measure an innate something called intelligence, what are we supposed to do with evidence that on average blacks, working-class people, and criminals score lower than others on IQ tests? Sterilize and kill low scorers? Put them in separate schools or institutionalize them at a young age? Keep them out of the country? Gottfredson does not argue for such drastic measures, although they've all been tried in the past, with intelligence theory to back them up. What Gottfredson posits we should do isn't quite clear, other than to be honest about what she sees as probable biological differences among races and classes. This leads her to knowing what she opposes—by her lights harmful and wasteful provisions in education or the workforce based on race or class—but only a vague sense of what should be done proactively.

"In fact, rather than seeking racial parity in all outcomes, we might do better by helping lower-IQ individuals of all races. . . . We might especially target individuals below IQ 80 for special support, intellectual as well as material," Gottfredson has written. She believes we should help them to survive and function, but not unnaturally force them up the educational and vocational ladder. People can reach these conclusions (or not) as they like, but they shouldn't look to intelligence research to help them make such decisions.

The theory of general intelligence is the very foundation of mainstream intelligence testing over the past century, but even the most ardent proponents of g will admit that it has not been unquestionably established. Take, for example, a quote from near the beginning of the controversial 1994 book *The Bell Curve*. "The evidence for a general factor in intelligence was pervasive but circumstantial, based on statistical analysis rather than direct observation. Its reality therefore was, and remains, arguable." Once that admission was disposed of quickly in two sentences up front in the book, however, the authors went on to discuss, for 845 pages, policy based entirely on the assumption that g exists, that it is measurable, and that it is innately and unevenly distributed among different socioeconomic classes and ethnicities. Until there is proof beyond statistical relationships of g's existence and measurability, society should not treat IQ tests as if they can meaningfully rank people along a continuum of innate intelligence. For the same reason, all inferences based on IQ test results about race differences are dangerously unfounded.

Afterword

The history of the use of IQ tests is appalling. IQ tests have often been used for the vilest purposes, no matter that many of their originators had lofty social goals in mind. Since World War II, their use has been more benign, but still not, in general, defensible. Their application in education, whether the eleven-plus in England and Wales or the Wechsler exams and the SAT in the United States, has been at best misguided. Considering that they do not test intelligence and have negligible ability to predict academic achievement, they have at the least been used to exclude many worthy individuals from access to an excellent education. At their worst, since they correlate so strongly with socioeconomic background, they have excluded those already most disadvantaged in society.

In spite of this, we as a society are still enamored of IQ tests and IQ scores. This easy acceptance is remarkable and discouraging, given the evidence brought together in this book. It is also easily understood. The notion that the IQ test is a measure of innate intelligence has simply worked its way into the general consciousness. It is broadly and unthinkingly accepted as a fact, even though it is untrue.

Perhaps the attractiveness of IQ tests lies in the notion that they are "scientific," and in the easy-to-use and misleading certainty of a single score. Psychologists often claim that what they do is science, but the use of statistics alone is not enough to support their claim. Conclusions of psychology do not have the force of physics; there is no engineering behind IQ tests that builds bridges that don't fall down and sends probes to Mars. Closer to home, their conclusions also do not have the force of molecular biology's explanations of biological mechanisms that lead to new drugs. Despite the usage as if it were true, when it comes to intelligence there is no direct measure or test of biological ability.

This problem of psychology's puffery and overselling is a result of the field's history. Psychology gained respectability, access, and power by selling IQ tests to institutions, by claiming that their tests could increase efficiency by measuring innate intelligence. Unlike psychotherapy, phrenology, and other psychological tools, IQ tests were not created to help individuals, even though psychologists billed them as glimpses into people's cores. Psychologists might have gained respect and access to society's various institutions— schools, militaries, businesses, law, hospitals, and governments— without claiming they could test something as profound as innate intelligence. The French government in the early part of the twentieth century, after all, asked Alfred Binet to sort schoolchildren despite his more modest claims, but his successors chose hubris, and we have suffered the consequences ever since.

The argument here is not that IQ tests are never useful; knowing that one job applicant has more general knowledge than another can be helpful. IQ tests can predict, with varying and debated degrees, that high scorers on average will perform better than low ones in certain settings. The problem is, though, that IQ tests' power to describe individuals' abilities is very rough, so when they are used in education, employment, or elsewhere, the tests incorrectly predict many peoples' future behavior. While the cutoff for enlisting in the U.S. military is an IQ of 80, there are undoubtedly people with IQs of 79 who would make terrific soldiers.

The answer to this problem is to figure out when institutional concerns are greater than individuals' interests. Surely, in the main, having an efficient military outweighs individual career concerns. And more broadly, why should we deprive employers of a tool that will improve their hiring and human resource decisions? Unless a test is patently harmful, there is no reason why businesses should be barred from using an imperfect tool until something better comes along. On the other hand, schools and the legal system should worry more about understanding each individual than considering educational and judicial efficiency. It's not clear from a score of 70, 80, or 110 what a person can and cannot learn or do, despite what psychologists and other experts have led us to believe over the past hundred years.

What should also not be lost in this story is that IQ tests were a great improvement over previous methods of selecting human beings (such as skull measuring) and even persistent ways of picking (such as nepotism), but it's time for psychologists and other intelligence experts to devise better tools. In the interim, they should stop trying to persuade the rest of us that they can test intelligence, because they can't, and such claims are dangerous. Thankfully, testing practices have improved in recent years (for example, one's tubes are no longer cut due to low scores), but intelligence tests themselves have remained essentially unchanged over the previous century. In 1905, Alfred Binet gave us a test that roughly gauged people's knowledge and mental abilities. More than a hundred years later, we're still waiting for the next jump forward.

Notes

PREFACE

xiii *"Why do we use stoves?"* (bolded language in original) Clarence Yoakum and Robert Yerkes, eds., *Army Mental Tests* (New York: Henry Holt, 1920) pp. 208, 261.

CHAPTER 1: THE PROBLEM WITH TESTING

1 *When Tim was just three* Tim is not his real name; his mother's name has been changed, as has the girl's in the waiting room.

4 *fewer than half of the students* School Matters, A Service of Standard & Poor's. http://www.schoolmatters.com/App/SES/SPSServlet/MenuLinks Request?StateID=9&LocLevelID=111&StateLocLevelID=378 &LocationID=9&CatID=-1&SecID=-1&CompID=-1&Site= (accessed November 8, 2005).

7 *"Any IQ estimate before"* Diane Coalson, senior research director, Wechsler Products, Harcourt Assessment, in discussion with author, July 29, 2005.

CHAPTER 2: THE ORIGINS OF TESTING

9 *a cousin of Charles Darwin* Nicholas Wright Gillham, *A Life of Sir Francis Galton: From African Exploration to the Birth of Eugenics* (Oxford, U.K.: Oxford University Press, 2001), pp. 13–22; Raymond Fancher, *The Intelligence Men: Makers of the IQ Controversy* (New York: W. W. Norton, 1985), pp. 18–19.

9 *"Whenever you can, count"* Daniel Kevles, *In the Name of Eugenics: Genetics and the Uses of Human Heredity* (Cambridge, Mass.: Harvard University Press, 1995), p. 7.

9 *As a young man, he suffered* Fancher, *The Intelligence Men*, pp. 23–24.

10 *He took a trip down the Nile* Gillham, *A Life of Sir Francis Galton*, pp. 47–58.

10 *"As regards the learned"* Ibid., p. 58.

10 *"The sub-interpreter was married"* Francis Galton, *Narrative of an Explorer in Tropical South Africa* (London: Ward, Lock, 1889), pp. 53–54. Gillham, *A Life of Sir Francis Galton*, pp. 75–76.

11 *"a single stroke,"*   Raymond Fancher, "Eugenics and Other Victorian 'Sec-
     ular Religions,'" in Christopher Green, Marlene Shore, and Thomas
     Teo, eds., *The Transformation of Psychology: Influences of Nineteenth-
     Century Philosophy, Technology, and Natural Science* (Washington, D.C.:
     American Psychological Association, 2001), p. 5.

11 *"a marked epoch"*   Francis Galton, *Memories of My Life* (London: Metheun,
     1908), p. 287. There were other factors contributing to his worrying,
     notably, and ironically for a man who would later become obsessed with
     human breeding, that he and his wife were unable to produce children.
     Fancher, "Eugenics and Other Victorian 'Secular' Religions," pp. 4–5,
     15–16.

12 *"I began by thinking"*   Fancher, *The Intelligence Men*, p. 30.

12 *"native chief[s]"*   Francis Galton, *Hereditary Genius: An Inquiry into Its Laws
     and Consequences* (New York: Horizon Press, 1952), pp. 327–328.

12 *"The number among the negroes"*   Ibid., p. 328.

13 *"inherit capacity, zeal"*   Ibid., p. 84.

14 *"America most certainly"*   Ibid., p. 40; Fancher, *The Intelligence Men*, p. 30.

14 *Galton's privileged background*   Fancher, *The Intelligence Men*, pp. 18–21.
     Some writers argue that Galton believed that nature mattered more
     than nurture (terms he coined) because of self-doubt. He hadn't done
     particularly well at Cambridge, didn't come from an old aristocratic
     family, and hadn't produced a child. He did, however, have successful
     relations and ancestors, in the form of Charles Darwin and illustrious
     businessmen. Adrian Wooldridge, *Measuring the Mind: Education and
     Psychology in England, c. 1860–1990* (Cambridge, U.K.: Cambridge Uni-
     versity Press, 1994), p. 75. Kevles, *In the Name of Eugenics*, pp. 8–9.

14 *"criminals, semi-criminals, loafers"*   Donald MacKenzie, *Statistics in Britain,
     1865–1930: The Social Construction of Scientific Knowledge* (Edinburgh:
     Edinburgh University Press, 1981), pp. 16–18.

15 *"found great industries"*   Ibid., p. 18.

15 *"Some dogs are savage"*   Francis Galton, "The Possible Improvement of
     the Human Breed under the Existing Conditions of Law and Senti-
     ment." Abstract of the Huxley Memorial Lecture delivered before the
     Anthropological Institute of Great Britain and Ireland, October 29, 1901.
     Galton.org. http://www.mugu.com/browse/galton/search/essays/pages/
     galton-1901-man-race-improvement_1.htm (accessed July 24, 2005).

15 *In a paper published in 1865*   Francis Galton, "Hereditary Talent and
     Character," *Macmillan's Magazine* 12 (1865): 157–166, 318–327. Dis-
     cussed in Fancher, *The Intelligence Men*, pp. 35–36.

16 *"public examinations, conducted"*   Fancher, *The Intelligence Men*, p. 35.

16 *"grace, beauty, health"*   Ibid., pp. 35–36.

16 *"The Sovereign herself"*   Ibid., p. 36.

16 *When working on a "beauty map"*   University College, London, still has a
     number of these odd little gadgets in their Galton Collection. See http://
     www.ucl.ac.uk/silva/museums/galton/index (accessed March 20, 2006).

17   *"It was a matter of surprise to myself"*   Francis Galton, "On the Anthropo-
     metric Laboratory at the Late International Health Exhibition," *Journal
     of the Anthropological Institute* 14 (1884): 205–218, 211.

18   *"The only information"*   Fancher, *The Intelligence Men*, p. 43.

18   *"Ladies rarely distinguish"*   Ibid.

19   *"One omission in the laboratory"*   Francis Galton, "On the Anthropometric
     Laboratory," p. 210. The Galton Collection at University College, Lon-
     don, includes head-measuring devices. At some point, therefore, he
     must have included the measurements.

19   *Galton was unsure about the relationship*   Fancher, *The Intelligence Men*, p. 42.

19   *"Aberdeenshire . . . a fact"*   Gillham, *A Life of Sir Francis Galton*, p. 213.

19   *four million Britons visited*   Annmarie Adams, *Architecture in the Family
     Way: Doctors, Houses, and Women 1870–1900* (Montreal: McGill-Queen's
     University Press, 1996), pp. 13, 14–16, 26–27. Gillham, *A Life of Sir
     Francis Galton*, p. 210.

20   *Galton believed that what people traditionally*   Fancher, *The Intelligence Men*,
     pp. 37–38.

21   *"all kindness"*   Francis Galton, "Hereditary Improvements," *Fraser's Mag-
     azine* 7 (1873): 129.

21   *"national conscience, like a new religion"*   Francis Galton, "Eugenics: Its
     Definition, Scope, and Aims," *American Journal of Sociology* 10 (1904): 5.

21   *"The way of nature has always"*   Ibid., p. 11.

21   *"It is worth pointing out"*   Ibid., p. 21.

22   Francis Galton, *Natural Inheritance* (London: Macmillan, 1889). For work
     on the correlation coefficient see Francis Galton, "Co-relations and
     Their Measurement, Chiefly from Anthropometric Data," *Proceedings of
     the Royal Society* 45 (1888): 135–45.

22   *While statistics certainly existed*   MacKenzie, *Statistics in Britain*, pp. 8–9.

23   *Galton had the statistics*   Ibid.

24   *One of Galton's most ardent*   Michael Sokal, "James McKeen Cattell and
     Mental Anthropometry: Nineteenth-Century Science and Reform and
     the Origins of Psychological Testing," in *Psychological Testing and Ameri-
     can Society: 1890–1930* (New Brunswick, N.J.: Rutgers University Press,
     1987), pp. 25–27.

25   *Cattell returned to the United States*   Sokal, "James McKeen Cattell and
     Mental Anthropometry," pp. 29, 32–33. Fancher, *The Intelligence Men*,
     pp. 46–47.

25   *At the end of the nineteenth century*   Michael Sokal, "Practical Phrenology
     as Psychological Counseling in the Nineteenth-Century United States"
     in Christopher Green, Marlene Shore, and Thomas Teo, eds., *The
     Transformation of Psychology: Influences of Nineteenth-Century Philosophy,
     Technology, and Natural Science* (Washington, D.C.: American Psycholog-
     ical Association, 2001), p. 27.

25   *Although phrenology paved*   Marlene Shore, "Psychology and Memory in
     the Midst of Change: The Social Concerns of Late-Nineteenth-Century

North American Psychologists," in Green, Shore, and Teo, eds., *The Transformation of Psychology*, pp. 63–64.

26   *Psychologists claimed to have*   Sokal, "James McKeen Cattell and Mental Anthropometry," p. 32.

26   *"believed that practical applications"*   Ibid.

26   *"delicacy of touch"*   Ibid., p. 39.

26   *Eventually, though, psychologists began*   Ibid., pp. 37–38. Fancher, *The Intelligence Men*, pp. 48–49.

27   *"Class standing correlated"*   Fancher, *The Intelligence Men*, p. 48.

28   *"receive the honour"*   Gillham, *A Life of Sir Francis Galton*, p. 340.

28   *"I have to live"*   Ibid.

Chapter 3: The Birth of Modern Intelligence Tests

29   *"the career of men"*   Raymond Fancher, *The Intelligence Men: Makers of the IQ Controversy* (New York: W. W. Norton, 1985), pp. 18–19.

29   *"curing" young Alfred*   Ibid., pp. 49–50.

30   *Over a period of twenty*   Fancher, *The Intelligence Men*, pp. 51–52, 54–56. Wolf, *Alfred Binet*, pp. 41, 46–50.

30   *"was learning to walk"*   T. H. Wolf, *Alfred Binet*, pp. 80–81.

31   *"to cut meat"*   Fancher, *The Intelligence Men*, pp. 59–61. Wolf, *Alfred Binet*, p. 84.

32   *Despite this theoretical breakthrough*   Fancher, *The Intelligence Men*, pp. 69–77, for details of the first test and why it was created.

34   *"It must be well understood"*   Ibid., p. 77.

34   *"one is six meters long"*   Leila Zenderland, *Measuring Minds: Henry Herbert Goddard and the Origins of American Intelligence Testing* (Cambridge, U.K.: Cambridge University Press, 1998), p. 96.

35   *"a position of some importance"*   Charles Spearman, *A History of Psychology in Autobiography*, vol. 1 (New York: Russell & Russell, 1961), p. 304.

35   *"a little village school"*   Ibid., p. 322.

35   *significant statistical relationships*   Spearman discovered that school grades correlated with each other at +.55; with the sensory measures the correlation was +.25, and the two groups correlated together at +.38. Fancher, *The Intelligence Men*, pp. 87–88.

36   *"by measuring promiscuously"*   Spearman, *A History of Psychology in Autobiography*, p. 324.

36   *"In such wise"*   Ibid.

36   *"One can . . . conceive"*   Fancher, *The Intelligence Men*, p. 95.

36   *In 1905, just a year*   Charles Spearman, "'General Intelligence': Objectively Determined and Measured," *American Journal of Psychology* 15 (1904): 201–292.

Chapter 4: America Discovers Intelligence Tests

39   *"My getting hold of Binet's"*   Leila Zenderland, *Measuring Minds: Henry Herbert Goddard and the Origins of American Intelligence Testing* (Cambridge, U.K.: Cambridge University Press, 1998), p. 92. All details of

Goddard first learning of Alfred Binet's test introducing it to America come from this excellent book.

40   *"Happiness first"*   Ibid., pp. 111–112.

40   *"We have a little secret"*   Ibid., p. 112.

40   *"were accustomed to talking"*   Ibid., p. 61.

40   *"Quaker Jail"*   Ibid., p. 20.

41   *"Fixed an electrical attachment"*   Ibid., p. 89.

41   *In the end, Goddard*   Ibid., p. 91.

42   *"No imbecile asylums"*   Ibid., p. 93.

42   *"Binet's lab. is"*   Ibid., pp. 92–93.

43   *"The vagueness of their"*   Ibid., p. 95.

44   *"a want of natural"*   Ibid., p. 79.

45   *"set of mental tests"*   Ibid., p. 99.

45   *"Here is a case"*   Ibid., p. 99.

46   *"Who is there that does not"*   Ibid., p. 103.

46   *"Mental testing produced"*   Paul Chapman, *Schools as Sorters: Lewis M. Terman, Applied Psychology, and the Intelligence Testing Movement 1890–1930* (New York: New York University Press, 1988), p. 12.

47   *"the girl problem"*   Wendy Kline, *Building a Better Race: Gender, Sexuality, and Eugenics from the Turn of the Century to the Baby Boom* (Berkeley: University of California Press, 2001), p. 15.

47   *"I do not believe that mental"*   Ibid., p. 37.

47   *"No amount of education"*   Zenderland, *Measuring Minds*, p. 175. Henry Herbert Goddard, *The Kallikak Family: A Study in the Heredity of Feeble-Mindedness* (New York: Macmillan, 1912). For a comprehensive discussion of the book, see "The Kallikak Family" in *Measuring Minds*, pp. 143–185.

48   *"even the defective"*   Zenderland, *Measuring Minds*, p. 160.

48   *"Subjective appreciation of mental"*   Ibid., p. 161.

49   *"After some experience"*   Goddard, *The Kallikak Family*, p. 15.

49   *"The surprise and horror"*   Ibid., p. 16.

49   *"conclusive proof"; "good members of society"*   Zenderland, *Measuring Minds*, pp. 171–173.

49   *"kept houses of ill fame"*   Ibid., p. 173. Goddard, *The Kallikak Family*, pp. 18–19.

50   *"loathsome unfortunate[s]"*   Goddard, *The Kallikak Family*, p. 101. Zenderland, *Measuring Minds*, p. 181.

50   *"He is indeed loathsome"*   Goddard, *The Kallikak Family*, p. 101.

50   *"How many are 12 less 3?"*   Ibid., p. 11.

51   *"This is a typical illustration"*   Ibid., pp. 12–13.

51   *"We need to hunt"*   Kline, *Building a Better Race*, p. 27.

51   *"such colonies [for the feebleminded]"*   Goddard, *The Kallikak Family*, pp. 105–106.

51   *Regardless of parental consent*   Michael D'Antonio, *The State Boys Rebellion* (New York: Simon & Schuster, 2004), p. 12.

52   *American schools grew rapidly*   Chapman, *Schools as Sorters*, pp. 39–43.

52   *"not only the truant"*   Ibid., pp. 42–43.

53 *The increases in numbers* Ibid., p. 48.

53 *Finally, on top of demographic* Zenderland, *Measuring Minds*, pp. 116–120. Chapman, *Schools as Sorters*, 41.

54 *"The 'science of heat"* Zenderland, *Measuring Minds*, p. 120.

55 *"there was a big difference"* Ibid.

55 *tested all the children in the district* Henry Goddard, "Two Thousand Normal Children Measured by the Binet Measuring Scale," *Pedagogical Seminary* 18 (June 1911): 232–233.

55 *"To a person familiar"* Zenderland, *Measuring Minds*, pp. 121–122.

55 *"native ability to do"* Ibid., p. 126.

56 *By 1912, just two* Ibid., p. 129.

56 *"We have not attempted"* Ibid.

56 *"to demand, as critics"* Lewis Terman, *The Measurement of Intelligence: An Explanation of and a Complete Guide for the Use of the Stanford Revision and Extension of the Binet-Simon Intelligence Scale* (Boston: Houghton Mifflin, 1916), p. 44.

56 *"three years or more"* Zenderland, *Measuring Minds*, p. 124.

57 *Teachers around the country* Ibid., pp. 141–142.

57 *By 1914 (just four* Chapman, *Schools as Sorters*, p. 36.

Chapter 5: Turning Back the Feebleminded

59 *"Pat, if I gave"* Phillip Cowen, *Memories of an American Jew* (New York: International Press, 1932), pp. 174–175.

60 *"imbeciles, feeble-minded and persons"* Leila Zenderland, *Measuring Minds: Henry Herbert Goddard and the Origins of American Intelligence Testing* (Cambridge, U.K.: Cambridge University Press, 1998), p. 266.

60 *"The day of the emigrants'"* Stephen Graham, *With Poor Immigrants to America* (New York: Macmillan, 1914), pp. 41, 44.

61 *"her common knowledge was meager"* E. K. Sprague, "Mental Examination of Immigrants," *Survey* (January 17, 1914): 467.

61 *"Should the immigrant appear"* Josette Harris, David Tulsky, and Maria Schultheis, "Assessment of the Non-Native English Speaker: Assimilating History and Research Findings to Guide Clinical Practice" in David S. Tulsky, et al., eds., *Clinical Interpretation of the WAIS-III and WMS-III* (San Diego: Academic Press, 2003), p. 347.

62 *"Facial expression may be"* Sprague, *Mental Examination of Immigrants*, p. 468.

62 *"The object is not"* Elizabeth Yew, "Medical Inspection of Immigrants at Ellis Island, 1891–1924," *Bulletin of the New York Academy of Medicine* (June 1980): 495.

63 *"An error which results"* L. L. Williams, "The Medical Examination of Mentally Defective Aliens: Its Scope and Limitations," *American Journal of Insanity* (January 17, 1914): 265. Zenderland, *Measuring Minds*, p. 270.

63 *"man walked into"* Zenderland, *Measuring Minds*, pp. 271–272.

64 *"cube imitation test"* E. H. Mullan, "Mentality of the Arriving Immigrant," *Public Health Bulletin No. 90* (1917; repr., New York: Arno Press, 1970), pp. 39–40.

64   *In 1911, two testers published*   W. Healy and G. M. Fernald, "Tests for Practical Mental Classification," *Psychological Monographs* 13, no. 54 (1911). Tulsky, et al., eds., *Clinical Interpretation of the WAIS-III and WMS-III*, pp. 65–67.

64   *The doctors on Ellis Island*   Howard Knox expressly acknowledged Binet in the introduction to his 1914 test. Howard A. Knox, "A Scale, Based on the Work at Ellis Island, for Estimating Mental Defect," *Journal of the American Medical Association* 62, no. 10 (March 7, 1914): 741.

64   *"justice, pity, truth"*   Ibid., p. 742.

64   *"the subject has never"*   Harris, Tulsky, and Schultheis, "Assessment of the Non-Native English Speaker," p. 355.

65   *"You ought to see"*   Cowen, *Memories of an American Jew*, p. 174.

65   *In 1908, only 186 people*   Zenderland, *Measuring Minds*, p. 273.

CHAPTER 6: THE TESTS THAT CHANGED THE WORLD

67   *Chemists, physicists, biologists*   Committee on Classification of Personnel in the Army, Adjutant General's Department, *The Personnel System of the United States Army*, vol. 1 (Washington, D.C., 1919), p. 53.

67   *improve soldiers' ability to aim*   Leila Zenderland, *Measuring Minds; Henry Herbert Goddard and the Origins of American Intelligence Testing* (Cambridge, U.K.: Cambridge University Press, 1998), p. 282. Committee on Classification of Personnel in the Army, *The Personnel System of the United States Army*, p. 54.

68   *The seven psychologists*   Daniel Kevles, "Testing the Army's Intelligence: Psychologists and the Military in World War I," *Journal of American History* 55, no. 3 (December 1968): 566.

68   *"I hope we can all"*   Richard Von Mayrhauser, "The Manager, the Medic, and the Mediator: The Clash of Professional Psychological Styles and the Wartime Origins of Group Mental Testing" in Michael Sokal, *Psychological Testing and American Society: 1890–1930* (New Brunswick, N.J.: Rutgers University Press, 1987), p. 129.

68   *"utter disgust"*   Ibid., p. 138.

69   *Working as a psychologist*   Ibid., p. 129.

69   *"moody, strong-willed, unsuggestible"*   Robert Mearns Yerkes, *History of Psychology in Autobiography*, vol. 2 (Worcester, Mass.: Clark University Press, 1930), p. 383.

69   *"physician, surgeon, or"*   Ibid.

69   *For Yerkes, the medical model*   Von Mayrhauser, "The Manager, the Medic, and the Mediator," pp. 137–138, 147.

70   *Yerkes tested people one-on-one*   James Reed, "Robert M. Yerkes and the Mental Testing Movement" in Sokal, *Psychological Testing and American Society*, p. 79.

70   *Scott, by contrast*   Von Mayrhauser, "The Manager, the Medic, and the Mediator," pp. 130–132.

70   *Yerkes thought intelligence tests*   Ibid., pp. 145–147.

71   *"I became so enraged"*   Ibid., p. 140.

71   *Scott was able to network*   Jacob Zabel Jacobson, *Scott of Northwestern: The Life Story of a Pioneer in Psychology and Education* (Chicago: L. Mariano, 1951), pp. 113–115.

72   *Worst of all, Yerkes*   Von Mayrhauser, "The Manager, the Medic, and the Mediator," p. 141.

72   *Doctors and psychiatrists at Boston*   Ibid., pp. 143–144.

72   *Yerkes hadn't yet made*   Zenderland, *Measuring Minds*, p. 283.

73   *With the conflagration*   Von Mayrhauser, "The Manager, the Medic, and the Mediator," p. 148.

73   *"to identify 'intellectually incompetent'"*   Paul Chapman, *Schools as Sorters: Lewis M. Terman, Applied Psychology, and the Intelligence Testing Movement 1890–1930* (New York: New York University Press, 1988), p. 67.

73   *"parts of the machine"*   Ibid.

74   *"It is safe to predict"*   Henry Minton, *Lewis M. Terman: Pioneer in Psychological Testing* (New York: New York University Press, 1988), p. 52.

74   *mainly urban, middle-class*   Ibid., p. 50.

74   *"Can you tell me"*   Ken Richardson, *The Making of Intelligence* (New York: Columbia University Press, 2000), pp. 31–32.

74   *He claimed that his test*   Minton, *Lewis M. Terman*, p. 49.

74   *"represent the level"*   Ibid., p. 54.

75   *"between 20 or 25 and 50"*   Lewis Terman, *The Measurement of Intelligence: An Explanation of and a Complete Guide for the Use of the Sanford Revision and Extension of the Binet-Simon Intelligence Scale* (Boston: Houghton Mifflin, 1916), p. 79.

75   *"explain the fact that"*   Wendy Kline, *Building a Better Race: Gender, Sexuality, and Eugenics from the Turn of the Century to the Baby Boom* (Berkeley: University of California Press, 2001), pp. 41–42.

75   *"the extent to which"*   Ibid., p. 42.

76   *"include[d] five tests practically"*   Robert Yerkes, ed., *Psychological Examining in the United States Army: Memoirs of the National Academy of Sciences* (Washington, D.C.: U.S. Government Printing Office, 1921), p. 299. Chapman, *Schools as Sorters*, p. 68.

76   *"Below are given the names"*   Frederick J. Kelly, "The Kansas Silent Reading Test," *Studies by the Bureau of Educational Measurement and Standards* (1915), n. 3. Discussed in Franz Samelson, "Was Early Mental Testing (a) Racist Inspired, (b) Objective Science, (c) A Technology for Democracy, (d) The Origin of Multiple-Choice Exams, (e) None of the Above? (Mark the RIGHT Answer)" in Sokal, *Psychological Testing in American Society*, pp. 118–119.

77   *(1) . . . be subject to only one entry*   Ibid., p. 119.

77   *"This piece of educational technology"*   Ibid., p. 123.

78   *Young adult men, of course*   Zenderland, *Measuring Minds*, p. 286.

78   *Ever after, psychologists such as*   Ibid., pp. 302–303.

78   *To prevent cheating*   Yerkes, ed., *Psychological Examining*, p. 9.

78   *"It was agreed"*   Ibid., p. 300.

78   *"empty—full," "vesper—matin"*   Zenderland, *Measuring Minds*, p. 286.

78   *"Why should food be chewed,"*   Yerkes, ed., *Psychological Examining*, p. 215.

79   *The Beta exam, on the other hand*   Ibid., pp. 235–258.

79   *"the correlations which the tests"*   Ibid., pp. 304–305.

80   *"avoid being too much influenced by his rank"*   Ibid., p. 425 (emphasis in original).

80   *"The results suggest"*   Joel Spring, "Psychologists and the War: The Meaning of Intelligence in the Alpha and Beta Tests," *History of Education Quarterly* 12, no. 1 (Spring 1972): 8.

80   *"scarcely more than a national constabulary"*   Committee on Classification of Personnel in the Army, *The Personnel System of the United States Army*, p. 27.

81   *In March 1917, the U.S. Army*   Ibid., p. 28.

81   *"among three and a half million"*   Ibid., p. 9.

81   *The army signed on*   Zenderland, *Measuring Minds*, p. 287.

81   *He had desperately wished for*   Yerkes, ed., *Psychological Examining*, pp. 11, 98, 300. Franz Samelson, "World War I Intelligence Testing and the Development of Psychology," *Journal of the History of the Behavioral Sciences* 13 (1977): 276.

81   *The recruits represented all ethnicities*   Meiron Harries and Susie Harries, *The Last Days of Innocence: America at War, 1917–1918* (New York: Random House, 1997), p. 127.

Chapter 7: Alpha and Beta

83   *"not looking for crazy"*   Daniel Kevles, "Testing the Army's Intelligence: Psychologists and the Military in World War I," *Journal of American History* 55, no. 3 (December 1968): 566.

83   *Foreign illiterates were often*   Robert Yerkes, ed., *Psychological Examining in the United States Army: Memoirs of the National Academy of Sciences* (Washington, D.C.: U.S. Government Printing Office, 1921), p. 379.

83   *And many white officers*   Ibid., p. 705.

83   *But the white examiners*   Franz Samelson, "World War I Intelligence Testing and the Development of Psychology," *Journal of the History of the Behavioral Sciences* 13 (1977): 279–280. James Reed, "Robert M. Yerkes and the Mental Testing Movement" in Michael Sokal, *Psychological Testing and American Society: 1890–1930* (New Brunswick, N.J.: Rutgers University Press, 1987), p. 85.

84   *"had been forced by superior"*   Samelson, "World War I Intelligence Testing," p. 280.

84   *fell asleep "en masse"*   Ibid.

84   *"relatively lower intelligence"*   Yerkes, ed., *Psychological Examining*, p. 706.

84   *"a splendid examination for negroes"*   Ibid.

84   *Without mentioning the test-taking*   Samelson, "World War I Intelligence Testing," p. 280.

84   *"mental meddlers," "pests"*   Kevles, "Testing the Army's Intelligence," p. 575.

84   *Camp commanding officers often*   Yerkes, ed., *Psychological Examining*, pp. 14–17.

85 *difference between psychiatrists and psychologists* Ibid., p. 97.

85 *"a board of art critics"* Kevles, "Testing the Army's Intelligence," p. 575.

85 *"exhibited keen interest"* Yerkes, ed., *Psychological Examining*, p. 15.

85 *doctors scored lower than other officers* Ibid., pp. 22–23, 97, 858–859.

86 *race, country of origin, salary before the war* Ibid., p. 124.

86 *"of great scientific interest"* Kevles, "Testing the Army's Intelligence," p. 574.

86 *"read and understand newspapers"* Leila Zenderland, *Measuring Minds: Henry Herbert Goddard and the Origins of American Intelligence Testing* (Cambridge, U.K.: Cambridge University Press, 1998), p. 288.

86 *They were also stunned* Ibid., pp. 288–289.

87 *"It appears that feeble-mindedness"* Ibid., p. 289. Yerkes, ed., *Psychological Examining*, p. 789.

87 *In some camps, examiners* Yerkes, ed., *Psychological Examining*, p. 790.

87 *Psychologists also thought* Zenderland, *Measuring Minds*, p. 289.

87 *The U.S. Army didn't care* Ibid.

88 *"the British colonel in the Boer War"* Kevles, "Testing the Army's Intelligence," p. 567.

88 *To bring the army up to date* Committee on Classification of Personnel in the Army, Adjutant General's Department, *The Personnel System of the United States Army*, vol. 1 (Washington, D.C.: 1919), pp. 10–11.

88 *"The old [personnel] system"* Ibid., p. 33.

88 *"I fully believe that"* Kevles, "Testing the Army's Intelligence," p. 570.

89 *"its pro rata share"* Ibid., p. 573.

89 *In the end, the army* Committee on Classification of Personnel in the Army, *The Personnel System of the United States Army*, p. 54.

89 *"Indeed, the low rank assigned"* Yerkes, ed., *Psychological Examining*, p. 98.

89 *Before the war was over* Kevles, "Testing the Army's Intelligence," p. 578. Reed, "Robert M. Yerkes," p. 85.

89 *awarded Walter Scott the only Distinguished* Richard Von Mayrhauser, "The Manager, the Medic, and the Mediator: The Clash of Professional Psychological Styles and the Wartime Origins of Group Mental Testing" in Michael Sokol, *Psychological Testing and American Society: 1890–1930* (New Brunswick, N.J.: Rutgers University Press, 1987), p. 151.

89 *"Velvet Joe"; "Why are cats useful animals?"* Zenderland, *Measuring Minds*, p. 286.

90 *"Altogether the testing at best"* Samelson, "World War I Intelligence Testing," p. 282 (emphasis in original).

91 *warred over small scraps of funding* Reed, "Robert M. Yerkes," pp. 81, 87.

92 *"demonstrated beyond question"* Paul Chapman, *Schools as Sorters: Lewis M. Terman, Applied Psychology, and the Intelligence Testing Movement 1890–1930* (New York: New York University Press, 1988), p. 1.

92 *"Before the World War"* Samelson, "World War I Intelligence Testing," p. 277.

92 *World War I allowed intelligence testing to grow* Reed, "Robert M. Yerkes," p. 76. Samelson, "World War I Intelligence Testing," pp. 275–276.

92 *"put psychology on the map"* Samelson, "World War I Intelligence Testing," p. 275.

92 *Terman and Yerkes' biggest accomplishment* Reed, "Robert M. Yerkes," p. 84.

92 *"bombarded by requests"* Chapman, *Schools as Sorters*, p. 78.

92 *"National Intelligence Tests"* M. E. Haggerty, L. M. Terman, E. L. Thorndike, G. M. Whipple, and R. M. Yerkes, *National Intelligence Tests: Manual of Directions* (Yonkers-on-Hudson, N.Y.: World Book, 1920), p. 3. Diane Ravitch, *Left Back: A Century of Failed School Reforms* (New York: Simon & Schuster, 2000), p. 137.

93 *"The army and the school"* Joel Spring, Psychologists and the War: The Meaning of Intelligence in the Alpha and Beta Tests," *History of Education Quarterly* (Spring 1972): 9.

93 *Colleges snapped up the Alpha* Ibid., p. 4.

93 *four hundred thousand copies of the third- to eighth-grade* Ravitch, *Left Back*, p. 137. Chapman, *Schools as Sorters*, p. 1.

93 *"The limits of a child's educability"* Ravitch, *Left Back*, p. 138.

94 *"subnormal" and the "unusually bright"* Haggerty, et al., *National Intelligence Tests*, p. 5.

94 *Terman broke the vocational guidance down* Ravitch, *Left Back*, p. 139.

94 *"ability grouping," "homogeneous grouping"* Chapman, *Schools as Sorters*, p. 2.

95 *"Most of us have the mind of a child of ten"* Roland Marchand, *Advertising the American Dream: Making Way for Modernity 1920–1940* (Berkeley: University of California Press, 1985), p. 66. Zenderland, *Measuring Minds*, p. 311.

95 *Cultural critics said* Zenderland, *Measuring Minds*, p. 311.

95 *"a multitude of features dedicated"* Marchand, *Advertising the American Dream*, p. 66.

95 *Henry Goddard started measuring the minds* Zenderland, *Measuring Minds*, p. 268.

96 *Yerkes used a bar chart* Yerkes, ed., *Psychological Examining*, pp. 693–697.

96 *46 percent of the men from Poland* Leon Kamin, *The Science and Politics of I.Q.* (Potomac, Md.: Lawrence Erlbaum Associates, 1974), p. 21.

96 *"I am not afraid to say anything"* Ibid.

97 *"We must face a possibility of racial admixture"* Ibid.

97 *"The steps that should be taken"* Ibid., p. 22.

CHAPTER 8: FROM SEGREGATION TO STERILIZATION:
CARRIE BUCK'S STORY

99 *In 1923* Paul Lombardo, "Three Generations, No Imbeciles: New Light on *Buck v. Bell*," *New York University Law Review* 60 (April 1985): 54.

99 *"wanted to have her committed"* Petitioner's Briefs and Records, Supreme Court of Appeals of Virginia, no. 1700, *Carrie Buck v. Dr. J. H. Bell* (June 1, 1925), p. 66.

100   *"residing with them an epileptic and feeble-minded person"*   Ibid., p. 30.

100   *"have cared for her"*   Ibid., p. 31.

100   *worked for the local streetcar company*   Paul Lombardo, e-mail message to author, July 7, 2005.

100   *"examined Carrie E. Buck and [found]"*   Petitioner's Briefs, p. 26.

101   *"How was the peculiarity manifested?"*   Ibid., pp. 22–26.

101   *"feeble-minded, or epileptic"*   Ibid., p. 27.

101   *The same day that the warrant*   Ibid., p. 28.

102   *"blind room"*   The Lynchburg Story: Eugenic Sterilization in America, video, directed by Stephen Trombley (New York: Filmmakers Library, 1993).

103   *"an illustration of the adage"*   Leila Zenderland, *Measuring Minds: Henry Herbert Goddard and the Origins of American Intelligence Testing* (Cambridge, U.K.: Cambridge University Press, 1998), p. 321.

103   *Only now, given the economic climate*   Phillip Reilly, *The Surgical Solution: A History of Involuntary Sterilization in the United States* (Baltimore: Johns Hopkins University Press, 1991), pp. 71–72.

103   *George Mallory, a poor, uneducated man*   All facts regarding and quotes from the *Mallory* case come from Lombardo, "Three Generations, No Imbeciles," pp. 40–45.

104   *"exposed to vicious and immoral influences"*   Ibid., p. 40.

104   *"Dear sir," he wrote*   Ibid., pp. 42–43.

104   *"I have your letter"*   Ibid., p. 43.

105   *"for the relief of physical suffering"*   Ibid., p. 44.

105   *"This is tort reform 1920s style"*   Paul Lombardo, in discussion with author, May 31, 2005.

106   *By March 1924, Strode had successfully*   Lombardo, "Three Generations, No Imbeciles," pp. 45–48.

107   *"as a matter of precautionary safety"*   Ibid., p. 48.

107   *He had examined her with the Stanford-Binet*   Petitioner's Briefs, p. 33.

107   *"native intelligence, not school knowledge"*   Lewis Terman, *The Measurement of Intelligence: An Explanation of and a Complete Guide for the Use of the Sanford Revision and Extension of the Binet-Simon Intelligence Scale* (Boston: Houghton Mifflin, 1916), p. 36.

107   *the Stanford-Binet measured vocabulary*   Ibid., p. 329.

107   *Priddy would have asked her to differentiate*   Ibid., pp. 324, 330–331.

107   *"her mother, Emma Buck"*   Petitioner's Briefs, p. 33.

108   *The board members charged Aubrey Strode*   Lombardo, "Three Generations, No Imbeciles," p. 50.

108   *never raised by any court*   Paul Lombardo, discussion, May 31, 2005.

108   *The colony hired a friend*   Lombardo, "Three Generations, No Imbeciles," p. 55.

109   *"passing through the place back and forth"* . . . *"Yes, sir, and the children less than that"*   Ibid., 52. Petitioner's Briefs, pp. 51–56.

110   *"passing work in the fourth grade"*   Petitioner's Briefs, pp. 56–60.

111   *"In the five years that"*   Lombardo, "Three Generations, No Imbeciles," p. 52. Petitioner's Briefs, pp. 54–55.

111 *"From your experience as a social worker"* . . . *"but just what it is, I can't tell"* Petitioner's Briefs, pp. 66–67.

112 *An out-of-town eugenics expert* Paul Lombardo, "Facing Carrie Buck," *Hastings Center Report* 33, no. 2 (2003): 16.

112 *"On that fact,"* . . . *much more likely to go wrong"* Petitioner's Briefs, p. 68.

113 *poor women's cheap labor available* Lombardo, "Three Generations, No Imbeciles," p. 60.

113 *"Now the demand for domestics"* . . . *"No, sir, none whatever"* Ibid. Petitioner's Briefs, p. 98.

113 *Carrie's case climbed its way* Lombardo, "Three Generations, No Imbeciles," pp. 55–56.

114 *"feeble minded white woman"* *Buck v. Bell*, 274 U.S. 200, 205 (1927).

114 *"Old man John Callicac [sic]"* Zenderland, *Measuring Minds*, p. 324.

114 *"It is better for all the world"* *Buck v. Bell*, p. 207. The line about three generations being enough instantly became famous and still is, even if people can't quite remember exactly what it's from. "It's one of the great sound bites of twentieth-century jurisprudence," said Paul Lombardo. "It's a bumper sticker. And it was used that way . . . all over the world." In fact, the pithy line quickly became a joke even back in its day. When the sole dissenting justice, Pierce Butler, would speak in public he would sometimes be introduced with the line "Three generations of imbeciles are enough, but Butler dissents."

"So it's a great line," said Lombardo, "but it's a throwaway line because it doesn't tell you anything." Paul Lombardo, discussion, May 31, 2005.

115 *"All they told me was that I had to get an operation"* Carlos Santos, "Historic Test Case," *Richmond Times-Dispatch*, February 17, 2002.

115 *"One decision that I wrote"* G. Edward White, *Justice Oliver Wendell Holmes: Law and the Inner Self* (Oxford, U.K.: Oxford University Press, 1993), p. 408.

115 *Indiana and North Dakota quickly passed* Reilly, *The Surgical Solution*, p. 88.

115 *In 1920, twelve states had passed* Ibid., pp. 100–101.

115 *In the 1930s, the brunt* Ibid., pp. 94–95.

115 *"the sterilization law was finally declared constitutional"* Ibid., p. 98.

115 *California, for instance, sterilized gays* Wendy Kline, *Building a Better Race: Gender, Sexuality, and Eugenics from the Turn of the Century to the Baby Boom* (Berkeley: University of California Press, 2001), pp. 54–55.

115 *California led the pack* Lombardo, "Three Generations, No Imbeciles," p. 31.

115 *In fact, the total figure of sterilizations* Reilly, *The Surgical Solution*, pp. 90, 96. Academics don't know exactly which state performed the last eugenic sterilization, or in what year. Even top government officials can be unaware that it's happened in their state fairly recently. Paul Lombardo once gave a speech in Virginia, unaware that Lynwood Holton, governor of Virginia from 1970 to 1974, was in the audience. When Lombardo announced that he had documentary evidence proving that a

Virginia hospital had performed involuntary sterilizations on patients in 1979, Holton was shocked: as governor, he had signed a directive ordering that such procedures were never to be performed again.

In 1991, the Virginia General Assembly apologized for the state's eugenic sterilization policies and placed a historic marker explaining Carrie Buck's trial roughly half a mile from where she is buried. Since then five other states also have apologized, although no state is seriously considering reparations. Paul Lombardo, discussion, May 31, 2005.

116 *"[She] was out in the country"* Ibid.

116 *"single-room cinderblock shed with no plumbing"* Lombardo, "Three Generations, No Imbeciles," p. 60.

116 *"even in her last weeks"* Ibid., p. 61.

116 *Lombardo even tracked down* Stephen Jay Gould, "Carrie Buck's Daughter," *Natural History* 93 (1984): 14–18.

116 *"The grade book I found"* Lombardo, "Facing Carrie Buck," p. 14.

117 *"I tried helping everybody"* Santos, "Historic Test Case."

117 *But the Nazis used* Buck v. Bell Stefan Kühl, *The Nazi Connection: Eugenics, American Racism and German National Socialism* (Oxford, U.K.: Oxford University Press, 1994), p. 41. Zenderland, *Measuring Minds*, p. 330.

117 *"Now that we know the laws of heredity"* Kühl, *The Nazi Connection*, p. 37.

Chapter 9: Nazis and Intelligence Testing

119 *Back in 1914, Harry Laughlin* Laughlin was maniacally prosterilization. In 1914, at the First National Conference on Race Betterment, he announced that fifteen million people over the next sixty-five years needed to be sterilized "to purify the breeding stock of the [white] race." Paul Lombardo, "Carrie Buck's Pedigree," *Journal of Laboratory and Clinical Medicine* 138 (2001): 279.

119 *"To one versed in the history"* Harry Laughlin, "Eugenical Sterilization in Germany," *Eugenical News* 18, no. 5 (September–October 1933): 89. Indeed, the Nazis took a shine not only to Laughlin's model statute, but also to the man himself. In 1936, for instance, the University of Heidelberg awarded him an honorary degree for his work in eugenics.

120 *"persons socially inadequate from defective inheritance"* Harry Laughlin, *Eugenical Sterilization in the United States* (Chicago: Psychopathic Laboratory of the Municipal Court of Chicago, December 1922), p. 446.

120 *"orphans, ne'er-do-wells, the homeless, tramps and paupers"* Ibid., p. 447.

120 *As a result, in addition to the feebleminded* Henry Friedlander, *The Origins of Nazi Genocide: From Euthanasia to the Final Solution* (Chapel Hill: University of North Carolina Press, 1995), p. 26.

120 *The statute aside, in terms* Ibid., p. 9.

120 *The law even required other medical professionals* Patricia Heberer (historian, United States Holocaust Memorial Museum), in discussion with author, July 7, 2004.

120   *Doctors denounced people in about 75 percent*   Friedlander, *The Origins of Nazi Genocide*, p. 27.

120   *By 1936 there were 205 of these courts*   Gisela Bock, "Nazi Sterilization and Reproductive Policies" in *Deadly Medicine: Creating the Master Race* (Washington, D.C.: United States Holocaust Memorial Museum, 2004), p. 69.

121   *In the years 1934 to 1936, they decided*   Friedlander, *The Origins of Nazi Genocide*, p. 28.

121   *Of the nine potential hereditary ailments*   Ibid., p. 31.

121   *included in everyone's medical file*   Patricia Heberer, discussion, July 7, 2004.

121   *As a result, the courts often*   Michael Burleigh, "Nazi 'Euthanasia Programs'" in *Deadly Medicine*, p. 131.

122   *"The tools of psychology, particularly those"*   Lewis Terman and Maud Merrill, *Measuring Intelligence* (Boston: Houghton Mifflin, 1937), p. ix.

122   *"What does Christmas signify?"*   All German intelligence test questions taken from Ursula H.'s medical file, Landesarchiv Berlin (A Rep. 003-04-04 Nr. 21), which was kindly provided to the author by the United States Holocaust Memorial Museum, Washington, D.C. They requested that Ursula's last name not be used.

123   *"Conduct during Interview"*   Friedlander, *The Origins of Nazi Genocide*, p. 32 (emphasis in original).

123   *A good example of how conduct influenced diagnosis . . . Schmidt went back to his job*   Ibid., p. 33.

124   *"Racial hygiene must always"*   Bock, "Nazi Sterilization and Reproductive Policies," p. 71.

124   *the Ann Cooper Hewitt trial*   Wendy Kline, *Building a Better Race: Gender, Sexuality, and Eugenics from the Turn of the Century to the Baby Boom* (Berkeley: University of California Press, 2001), pp. 107–124.

125   *But in Germany, two-thirds*   Bock, "Nazi Sterilization and Reproductive Policies," p. 78.

125   *By the end of World War II*   Ibid., pp. 62, 75.

125   *The Germans had been debating killing*   Burleigh, "Nazi 'Euthanasia Programs,'" pp. 127–128.

126   *"We have seen more than once"*   *Buck v. Bell*, p. 207.

126   *"If Germany were to get a million"*   J. Noakes and G. Pridham, eds., *Nazism 1919–1945: Foreign Policy, War, and Racial Extermination: A Documentary Reader. Nazism Series*, vol. 3 (Exeter, U.K.: Exeter University Publications, 1988), p. 1002.

127   *"You Are Sharing the Load!"*   Robert Proctor, *Racial Hygiene: Medicine under the Nazis* (Cambridge, Mass.: Harvard University Press, 1988), fig. 37.

127   *German students were indoctrinated*   Ibid., p.184.

127   *"Would you . . . if you were a cripple"*   Ibid., p. 183.

128   *"natural and God-given inequality of men"*   Ibid., p. 181.

128   *the Nazis would kill well over two hundred thousand*   Henry Friedlander, "From Euthanasia to the Final Solution" in *Deadly Medicine*, p. 163.

128   *The example of a girl from Berlin*   All details of Ursula H.'s story are from
      her medical file, Landesarchiv Berlin (A Rep. 003-04-04 Nr. 21).

129   *60 percent of the people the Nazis sterilized*   Bock, "Nazi Sterilization and
      Reproductive Policies," pp. 78–79.

136   *After the war, witnesses said . . . "but that Hitler will go to hell"*   Friedlander,
      The Origins of Nazi Genocide, pp. 170–171.

137   *"patients who caused extra work"*   Ibid., p. 160.

137   *Inmates were forced to work*   Ibid., p. 166.

137   *When the Russians arrived at Meseritz-Obrawalde*   Michael Burleigh, *Death
      and Deliverance: "Euthanasia" in Germany 1900–1945* (Cambridge, U.K.:
      Cambridge University Press, 1994), pp. 269–270.

138   *By the end, the Germans were killing "asocials"*   Burleigh, "Nazi 'Euthanasia'
      Programs,'" p. 152.

138   *Historians are confident*   Patricia Heberer, e-mail message to author, June
      16, 2006.

CHAPTER 10: THE ELEVEN-PLUS IN THE UNITED KINGDOM

139   *they only empowered local authorities to sequester*   Gillian Sutherland, *Ability,
      Merit, and Measurement: Mental Testing and English Education 1880–1940*
      (Oxford, U.K.: Clarendon Press, 1984), pp. 39–40, 87–89.

140   *In the early to midtwentieth century, Burt*   Adrian Wooldridge, *Measuring
      the Mind: Education and Psychology in England c. 1860–1990* (Cambridge,
      U.K.: Cambridge University Press, 1994), p. 94.

140   *Cyril Burt and many of his fellow psychologists*   Ibid., p. 164.

140   *Indeed, as early as 1926, Burt had testified*   Ibid., p. 225.

141   *"It appears that well over 20 per cent"*   Cyril Burt, "Intelligence and Social
      Mobility," *British Journal of Statistical Psychology* 14 (May 1961): 23.

141   *There was a third alternative, called a technical school*   Wooldridge, *Measur-
      ing the Mind*, p. 260.

141   *"Intellectual development during childhood"*   Sutherland, *Ability, Merit, and
      Measurement*, p. 153. Wooldridge, *Measuring the Mind*, p. 237.

141   *"impervious to cramming"*   Wooldridge, *Measuring the Mind*, pp. 227–228,
      237–238.

142   *The eleven-plus wasn't just one test*   Sutherland, *Ability, Merit, and Measure-
      ment*, p. 189. Wooldridge, *Measuring the Mind*, p. 251.

143   *"In a box of oranges"*   Glamorgan Education Authority, "Entrance Exami-
      nation to Grammar Schools" (March 15, 1955), Arithmetic, No. 12.

143   *"Dressing a doll"*   Ibid., Essay, Nos. 1–3.

143   *"(1) How often had Juan"*   Ibid., General Composition, No. 1, (1) and (10).

143   *"(10) Sorrow is to tears"*   Ibid., General Composition, No. 4 (a)(10).

143   *"If you don't buck your ideas"*   Patricia Morgan, in discussion with author,
      November 8, 2004.

144   *"I can see the paper"*   Joan Murdoch, in discussion with author, October 7,
      2004.

145   *"run away to sea"*   Wooldridge, *Measuring the Mind*, p. 260.

145   *Take Mike Clements, for instance*   Details of Michael Clements's life come
       from two discussions with author, December 4, 2004, and May 11, 2005, as
       well as a series of e-mails from the end of 2004 through the summer of 2005.

148   *In 1947, the government needed to provide 1.15 million*   Wooldridge, *Mea-
       suring the Mind*, p. 260.

148   *By design, most students failed the eleven-plus*   Ibid., p. 261.

148   *higher proportions of semiskilled and unskilled laborers*   Ibid.

149   *"Some headmasters have moulded"*   Brian Simon, *Intelligence Testing and the
       Comprehensive School* (London: Lawrence & Wishart, 1958), p. 17.

149   *Teachers had to decide*   Ibid., p. 13.

150   *"Children born between September and December"*   Wooldridge, *Measuring
       the Mind*, p. 334.

150   *"road sweeper material"*   Clements, discussions.

150   *"it is the duty of the community, first"*   Wooldridge, *Measuring the Mind*, p.
       204.

151   *"Are you sure that's really"*   Clements, discussions.

151   *"We were just bunged into"*   Ibid.

151   *In the 1950s, one critic concluded*   Simon, *Intelligence Testing and the Compre-
       hensive School*, p. 82.

151   *For starters, only 10 percent of grammar school students*   Ibid., p. 21.

152   *"one of the best medical researchers in the country"*   David Barnes (doctor,
       Atkinson Morley's Hospital, London), in discussion with author, Novem-
       ber 23, 2004.

152   *"The friends that I had"*   John Bevan, in discussion with author, November
       9, 2004.

152   *IQ scores of lower-working-class kids*   Wooldridge, *Measuring the Mind*, pp.
       275–276.

153   *Fifteen years after World War II*   Ibid., p. 277.

153   *"The condition of the home"*   Ibid., pp. 275–276.

153   *"The children who did go were usually an only child"*   Betty Shepherd, e-mail
       message to author, January 6, 2005 (emphasis in original).

154   *Of middle-class children with IQs*   Wooldridge, *Measuring the Mind*, p. 326.

154   *"If you went on to the grammar school"*   Bevan, discussion, November 9, 2004.

154   *"if the IQ had been made the single criterion"*   Wooldridge, *Measuring the
       Mind*, p. 329.

155   *" 'If it's the last thing I do' "*   Ibid., pp. 330–332.

155   *"a large blob of ink"*   Simon, *Intelligence Testing and the Comprehensive
       School*, p. 19.

156   *"so volatile and dynamic"*   Clements, discussions.

157   *"My firm belief, more so now"*   Ibid.

CHAPTER 11: INTELLIGENCE TESTING AND THE DEATH
PENALTY IN THE UNITED STATES

159   *Poor people, welfare recipients, criminals behind bars*   Richard Herrnstein and
       Charles Murray, *The Bell Curve: Intelligence and Class Structure in American*

Life (New York: Free Press, 1994), pp. 369–386. L. S. Gottfredson, "Why g Matters: The Complexity of Everyday Life," *Intelligence* 24, no. 1 (1997): 79–132.

159   *High scorers, on the other hand*   L. J. Whalley and I. J. Deary, "Longitudinal Cohort Study of Childhood IQ and Survival up to Age 76," *British Medical Journal* 322 (2001): 1–5.

159   *"diminished capacities to understand and process"*   *Atkins v. Virginia*, 536 U.S. 304, 318 (2002).

160   *"To the extent there is serious disagreement"*   Ibid., 317.

161   *"And the [school] transcript says placed in fifth"*   Testimony of Evan Nelson at trial, transcription, *Commonwealth of Virginia v. Daryl Renard Atkins*, Case No. 96-8229(6), February 14, 1998, p. 112.

161   *"I went and lay on my front porch"*   Beverly Williams, "Murder Suspect Will Face 24 Charges: 10 Victims of Spree Describe Crimes," *Newport News (Va.) Daily Press*, October 26, 1996.

161   *"We was drinking and smoking weed"*   William Jones, transcription, *Commonwealth of Virginia v. Daryl Renard Atkins*, February 12, 1998, p. 106.

162   *"We have a great clientele"*   Carol Owens, in discussion with author, May 3, 2005.

162   *"I had brought my dollar and fifty"*   Jones, transcription, p. 113.

163   *"Move over, let my friend drive"*   Ibid., pp. 117–118.

163   *"Take it [the money]"*   Ibid., p. 122.

163   *They pulled up at the drive-through ATM*   Frederick Troy Lyons (investigator, York County Sheriff's office), transcription, *Commonwealth of Virginia v. Daryl Renard Atkins*, February 10, 1998, pp. 197–198.

163   *"Yes, yes," Jones recalled*   Jones, transcription, p. 129.

164   *He had a grandfather*   Phillip Atkins (defendant's grandfather), transcription, *Commonwealth of Virginia v. Daryl Renard Atkins*, February 10, 1998, pp. 155–156.

164   *He shot Nesbitt*   George Rogers (defense attorney), transcription, *Commonwealth of Virginia v. Daryl Renard Atkins*, February 10, 1998, p. 179.

165   *Atkins, however, was easy to find*   Lyons, transcription, p. 210.

165   *because Atkins performed so poorly*   Nelson, transcription, pp. 138–139.

165   *"the standard IQ test for adults here in the United States"*   Ibid., p. 96.

165   *Harcourt Assessment, which publishes the tests*   Matthew Slitt (public relations, Harcourt Assessment), in discussion with author, July 21, 2005.

165   *The largest use today*   Diane Coalson, in discussion with author, July 29, 2005.

166   *"That means that he falls in the range"*   Nelson, transcription, p. 96.

166   *"harder to reason"*   Ibid., p. 116.

166   *Atkins appealed to the Virginia Supreme Court*   *Atkins v. Commonwealth of Virginia*, 510 S.E. 2d 445 (Va. 1999).

166   *"his vocabulary and syntax"*   Stanton Samenow, U.S. Supreme Court Record, *Atkins v. Virginia*, August 18, 1999, pp. 330–331.

167   *"not willing to commute Atkins' sentence"*   *Atkins v. Commonwealth of Virginia*, 534 S.E. 2d 312 (Va. 2000), p. 321.

167 *This comported with U.S. Supreme Court precedent* Penry v. Lynaugh, 492
     U.S. 302 (1989).

168 *"When I saw him [for the first time]"* Evan Nelson, U.S. Supreme Court
     Record, *Atkins v. Virginia*, August 18, 1999, p. 240.

168 *"He stated that 'oath' meant a promise"* Robert S. Brown, U.S. Supreme
     Court Record, *Atkins v. Virginia*, June 30, 1999, p. 330.

168 *Researchers estimate that children* Joseph Fagan and Cynthia Holland, "Equal
     Opportunity and Racial Differences in IQ," *Intelligence* 30 (2002): 364.

169 *in February 2005, they even filed a motion* Motion for order limiting testi-
     mony on mental retardation issues to Virginia's statutory definition,
     Commonwealth of Virginia v. Daryl Renard Atkins, February 2005, p. 2.

169 *In June 2006, however, the Virginia Supreme Court* "Court Orders New
     Trial for Death Row Inmate," *Los Angeles Times*, June 9, 2006.

Chapter 12: What Do IQ Tests Really Measure?

171 *"Human differences have enormous social"* Linda Gottfredson, e-mail mes-
     sage to author, December 13, 2004.

171 *intelligence as "some innate ability"* Testimony of Evan Nelson at trial,
     transcription, *Commonwealth of Virginia v. Daryl Renard Atkins*, Case
     No. 96-8229(6), February 14, 1998, p. 98.

172 *The verbal section of the WAIS* See generally Corwin Boake, "From the
     Binet-Simon to the Wechsler-Bellevue: Tracing the History of Intelli-
     gence," *Journal of Clinical and Experimental Neuropsychology* 24, no. 3
     (2002): 383–405.

172 *"When someone has offended you"* Raymond Fancher, *The Intelligence Men:
     Makers of the IQ Controversy* (New York: W. W. Norton, 1985), p. 73.

172 *Freezing water bursts pipes because* Clarence Yoakum and Lewis Terman,
     eds., *Army Mental Tests* (New York: Henry Holt, 1920), p. 209.

172 *"What is the thing to do if a water pipe"* Nelson, transcription, p. 103.

173 *In the 1880s, for instance, Francis Galton* Boake, "From the Binet-Simon to
     the Wechsler-Bellevue," p. 384.

173 *"a fly and an ant"* Fancher, *The Intelligence Men*, p. 73.

173 *"Degree of abstractness should be evaluated"* Alan Kaufman and Elizabeth
     Lichtenberger, *Essentials of WAIS-III* (New York: John Wiley & Sons,
     1999), pp. 89, 96.

173 *Of the seven verbal subtests* Ibid., p. 52.

175 *"were all right"* David S. Tulsky, Donald H. Saklosfske, and Joseph Ricker,
     "Historical Overview of Intelligence and Memory: Factors Influencing the
     Wechsler Scales" in David S. Tulsky et al., eds., *Clinical Interpretation of the
     WAIS-III and WMS-III* (San Diego: Academic Press, 2003), pp. 23–26.

175 *"people go, that looks just like a Wechsler item"* Jack Naglieri, in discussion
     with author, April 28, 2005.

175 *Like Alfred Binet and Charles Spearman before him* Kaufman and Lichten-
     berger, *Essentials of WAIS-III*, p. 3.

176 *"certainly it is not something which can be expressed"* Tulsky, Saklosfske, and
     Ricker, "Historical Overview of Intelligence and Memory," p. 27.

176 *"the only important or paramount factor"* Ibid.

177 *"These questions are very important"* Nelson, transcription, p. 104.

177 *Depending on something as arbitrary* Joseph Fagan and Cynthia Holland, "Equal Opportunity and Racial Differences in IQ," *Intelligence* 30 (2002): 362, 364.

178 *Arthur Jensen, a famous University of California psychologist* James Flynn, "Searching for Justice: The Discovery of IQ Gains over Time," *American Psychologist* 54, no. 1 (January 1999): 7.

178 *"Take a woman with an IQ of 110"* Ibid.

178 *The results of two other studies involving Ravens* Ibid., pp. 6–7.

179 *"How reasonable is it to assume"* Ibid., pp. 7–8.

179 *Interestingly, scores from education-reliant tests* Ibid., p. 8.

179 *"Massive IQ gains cannot be due"* James Flynn, "Massive IQ Gains in 14 Nations: What IQ Tests Really Measure," *Psychological Bulletin*, 101, no. 2 (1997): 189.

180 *"psychologists should stop saying"* Ibid., p. 188.

CHAPTER 13: ALTERNATIVES TO IQ

182 *"No, I don't think so"* Howard Marks, in discussion with author, February 7, 2005. All Marks's quotes are from the same interview.

183 *The most famous alternative theory* Howard Gardner, *Frames of Mind: The Theory of Multiple Intelligences* (New York: Basic Books, 1983).

183 *Gardner's theory of multiple intelligences* Howard Gardner, *Intelligence Reframed: Multiple Intelligences for the Twenty-First Century* (New York: Basic Books, 1999), pp. 35–41.

184 *As the years progressed, Gardner* Ibid., pp. 41–64.

184 *"Intelligences are not things that can be seen or counted"* Ibid., p. 34.

185 *The trend has done nothing but continue* Cathi Cohen, *Raise Your Child's Social IQ: Stepping Stones to People Skills for Kids* (Silver Spring, Md.: Advantage Books, 2001). Daniel Goleman, *Emotional Intelligence: Why It Can Matter More Than IQ* (New York: Bantam Books, 1995).

185 *"Intelligence is what the tests test"* Edward Boring, "Intelligence as the Tests Test It," *New Republic* (June 6, 1923), p. 35.

186 *"At least where I grew up"* Robert Sternberg, in discussion with author, November 11, 2004. All Sternberg quotes are from this interview unless otherwise indicated.

186 *Sternberg dedicated his book* Robert Sternberg, *Successful Intelligence: How Practial and Creative Intelligence Determine Success in Life* (New York: Plume, 1997).

187 *"the ability to achieve success"* Robert Sternberg, the Rainbow Project Collaborators, and the University of Michigan Busines School Project Collaborators, "Theory-Based University Admissions Testing for a New Millennium," *Educational Psychologist* 39, no. 3 (2004): 185–198.

187 *"The analytical aspect is used to solve problems"* Sternberg, *Successful Intelligence*, p. 47.

187 *He also publishes copiously* Ibid., p. 12.

188 *"is a stupid concept if you think about it"* Jack Naglieri, in discussion with author, April 28, 2005. All Naglieri quotes are from this discussion.

CHAPTER 14: THE SAT

191 *In 1954, twenty-five hundred white students boycotted* Raymond Wolters, *The Burden of Brown: Thirty Years of School Desegregation* (Knoxville: University of Tennessee Press, 1984), p. 12.

191 *"economically disadvantaged"* School Matters, a Service of Standard & Poor's. http://www.schoolmatters.com/app/location/q/stid=9/llid=118/stllid=376/locid=1027368/catid=-1/secid=-1/compid=-1/site=pes (accessed May 23, 2006).

191 *The Environmental Protection Agency calculates* "Saving Their Community," *60 Minutes*, April 24, 2005. http://www.cbsnews.com/stories/ 2005/04/ 21/60minutes/main690002.shtml (accessed May 23, 2006).

192 *"Their morals, values are disheartening"* Wensworth E. Lovell, in discussion with author, February 2005.

194 *"I'm definitely not one to just"* Jimmy D'Andrea, in discussion with author, February 18, 2005.

197 *As we rely more* College Board, Sample SAT Reasoning Test, 2004, Section 5, Question 20, www.collegeboard.com.

197 *The Portuguese musical tradition* Ibid., Section 5, Question 11.

199 *About half a dozen Washington* Alicia Abell, "Getting In," *Washingtonian* (November 2002). http://www.washingtonian.com/schools/private/gettingin.html (accessed July 28, 2005).

199 *Almost 80 percent are white* School Matters. http://www.schoolmatters .com/app/location/q/stid=21/llid=118/stllid=197/locid=944893/catid=-1/secid=-1/compid=-1/ site=pes (accessed May 23, 2006).

200 *"cool to be smart"* Suzanne Coker, in discussion with author, February 8, 2005.

200 *"When you have such good"* Dr. Alan Goodwin, in discussion with the author, February 22, 2005.

202 *Carl Brigham, a young officer* Nicholas Lemann, *The Big Test: The Secret History of American Meritocracy* (New York: Farrar, Straus, & Giroux, 1999), pp. 30–31.

202 *Brigham claimed the questions* David F. Lohman, "Aptitude for College: The Importance of Reasoning Tests for Minority Admissions," in *Rethinking the SAT: The Future of Standardized Testing in University Admissions* (New York: RoutledgeFalmer, 2004), p. 44.

202 *On the old 1,600-point SAT* Manuel Gómez, "Remarks on President Atkinson's Proposal on Admissions Tests," in *Rethinking the SAT*, p. 38.

203 *After extensive study of its student body* Saul Geiser and Roger Studley, "UC and the SAT: Predictive Validity and Differential Impact of the SAT I and SAT II at the University of California" in *Rethinking the SAT*, p. 130.

203 *The exam doesn't predict college grades* Richard Atkinson, "Achievement versus Aptitude in College Admissions" in *Rethinking the SAT*, p. 19.

203　*more than seven hundred colleges and universities*　Fair Test, "New Fairtest Analysis Finds: More Than 700 4-Year Colleges Do Not Use SAT I or ACT Scores to Admit Substantial Numbers of Bachelor Degree Applicants." http://www.fairtest.org/pr/Opt_PR_1003.html (accessed May 19, 2006).

204　*"a class of twelve-year-old students"*　Richard Atkinson, "Standardized Tests and Access to American Universities" (speech, 2001 Robert H. Atwell Distinguished Lecture, eighty-third annual meeting of the American Council of Education, Washington, D.C., February 18, 2001).

204　*The day before his speech*　Michael A. Fletcher, "Key SAT Test under Fire in Calif.: University President Proposes New Admissions Criteria," *Washington Post*, February 17, 2001.

204　*Similar articles appeared*　Richard Atkinson, "College Admissions and the SAT: A Personal Perspective," *Voice of San Diego*, May 11, 2005. http://www.voiceofsandiego.org/site/pp.asp?c=euLTJbMUKvH&b =677795 (accessed July 12, 2005).

204　*students in California represented*　Justin Ewers, "It's Bigger—Is It Better?," *U.S. News & World Report*, March 14, 2005.

205　*"the UC data show"*　Atkinson, "Achievement versus Aptitude in College Admissions," p. 18.

206　*"I was certainly not chosen"*　Gaston Caperton, "Striving for Excellence in Education," *Views and Visions: A Newsletter for Clients and Friends*, Bowles, Rice McDavid, Graff & Love, Summer 2001, p. 20.

206　*"Why would I be interested"*　Ibid., p. 1.

206　*"I was amazed"*　Ibid., pp. 1, 17.

207　*"It's worth noting"*　Nicholas Lemann, "A History of Admissions Testing" in *Rethinking the SAT*, p. 8.

207　*"The decision to include"*　Atkinson, "Achievement versus Aptitude in College Admissions," p. 18.

208　*"This [new] test is really going to create"*　John Cloud, "Inside the New SAT Test," *Time*, October 19, 2003. http://www.time.com/time/covers/ 1101031027/index.html (accessed May 22, 2006).

209　*turned into cash-register music*　Michael Dobbs, "New SAT a Boon for Test-Prep Business: Expensive Coaching Debated as Students Prepare for Revised Exam," *Washington Post*, March 7, 2005.

209　*"I discovered that I could guess"*　David Owen, "The S.A.T.'s Watchdog," *New Yorker*, April 3, 2006, p. 32. See also Michael Winerip, "SAT Essay Test Rewards Length and Ignores Errors of Fact," *New York Times*, May 4, 2005.

209　*"I believe this is an ideal"*　Richard Atkinson, "College Admissions and the SAT," *American Psychological Society* 18, no. 5 (May 2005). http://www .psychologicalscience.org/observer/getArticle.cfm?id=1779　(accessed August 30, 2005).

209　*"I admire Caperton greatly"*　Ibid.

210　*There, in recent years, parents*　Carol Blum (director, High School Instruction, Montgomery County Public Schools), in discussion with author, February 15, 2005.

210   *Anacostia students scored a 1042*   District of Columbia Public Schools, Office of Educational Accountability.

211   *"I have been told that"*   Dr. Alan Goodwin, e-mail message to author, May 10, 2006.

211   *his students scored 1884*   Clare Von Secker, "Participation and Performance of the Montgomery County Public Schools Class of June 2006 on the New SAT," *Research Brief, Department of Shared Accountability* (August 2006). http://www.sharedaccountability.mcpsprimetime.org/reports/ list.php?Options=&Set=Tests (accessed February 8, 2007).

211   *he has an exam based on "successful intelligence"*   Robert Sternberg, "Theory-Based University Admissions Testing for a New Millennium," *Educational Psychologist* 39, no. 3 (2004): 189, 190.

211   *After trying out their test on students nationwide*   Ibid., p. 192.

212   *After World War II, the LSAT*   William LaPiana (Rita and Joseph Solomon Professor, New York Law School), "A History of the Law School Admission Council and the LSAT," keynote address, 1998 Law School Admission Council annual meeting, p. 8.

213   *"After controlling for family income"*   Atkinson, "Achievment versus Aptitude in College Admissions," p. 19.

213   *"There's a danger that making"*   Cloud, "Inside the New SAT Test."

CHAPTER 15: BLACK AND WHITE IQ

215   *In the main, studying different "races'" IQs is not considered*   Graham Richards, "'It's an American Thing': The 'Race' and Intelligence Controversy from a British Perspective" in Andrew S. Winston, ed., *Defining Difference: Race and Racism in the History of Psychology* (Washington, D.C.: American Psychological Association, 2004), pp. 137–169.

216   *"is the conservative wing"*   Earl Hunt, in a telephone discussion with author before the ISIR Conference, November 30, 2004.

217   *by adulthood our genes determine 80 percent*   Thomas J. Bouchard, "Genetic Influence on Human Psychological Traits: A Survey," *Current Directions in Psychological Science* 13, no. 4 (2004): 148–151.

217   *"Look, there is a perfectly legitimate discussion"*   Hunt, discussion, November 30, 2004.

218   *There is ample opposition, perhaps overwhelmingly*   Richards, "'It's an American Thing,'" p. 150.

218   *"You're a Celt"*   Ibid.

219   *"There is no direct biological test"*   Roger Pearson, *Race, Intelligence, and Bias in Academe* (Washington, D.C.: Scott-Townsend, 1991), p. 16.

220   *"Compensatory education has been tried"*   Arthur R. Jensen, "How Much Can We Boost IQ and Scholastic Achievement?," *Harvard Education Review* 39, no. 41 (October 9, 1969): 2.

220   *"we are left with various lines of evidence"*   Ibid., p. 82.

220   *"Blacks and whites differ in IQ by 15 points"*   Joseph Fagan, "Race, Language, and Information Processing," lecture, Fifth Annual International Society of Intelligence Research, New Orleans, December 4, 2004.

221 *"spoke another language"* Joseph Fagan didn't respond to subsequent inquiries from the author for examples of black English words.

221 *words he presumed they didn't know already, such as "venter"* J. F. Fagan and C. R. Holland, "Equal Opportunity and Racial Differences in IQ," *Intelligence* 30 (2002): 364.

222 *"e.g., age, sex, parent education, community setting, and region"* Jack A. Naglieri, "Current Advances in Assessment and Intervention for Children with Learning Disabilities" in T. E. Scruggs and M. A. Mastropieri, eds., *Advances in Learning and Behavioral Disabilities: Identification and Assessment,* vol. 16 (Oxford, U.K.: Elsevier Science, 2003), p. 177.

222 *Psychologist Robert Sternberg, at Yale* Robert Sternberg, "Theory-Based University Admissions Testing for a New Millennium," *Educational Psychologist* 39, no. 3 (2004), pp. 191–192.

223 *"insufficient familiarity with standard English"* Frank Miele, *Intelligence, Race, and Genetics: Conversations with Arthur R. Jensen* (Boulder, Colo.: Westview, 2004), pp. 129–130.

223 *"Failure has plagued the many programs based on 'reverse discrimination'"* Pearson, *Race, Intelligence, and Bias in Academe,* p. 12.

224 *"It hardly needs to be emphasized that when charity organizations help* Lewis Terman, *The Measurement of Intelligence: An Explanation of and a Complete Guide for the Use of the Stanford Revision and Extension of the Binet-Simon Intelligence Scale* (Boston: Houghton Mifflin, 1916), p. 18.

225 *"some kind of devil"* Linda S. Gottfredson in discussion with author, December 3, 2004. All Gottfredson quotes are from this interview unless otherwise noted.

225 *Taken together, the photos had a rogues' gallery* John Sedgwick, "The Mentality Bunker," *GQ* (November 1994): 228–235.

227 *"to master the elementary school curriculum"* Linda S. Gottfredson, "Social Consequences of Group Differences in Cognitive Ability (Consequencias Sociais das Diferencas de Grupo em Habilidade Cognitiva)," in C. E. Flores-Mendoza and R. Colom, eds., *Introducau a Psicologia das Diferncas Individuais* (Porto Allegre, Brazil: ArtMed, 2006), p. 28.

227 *By about 1980, however, the average black IQ score* Richards, " 'It's an American Thing, '" p. 155.

228 *"In fact, rather than seeking racial parity"* Linda S. Gottfredson, "What if the Hereditarian Hypothesis is True?," *Psychology, Public Policy, and Law* 11, no. 2 (2005): p. 318.

229 *"The evidence for a general"* Richard Herrnstein and Charles Murray, *The Bell Curve: Intelligence and Class Structure in American Life* (New York: Free Press, 1994), p. 3.

Index